Leading the Race

Leading the Race

The Transformation of the Black Elite in the Nation's Capital, 1880–1920

Jacqueline M. Moore

University Press of Virginia
Charlottesville and London

The University Press of Virginia
© 1999 by the Rector and Visitors of the University of Virginia
All rights reserved
Printed in the United States of America
First published 1999

∞ The paper used in this publication meets the minimum requirements of the American National Standard for Information Sciences—Permanence of Paper for Printed Library Materials, ANSI Z39.48-1984.

Library of Congress Cataloging-in-Publication Data
Moore, Jacqueline M., 1965–
  Leading the race : the transformation of the Black elite in the nation's capital, 1880–1920 / Jacqueline M. Moore.
    p.   cm.
  Includes bibliographical references (p.   ) and index.
  ISBN 0-8139-1903-7 (cloth : alk. paper)
  1. Afro-Americans—Washington (D.C.)—Social conditions—19th century.   2. Afro-Americans—Washington (D.C.)—Social conditions—20th century.   3. Elite (Social sciences)—Washington (D.C.)—History—19th century.   4. Elite (Social sciences)—Washington (D.C.)—History—20th century.   5. Washington (D.C.)—Race relations.   6. Washington (D.C.)—Social conditions—19th century.   7. Washington (D.C.)—Social conditions—20th century.
E185.93.D6M66   1999
305.8960753—dc21   99-31004
                                                            CIP

CONTENTS

Acknowledgments	vii
Introduction	1
ONE The Washington Black Elite: An 1880s Overview	9
TWO The Family	33
THREE Culture and Leisure	51
FOUR The Church	70
FIVE Primary and Secondary Education	86
SIX Howard University and Higher Education	111
SEVEN Occupation and Enterprise	132
EIGHT Charitable, Professional, and Fraternal Organizations	161
NINE Race and Racial Uplift	187
Notes	215
Bibliography	241
Index	249

ACKNOWLEDGMENTS

To quote a cliché: I owe many debts of gratitude to many people for this work, but the faults are all my own. My thanks go first and foremost to Louis R. Harlan, who waded through many drafts and whose constant advice and careful editing have been invaluable. I only hope he is pleased with the results and that I have improved since the beginning of it all.

I owe thanks to Robyn Muncy for helpful discussions on the history of women and families at the turn of the century and for her careful and thoughtful criticism of the manuscript. Bart Landry has my undying gratitude for taking an entire afternoon to discuss social classes and status groups with me. My thanks go also to Ira Berlin and Al Moss for their help in refining my topic and advice on sources. Leslie Rowland has been a constant source of sound advice on both theoretical approaches to a manuscript and practical advice on becoming a professional historian. Esme Bhan was a friend, mentor, adviser, critic, and encyclopedic source of information on the black elite of the District of Columbia throughout the entire process of research and writing the dissertation on which this book is based.

The staff of several research facilities have helped me find documents and gain access to them. The staff of the Manuscript Division of the Library of Congress was particularly helpful in allowing me to see original documents when the microfilm was of poor quality. I owe the most thanks to the incomparable staff of the Moorland-Spingarn Research Center at Howard University. Time and again individuals went out of their way to help me find the information I needed. I particularly thank Joellen ElBashir in the Manuscript Division for her timely help with permissions and Donna Wells in the Prints and Photographs Division for her knowledgeable assistance.

The Moorland-Spingarn manuscript collection is an incomparable collection of papers of African Americans, thanks largely to the efforts of Dorothy Porter, who encouraged members of the Washington black community to donate their papers. The scope of the collection is such that I found enough material for several books, and yet still feel that I have not exhausted its resources. This explains the seeming sparseness of the bibliography.

A number of people have helped me clarify my ideas and reviewed parts of the work, including Nina Mjagkij, whom I credit for helping me to get a thesis and who kept me sane through the publishing process; Michael Parker, who reviewed the final chapter of the dissertation on which this book is based; Richard Holway, who dealt with my neuroses; Maribeth Corrigan; Doug Pielmeier; Marie Schwartz; and Ann-Marie Przybyla. Special thanks to Ann-Marie and Helen Rupp for checking some of my notes. I also thank *Jeopardy!* for the "fellowship" that enabled me to finish the dissertation on which this book is based, Austin College for having faith that I would finish when I wasn't so sure myself, my father for his constant encouragement, and my mother for her support. To John, thanks for everything.

Leading the Race

Introduction

For many years research in black history focused primarily on slavery, Emancipation, and Reconstruction. Studies of the turn-of-the-century black experience emphasized the rise of Jim Crow in the South and the debate over racial leadership between Booker T. Washington and W. E. B. Du Bois. Only recently have historians begun to focus on the urban experiences of African Americans. The first works in this field concentrated largely on the Great Migration and the rise of the ghetto. Such studies focused on the inability of blacks to overcome discrimination, and largely treated them as passive victims. Beginning in the mid-1980s historians started to emphasize that African Americans have played active roles in shaping their lives, and that the external pressure of racism is only one element in the black experience. Nonetheless, most black urban studies have focused on working-class institutions and culture. Social historians assumed that there was little more to say on the topic of black leaders, who, after all, made up such a small percentage of the black population.

Discussions of the black elite, when they occurred, inevitably focused on their exclusivity and dominance of black institutions. The implication was that the elite served only their own interests, and that their control precluded constructive efforts to improve the status of the race. In the past few years, however, a new group of historians has begun to reexamine the role of the black elite at the turn of the twentieth century, incorporating the work of social historians on class and gender and thus presenting a more complex picture. Recently the historian Joe W. Trotter, in a survey of black urban historiography, highlighted the need for such a reevaluation.[1] It is in this vein that I examine how the self-interest of the black elite and the needs of the black community interacted in Washington, D.C., the center of black society at the turn of the century.

Unlike studies focusing on race relations, which see the Progressive Era as the nadir for African Americans, or studies of internal divisions within the black community, which emphasize attempts of members of the elite to distance themselves from the masses, this work shows how both external and internal pressures drew the elite closer to the masses and helped them to become true race leaders.

At the turn of the century open protest was dangerous, and so many see elite blacks as retreating into their own exclusive world, giving up a fight they had begun during Reconstruction. In reality elites were actively involved in building up the black community. It is true that immediately after Reconstruction they concerned themselves with creating social distinctions, but objective conditions forced a transformation of the black elite into a racially conscious group. What had been attempts at gaining individual rights were translated through the rise of Jim Crow to gaining rights as a group. In this process, institution building was key.

In order to study the transformation process in detail, it is necessary to use a case study approach. In this way we can see how the experiences of one community shaped the actions of its members and study key institutions in greater depth. Washington, D.C., can serve as a prototype for other communities because of its central importance at the turn of the century, and because Washington's black elite had such strong ties with elite blacks in other cities around the country. Indeed, individual members of Washington's elite were often transients, as black officeholders and their families came to the capital for the duration of their appointments and then returned to their home states with changes in administrations. Few could escape Washington without being influenced by the activities of its leading men and women, which would be equaled in brilliance only by the elite of Harlem in the 1920s. Thus in Washington we have the benefit of close scrutiny with the likelihood of greater significance because of the centrality of Washington's black society to the national community.

Social discrimination has always existed in both black and white communities. Even during slavery, the African American community made distinctions between slaves and freemen, between house and field slaves, between rural and urban people. Although whites did not generally recognize these distinctions, the growth of a black elite in the nineteenth century ensured the emergence of black leaders both before and during Reconstruction. Emancipation brought many changes in social status for blacks, and the late nineteenth century was a confusing period for the black community as it sought to confront the new problems of an industrial society and the rise of racism and looked to its leaders to show the way.

Between 1880 and 1920 the small group of African Americans that made up the black social elite in Washington faced many challenges to their social and economic status. The rise of segregation and disfranchisement of African Americans in the South led to disillusionment with the ideals of Reconstruction, which had held out the promise of biracial cooperation and assimilation. The Organic Act of 1879 effectively disfranchised the District of Columbia by ending home rule, thereby cutting what few political ties existed between blacks and whites in the city. Washington became two distinct communities, one white, one black, the black one struggling for identity and control of the few matters that were left in its hands. That struggle was particularly intense because it coincided with the rise in racism at the turn of the century. In the eyes of many of the whites who controlled the administration of the District, African Americans were incompetent to manage their own affairs. In the process of gaining control of their public institutions and professional lives and trying to maintain their social status, the black social elite created new strategies of racial advancement that tied them inseparably to the black community while establishing a firm foundation for a black leadership class. In short, what occurred between 1880 and 1920 within the black social elite in Washington was nothing short of a transformation in self-definition.

In 1880, elite blacks based their social status on their ties with prominent whites, their skin color, and their family backgrounds. They were obsessed with being seen as distinct from the race and therefore acceptable to the white community. Their primary concern was their own assimilation. They soon discovered, however, that whites did not make the same social distinctions that they so carefully cultivated. They found it necessary to turn to the black community for approval, and to get this approval they had to demonstrate genuine concern for the race. They accomplished this feat by building institutions to serve a segregated black community and by acquiring more substantial qualifications for leadership. By 1920 they had formed a firmer foundation for social status based on income, education, and the creation of independent institutions. They could now associate with less fortunate members of their race without risking their social status. Superficial distinctions that were common in the 1880s remained within elite social circles, but entrance into the elite was now more open to men and women of exceptional abilities and achievements; the criterion was now merit rather than family background or skin color. The transformation of the black elite paralleled the transformation of objective conditions such as the rise of racism and the increasing opportunities for education and business enterprise. It is this transformation that this book addresses.

The chapters are organized around the institutions that had the greatest influence on black elite values and their transformation. The first three chapters provide an overview of the Washington black elite in the 1880s and discuss family relationships and cultural and leisure activities. These chapters show the objective conditions in Washington as well as the foundations of elite values, and begin to indicate how these values were transformed. Chapters 4 through 6, on the church, primary and secondary education, and higher education, outline the stages of the transformation in elite definitions and approaches to racial uplift and show how the elite realized that dependence on the white community only meant white control of racial endeavors. The last three chapters, on occupation and enterprise; charitable, professional, and fraternal organizations; and race and racial uplift, show how the principles of racial solidarity and commitment to racial uplift became integral parts of black elite livelihoods, and discuss the rise of a new racially conscious elite.

Since objective characteristics that determine social class do not readily apply to the black elite in this period, identifying members of the black elite is more a sociological problem than a statistical one. All held the respect of members of the black working classes for their accomplishments or affiliations. All received prominent mention in the social columns of the black press and most received attention from the white community. Further clues to their inclusion in the black elite were their involvement with certain prominent social circles, affiliation with elite churches or organizations, and employment within respected institutions within the black community. In short, the black Four Hundred, as the black press sometimes called them, made every effort to distinguish themselves from the black masses socially, and succeeded so well that they attained a publicly recognized status.

Within Washington's black elite were both major players and minor figures. Some African Americans gained prominence only in one aspect of their lives, others in all of them. National status was not a prerequisite for local status, although it did help. Both Perri W. Frisby and Robert H. Terrell were black attorneys in the District, but while Frisby gained prominence in the black professional community through his work in establishing the black District bar association, he did not have the prominence in national circles that Terrell enjoyed. Nonetheless, both moved in the same elite social circles in Washington.

Nannie Helen Burroughs was proof that superficial characteristics often determined entrance to elite social circles. She gained national leadership status through her work for the Baptist church and her many reform activities. Yet her unremarkable social background and her prominent African features gave her a social taint that denied her total acceptance by the District's black aristocrats. Her position was secure in the subelite of Washington charitable workers, but Burroughs did not seek acceptance, nor was she accepted, among Washington's black social elite.

Affiliation with certain institutions might bring otherwise undistinguished African Americans into the elite, but only in a limited sense. Being a professor at Howard University might give one access to certain social rank, for example, but it did not ensure inclusion in all aspects of elite life without considerable other contributions to black society, such as those of Carter G. Woodson and Kelly Miller. Gaining a small appointment in the federal government was a mark of status, but it did not entitle one to the same consideration as Senator Blanche K. Bruce or the former consul in Santo Domingo, Archibald Grimké. Consequently, Washington's black elite consisted of several subelites centered on elite institutions that gave members prominence in Washington, and a few families that could claim national prominence, such as the Grimkés, Terrells, and Bruces.

Elite blacks felt contradictory pressures that led them both toward and away from the larger black community. The generation of black leaders that rose to prominence during Reconstruction and the 1880s had faith that the race would ultimately be assimilated into white society. As educated men and women and, in many cases, with ancestral ties to the white community, elite blacks fully expected that they would be the first to be accepted as equals. Since they expected that the entire race would eventually achieve equal status, the black elite hoped to distinguish itself from the black masses so as to retain its superior social status in the community at large. As the government's and the public's commitment to the ideals of Reconstruction declined, however, assimilation became increasingly unlikely, and the dramatic rise of racism in the 1890s came as a great shock to the black elite.

Increasing racism and segregation in the 1890s led to changing strategies for racial uplift and economic undertakings. Dependent on the white community for patronage in official appointments and investment in business opportunities, elite blacks had to find ways to express themselves without angering their patrons. The increase in segregation made the elite more dependent on the patronage of the black community, since few whites would patronize black businesses or consult black professionals. This new dependence on the black working classes brought different priorities for elite blacks. Whereas earlier they had welcomed ties to the white community and white patronage, now they realized that this patronage kept blacks in a subordinate position. Black elite women felt particularly vulnerable to the new racism and saw general racial uplift as the best solution. Since there was little hope of gradual assimilation, elite blacks now sought to free themselves from dependence on the white community so that they could speak openly against inequalities. They created institutions that united the black community and strengthened its independence. They reluctantly adopted the rhetoric of racial solidarity to protect their own status, which had come increasingly to depend on the perceptions of the black community alone. They worked to consolidate their social and economic status by training in the professions and by encouraging black capitalism.

The children of this social elite who came to prominence in the early twentieth century were more secure in their position, expected a certain measure of success, and believed it was the responsibility of the elite to lead the race to better things. Having never lived at a time when assimilation seemed a possibility, this younger generation accepted the rhetoric of racial solidarity as a reflection of reality. They trained for careers that would help the black community achieve independence from white society. They initiated movements for general racial uplift rather than concentrating solely on personal gain. Building on the strength of the independent black institutions that their forebears had created, they worked more openly for racial justice. With the rise of a united and independent black community in Washington, the black elite chafed under the nonconfrontational strategies of racial advancement that their predecessors had pursued. With the death and decline of the older generation of leaders, the newly politicized elite initiated open protest against racial discrimination and truly assumed the mantle of race leaders.

Although some blacks criticized Washington society as shallow and caste-oriented, for good or ill it served as an example for black communities everywhere. Several articles appeared in black journals over the years either romanticizing, criticizing, or defending this capital of black culture. Three of the black newspapers with the largest nationwide circulation, the *New York Age,* the *Detroit Plaindealer,* and the *Indianapolis Freeman,* ran regular columns on Washington society. Washington elite blacks had extensive friendship and business networks nationwide that spread the influence of their experiences. Many elite blacks came to Washington later in life and kept strong ties, if not financial concerns, in their home states that strengthened these networks. For example, newspapers always referred to Blanche K. Bruce as "Bruce of Mississippi," despite his almost thirty-year residence in Washington, and most of the elite retained their home state identifications even after long-term residency in the District. Other members of Washington's black elite were transients, arriving in Washington to accept a government appointment, to study at Howard University, or to teach in the school system. These people stayed long enough to absorb the culture and then returned to their home towns to spread this culture. Obviously Washington was not typical, but it became a model for black Americans, whether positive or negative.

Historians such as August Meier, Kenneth Kusmer, Allan Spear, and Willard Gatewood have all discussed the rise of a black professional leadership class in the twentieth century. Most of these historians see a clear break in personnel between this class and the aristocratic elite that preceded it. They see the rise of the new leaders as being due in part to the increase in the numbers of African Americans in northern cities after the Great Migration, which enabled blacks to maintain a livelihood in the professions. The professionals, with their larger incomes and greater claims to leadership abilities, displaced the old elite, which then faded from sight. Willard Gatewood makes a clear distinction between what he calls the aristocracy of color and this new leadership class by excluding the latter from his study of the black elite. In particular, in his discussion of Washington, D.C., Gatewood refers to the competition between "old cits" and the newly arrived professionals and intellectuals centered on Howard University.[2]

In truth these distinctions are not so clear-cut. I believe the change in leadership occupations reflected not the arrival of new actors on the scene but changing objective conditions that blurred the distinctions between the aristocracy and the professionals. The change was a matter more of generations than of dynasties. The children of aristocratic families trained, under the advice of their parents, to take on careers best suited for the realities of segregation and twentieth-century life. Many of the aristocrats actually became the professionals and racially conscious businessmen who took over community leadership. Although new families did gain elite status as a result of increased educational opportunities and a decline in the need for superficial qualifications for membership, there was more continuity between the groups in Washington than has previously been suggested. It was not that the old elite was displaced, it was that in the process of coming to terms with new realities, the black elite redefined itself on a more permanent foundation.

With the rise of a black professionally oriented elite situated on a more substantial economic and educational base, factors such as skin color and family connections declined in importance, although families that had traditionally held elite status were better able to provide opportunities for their offspring to succeed. The aristocratic ideal declined in favor of an ideal of leaders with tangible assets based on their abilities, not their birth. This transformation paralleled the decline of aristocratic elites in the nation as a whole, and was the mark of the emergence of a modern society.

For the black elite in Washington, however, an additional factor entered the equation of social status, perhaps as a part of the legacy of the reform tendencies of the Progressive Era. By the end of World War I, involvement in efforts for racial uplift had become a key part of elite status. Elite blacks no longer distanced themselves from the masses politically, but identified many common racial goals. These people were not saints and certainly still preferred to maintain a certain social distance, but they realized that they had more in common with other members of their own race than with elite whites.

By 1920, blacks had built a solid community base from which to speak out against racial injustice. This new reality was due in large part to the activities of elite blacks in the previous forty years, and it enabled African Americans to move beyond assimilation to protest. At no time in this period were elite blacks complacent about their lot. Publicly, they may have generally preached a conservative approach, but privately each was seeking a way to improve their conditions within restricted circumstances. This search often created intense conflicts over strategies for racial advancement that at times appeared to be petty personal vendettas. The resolution of these conflicts, however, or sometimes the conflicts themselves, spurred elite blacks toward their goals. In the process, elite blacks lost faith in assimilation and turned to leading the race.

ONE

The Washington Black Elite
An 1880s Overview

In the 1880s, Washington had a large and cohesive black social elite, among them some of the most influential African Americans in the country. After the Civil War, many blacks migrated to Washington seeking opportunities. They found them in the federal government and in trades, particularly those catering to the black community. The nation's capital attracted many race leaders who lobbied the black cause before Congress, formed national organizations, and found convivial companionship among others of similar social status. Blacks and whites rightly recognized the city as the center of black culture long before New York's Harlem rose to prominence in the 1920s.

Washington's black society was the subject of many conflicting opinions. Viewed alternatively as "the Athens of colored America" and "a huge shell filled with fish flesh and fowl and foul" with "the vandal axe at the root," Washington was either the downfall or the salvation of black America.[1] Early critiques clearly showed the insubstantial nature of black social status. One of the earliest and most damning critiques came in 1877 from John E. Bruce, a syndicated columnist from New York known as Bruce Grit. Bruce held Washington's early black aristocrats up to ridicule for their shallowness and meaningless distinctions. According to Bruce, the District's black society would "never be anything—except nothing—of the flimsiest and poorest, weakest and meanest quality at that." He noted that the citizens took great stock in whether one had been free before the war or emancipated. He accused black society members of a love of display and an overwhelming desire to be reckoned among leading citizens. Bruce observed that a certain exclusive social club would never accomplish anything because its members had caught "the disease called the 'Big Head' before their enterprises fully matured."[2] As in all of Bruce's caustic commentaries, he spared few feelings.

The Washington *Bee* attributed the pomposity of black society in the 1880s to the perpetual influx of office seekers. These people, according to the *Bee*, were usually unintelligent, incompetent, overly bombastic, and given to chronic gambling.[3] More permanent denizens were even relieved when Democrats began removing black appointees from the government in the late 1880s. Commenting on the sad state of affairs, Alexander Crummell wrote: "Our Democratic friends are weeding t[he]. departments of col'd employees, both clerks & messengers: & so col'd society is fading out, 'small by degrees & beautifully less.' I think too that I perceive that society begins to take a 'sober coloring' fr[om] t[he]. eliminating processes of an adverse administration. There are indeed fools, still abiding with us, who imitate t[he]. style & fashion of 5th Ave. Millionaires. But thank God there are fewer than ever."[4]

The office-seeking process was enough to demoralize anyone who spent much time in Washington. The black intellectual Richard T. Greener felt that he had wasted his years in Washington in various squabbles and disappointments, and found that once he was away from the city, he no longer cared about such matters. Yet he still told Francis J. Grimké, minister of the Fifteenth Street Presbyterian Church, that Washington was "a good place, I am convinced, for you, much better than a similar place south or west."[5] Booker T. Washington avoided the city as much as possible. "The office seeking atmosphere which seems to pervade the whole city disgusts me so very much," he wrote to Grimké, "that I can rarely stay there longer than I am absolutely compelled to do so."[6] Despite Washington's professed dislike of the city, he was a frequent visitor, as were many of the nation's black leaders who had causes to promote.

Nonetheless, the District had a good foundation for a social elite among its black residents. A few families had provided community leadership for several generations. The Wormleys began with a livery business in the early 1800s, progressed to catering, and ended as hoteliers during Reconstruction. The Syphaxes, who claimed descent from Martha Washington's grandson, were active in education in the District, and William Syphax was instrumental in creating the black high school in 1870. The Shadds, Francises, and Grays all began as restaurateurs and caterers, then educated their children to become doctors and pharmacists. Prominent in Washington black society in her later life, Mary Ann Shadd Cary became a teacher in Pennsylvania and New York before moving to Canada, where she established the *Provincial Freeman*, the first paper edited by a black woman in North America. She moved to Washington and began teaching in the Lincoln Industrial School, and in 1883 got a law degree from Howard University.[7]

Probably the most distinguished family in the District was that of John F. Cook. Cook established private schools for blacks in the mid–nineteenth century. By the 1880s, his son George F. T. Cook was serving as superintendent of the District's black public schools, a job he would hold for twenty-five years. John F. Cook Jr., who would ultimately serve as a trustee of Howard University for thirty-five years and as tax collector in the District, was thought to be the richest African American in Washington, partly as a result of his real estate investments. George W. Cook would serve as registrar of Howard University for ten years as part of his forty-year affiliation with the institution. Samuel LeCount Cook was on his way to becoming a prominent physician. Members of the Cook family served on the Board of Education and the Board of Trade, and held many other prominent positions.

Another well-known Washington family, the Terrells, originally hailed from Virginia. Harrison Terrell served as nurse-companion to Ulysses S. Grant, worked for the banker George W. Riggs, and served in the Department of the Interior for twenty years. His son, Robert H. Terrell, graduated from Harvard, would teach at M Street High School and later become its principal, and was getting a law degree at Howard University. Terrell would complete his law career as a municipal judge. His future wife, Mary Church, who moved to Washington in the late 1880s and was teaching Latin at M Street when they met, was the daughter of one of the first black millionaires, Robert R. Church of Memphis.[8]

The Grimké family consisted of the noted author and lecturer Archibald H. Grimké; his activist minister brother, Francis J. Grimké; Francis's wife, Charlotte Forten Grimké, the famous abolitionist granddaughter of James Forten of Philadelphia; and Archibald's daughter, Angelina Weld Grimké, named for her white great-aunt, Angelina Grimké, who married the abolitionist Theodore Weld. All of the Grimkés achieved national recognition for their racial uplift efforts.

The backbone of the elite consisted of families that had distinguished backgrounds, in Washington or elsewhere, and achieved prominence in each generation. Thus Ionia Rollin Whipper, "a staunch figure in Washington's black haute bourgeoisie," was the daughter of Frances Rollin, one of the beautiful Rollin sisters of Charleston, South Carolina, all of whom were activists for the cause of women's rights, education, and civil rights for blacks during Reconstruction. Their father, William Rollin, had been a businessman of some note, and had avoided many of the humiliations that even free blacks had had to face.[9] Other notable District family names included Purvis, Cardozo, Menard, McKinlay, and Murray.

Three major black politicians made their homes in Washington at the end of the nineteenth century. P. B. S. Pinchback, a black political broker and former acting governor of Louisiana, spent much time in the District and moved permanently to Washington in 1893; he remained there until his death. His daughter Nina lived in the District, and her son Jean Toomer would later portray Washington black society life in his novel *Cane*.[10] Blanche K. Bruce, of Mississippi, the first black U.S. senator to serve a complete term, also remained in Washington after Reconstruction. He married a society woman from Cleveland, Josephine Willson, and the two entertained frequently. Their son, Roscoe Conkling Bruce, named in honor of the senator who escorted Blanche K. Bruce to his seat in the Senate, went on to become a Harvard graduate and assistant superintendent of colored schools.

The District's most famous black denizen was Frederick Douglass, who lived at Cedar Hill, his home in Anacostia. He inspired others of the black Four Hundred to move to Anacostia, and was regarded as the leader of black society until his death in 1895. Though Douglass preferred to avoid the more vacuous socialites, he did entertain select groups and participated in cultural programs. His sons by his first marriage, Lewis and Charles, were even more prominently involved in Washington society than their father. These families and a few others served as the foundation for Washington's black elite.

In the 1880s, Washington's elite blacks wished recognition of their elite status in the white community. For this reason they felt the need to distinguish themselves from the rest of the black community through their manners and behavior. They also felt the need to correct what they considered unsuitable behavior that reflected poorly on the race. They preached etiquette to the masses in the local newspapers. The great debate over elite involvement in Emancipation Day celebrations was a part of this tendency to stress etiquette. Throughout the 1880s they scorned the overenthusiastic crowds, and by the early 1890s, black elites complained that the parades had become too rowdy and stereotypically disorganized among the masses to be dignified by their participation. Gradually all the important people dropped out of the organizational committees.[11]

Distaste for working-class behavior would continue through the turn of the century. In 1898 the *Bee* stated that one of the obstacles to race progress was indifference to appearances at home and in the streets, especially the habit of hanging one's head out of a window. "The habit, however, is confined mainly to the more ignorant class, who while they are no less intelligent than the average white person, are discriminated against for the very good reason that they do not observe proper appearances in their homes and not merely because they are colored." The editor, W. Calvin Chase, went so far as to say that if blacks would cease the offensive practice, they could obtain better housing. The *Bee* also admonished parents who sent their children out to Marine Band concerts "with bare feet, hair not combed, faces not washed, and what is more, these children behave the more rudely and unbecomingly than any of the rest."[12]

Another way in which the Four Hundred attempted to distinguish themselves from the black masses was through refinement and by avoiding conspicuous consumption. The elite scorned the gaudy furnishings and outrageous manners common among the nouveau riche and social climbers, and praised simple good taste. Elite blacks still considered appearances important, nonetheless; as Archibald Grimké reminded his brother and sister-in-law when they were preparing his daughter for boarding school, a friend of Angelina's had advised him that "the treatment which will be accorded her by all will be at once felt favorably if she be well dressed. If she appears at once to be a young girl of refined manners & tastes & used to the best Society, & this the general style of her dress contributes much to [prove], she will be treated quite differently [than] if her dress were indicative of a lower position in the social scale, & other associations."[13] Mary Church Terrell also realized the importance of appearances when she wrote: "Alas I can never finish shopping & spending money all the time but the children must appear well and so must I."[14]

In purely social activities the elite blacks tried to distance themselves from the black masses as much as possible. They established exclusive social circles and passed their recreational time in stereotypical elite activities: they indulged their tastes and demonstrated their cultural refinement by patronizing the theater, attending lectures, and sponsoring musical programs. Though excluded from most white social circles, elite blacks adopted the "genteel performance" that most elite whites practiced at the turn of the century. They belonged to exclusive clubs, vacationed in secluded resorts, and created a culturally and intellectually stimulating social life in the District.

In the 1880s, black society members sometimes ate lunch or dinner at public restaurants. Lunching at the restaurant underneath the House of Representatives was a privilege only the elite dared exercise. In the early eighties the problem appeared to be discrimination against black patrons by black waiters. The *Bee* reported that blacks who dined at the restaurant received better treatment from the white waiters.[15] This discourtesy, extended to men and women alike, was upsetting and divisive to the black community, but the black waiters had their reasons. In the 1860s and 1870s a black waiter in a predominantly white restaurant, particularly a headwaiter, had a status comparable to that formerly enjoyed by house slaves vis-à-vis field slaves. These waiters gained prestige in proportion to the importance of their white clientele. To have then to serve another black person was a reminder of their true status as servants, and undoubtedly did damage to the waiter's self-image. This impression was furthered by white bosses who did not mind alienating black customers. Hence the reluctance to serve black patrons.

Excluded from white social clubs, the elite blacks inevitably formed their own. One of the earliest elite social clubs, formed during Reconstruction, was the Lotus Club, composed largely of mulatto servants, waiters, and coachmen. The group attempted to keep out full-blooded blacks, but since many of these people held important positions, the group decided to widen its membership. Most members of the Lotus Club were newcomers to Washington who hoped to replace the old citizens as the new social elite. The club had close connections to the management of the Freedmen's Bank. It was the subject of much criticism by the press, particularly by the *Bee,* and it soon disbanded. W. Calvin Chase noted that a few members, such as William H. Bruce, John F. Cook, and George F. T. Cook, had retained their dignity by recognizing that the criteria that the Lotus Club used to identify society members were so arbitrary that they allowed people of dubious moral reputation to join the elite.[16]

Other early social clubs, such as the Sparta Club, the Columbia Social Club, and the Diamondback Club, were less pretentious. In the late 1880s, the two key social clubs in the city were the Manhattan, established in 1888, and the Acanthus, started in 1889. The Manhattan Club consisted mostly of newer residents in the District, and the Acanthus Club catered largely to longtime residents.[17]

Formal and informal elite organizations devoted to the arts continued social distinctions. In the 1880s, the musical Carreno Club was "exceedingly careful in admitting to membership only those who [were] congenial in taste and of established social standing." The group performed works by Beethoven, Chopin, Josephy, and Gottschalk. On Friday nights a similarly refined but informal Art Club met at the home of Francis and Archibald Grimké. The group met from eight to ten P.M. to discuss such subjects as Italian art, and assigned readings on which members were quizzed.[18]

Elite blacks also formed exclusive literary organizations. Students at Howard University had formed the Eureka Literary Society in 1872. At first the "Literary" in the club's name was an overstatement, but within a decade the members had begun to debate substantial topics. Another of the earliest serious scholarly circles in Washington was the Chautauqua Literary Scientific Circle, founded in December 1882. The group, which included the black bibliophile John W. Cromwell, discussed both history and race topics.[19]

Not all literary societies—or "literaries," as they were known—were devoted exclusively to race topics. Perhaps the crème de la crème of literaries in the early 1880s was the Monday Night Literary Society. The closing meeting of the 1882–83 season was held at Cedar Hill by invitation of Frederick Douglass himself. Among those attending were notables from the local schools, Howard University professors, and representatives of leading families such as the Cooks and Grimkés. The meeting lasted from 4 to 8 P.M. on the croquet lawn and grounds, and in addition to hearing a review of the year's activities, the guests were entertained with music and supper until 10 P.M. Francis J. Grimké presided.[20]

Conspicuously absent from this group was John W. Cromwell, who probably was referring to the Monday Night Literary when he wrote of a certain group that discussed only literature in its parlors and drawing rooms and had no real impact on the race. In order to join, said Cromwell, you had to be of a certain social group. "There was no large class who had acquired the habit of listening quietly from week to week to papers of unusual literary and scholarly merit and then witnessing merciless assaults upon them to be parried with skill or repulsed with thrilling eloquence."[21]

This vacuum was filled with the establishment of the Bethel Literary and Historical Society. Focusing largely on racial topics, the Bethel Literary foreshadowed later developments within the black elite. Founded in 1881 as an adjunct of the Union Bethel African Methodist Episcopal (AME) Church, the organization did much to raise the elite's consciousness of their common bonds with their race, but it was one of the few organizations of the 1880s to do so, while still maintaining the genteel performance.

Many values that the members of the black elite passed on to their children were reinforced by the ministers of the churches they chose to attend. Prominent African Americans joined for worship in several exclusive churches distinguished by their membership and frequent mention in the black press. The Fifteenth Street Presbyterian Church, where Francis J. Grimké served as pastor after 1878, was probably the premier religious establishment in the city, but elites also attended the Union Bethel AME, which became the Metropolitan AME; the Nineteenth Street Baptist; St. Luke's Protestant Episcopal, where Alexander Crummell was minister; and several smaller churches. The few Catholic elites attended St. Augustine's. All of these churches were located in the more exclusive black sections of Northwest Washington. The churches played an important role in the lives of the black elite. Most attended services regularly, participated in church activities, and belonged to church-affiliated groups. Since church affiliation was closely allied to social status, the attitudes and programs of elite churches reflected the situation of the black elite.

In the 1880s debate centered on differentiating elite churches from those of the black masses, part of the effort to achieve assimilation. Since the black minister was often the leader of his community, elite blacks sought to install ministers who reflected the increased educational opportunities for the race. They wanted a religion that would speak to earthly as well as spiritual issues, and hoped to move beyond the old-time slave religion with its emphasis on rewards in the world to come.

The path to the formation of elite congregations followed that of the development of the elite itself. After Reconstruction, the black church had been the leading source of information on how to better oneself. The church played the role of teacher of morals to the masses, and the minister was expected to set the example. Elite black churches became preoccupied with the manners and morals needed to distance oneself from the lower elements of black society, and were particularly obsessive about setting an example of proper conduct. Black elite churchgoers were encouraged in these ideas by their contact with white northern missionaries who believed that the only way the "Negro Problem" could be solved was through teaching blacks the correct morals and rules of behavior.

By stressing proper behavior, the elite churches hoped to distinguish themselves from the more emotional working-class black churches, to which whites pointed as typical indications of why blacks could never assimilate with sedate white society. Washington's elite black ministers and their congregations constantly tried to impress upon the white community that they were different from other blacks, that not all blacks were given to loud emotional outbursts and fainting spells in church. If they demonstrated that religious practices were no more remarkable in black churches than in white, then surely whites would accept them as social equals. Besides, intellectual sermons and sedate services provided yet another way to distinguish the elite from the nonelite. Episcopal and Presbyterian churches, which stressed sedate worship, held great appeal for elite blacks.

It is therefore not surprising that in 1923, when Francis J. Grimké outlined what his goals had been when he took up the pastorate at Fifteenth Street Presbyterian in 1878, he emphasized the church's role in setting a moral example. It is also not surprising that the moral values he embraced were largely those of white Victorian America. He had sought to be, among other things, a strong advocate of temperance, a practice he himself had long followed. He had sought to make the home "the center of all that is best and noblest in thought and sentiment, in character and life; of the careful, painstaking, conscientious effort on the part of parents to train their children." He had tried to create a healthy moral public sentiment and encourage purity in the community. He had stressed the importance of punctuality and regular church attendance. He had tried to avoid internal dissention and to stand up for the rights of African Americans. He encouraged the development of the race through the building of individual character. He had both taught these principles and tried to live his own life in accordance with them.[22] Character was the key to racial uplift, as Grimké saw it. Without respectability and self-respect, the race could not be expected to rise.

The records of the Fifteenth Street Presbyterian and the Metropolitan AME make it clear that they closely monitored the behavior of their communicants in the late nineteenth century. The boards of both churches frequently held discussions about the "spiritual condition" of the institutions as well as their financial situation.[23] The boards also settled disputes between members of the congregations. It was the job of the church to minimize divisions in the community and keep them from becoming public embarrassments. By monitoring the behavior of their congregations, elite churches were able to create distinct characters that reflected the attitudes of the black elite as a whole.[24]

Elite churches were distinct from mass churches in several ways. Most tended to be urban churches with large congregations. As such they were less likely to have white supervision and more likely to concentrate on the immediate needs of the congregation. Whereas the rural church focused on preparing for the next world, the urban church focused on making this world a better place. Urban elites criticized rural ministers for retreating to folk religiosity, with its emotional excesses. They saw that type of religion as escapism that weakened the social protest efforts of their own churches. Not for them the shouts and spiritual enthusiasm at which the whites sniggered.[25]

The distinction between rural and working-class emotional theology and that of the urban elite rational churches was the central debate within elite churches in the 1880s in Washington. Increasingly the District's black church members were educated professionals who demanded more from their ministers than jeremiads and emotionalism. Since many of the elite were formerly free blacks, they had begun to assimilate the white churches' standards of behavior. They wanted intelligent sermons, staid music, and less ostentatious collection methods. And since they felt more in control of their personal status, they wanted fewer warnings against personal sin and more ideas about how to reform the behavior of others.[26] Churches became increasingly divided between conservatives, who clung to the old-time religion, and progressives, who looked for a more intellectual way to worship. Elite blacks fell largely in the progressive category, as having an intellectual minister was one more way to distinguish themselves from the masses.

At St. Luke's Protestant Episcopal Church the congregation had already moved in this direction under the leadership of its intellectual minister, Alexander Crummell. St. Luke's had, as a result, become the ideal for elite churches to follow in Washington. The same debate within Union Bethel AME, however, led to a split in the congregation and the ultimate reorganization of the church as Metropolitan AME.

As a mainstream church known for its more sedate style of worship, Union Bethel AME attracted many members of Washington's black elite.[27] The

Simms family was prominent in its membership. John A. Simms Sr. and his wife, Martha Ann Simms, were devoted founding church members, and John A. Simms Jr. was class leader, trustee, and president of the choir.[28] The Simmses, as one of Washington's leading black families, tried to ensure that the church reflected the needs of its congregation, and so became involved in the controversy over the pastorate of the Reverend John W. Stevenson and the completion of a new church.

John W. Stevenson was transferred from the New Jersey Conference to Union Bethel AME in 1880 for the specific purpose of building a new church and raising money for it. No one could question his ability to raise funds, but his methods "occasioned much friction and disgust in Washington."[29] The more progressive church members frowned on blatant fund-raising and the erection of grand edifices as signs of a backward church, concerned only with its own importance rather than with the well-being of its members. Stevenson catered to the more conservative, less "cultured" members of the congregation. After one year, a committee petitioned Bishop Daniel Alexander Payne and the Baltimore Annual Conference for Stevenson's removal, believing that his return would "be detrimental to the church, both financially and spiritually." No official complaint was made against the pastor, however, and Payne did not give the committee a hearing.[30]

The elite members of the congregation were so dissatisfied that at least 150 of them severed their ties with Union Bethel. Sixty-three of these people left to form what would become Plymouth Congregational Church. In 1882, Plymouth Congregational attached itself to the New Jersey Association of Congregational Churches, and in 1887 built a new church at the corner of 17th and P Streets. Sterling N. Brown took over the church as minister in 1889, by which time the church had truly evolved from the Methodist to the Congregational theology. Others who left Union Bethel joined the Israel Colored Methodist Episcopal (CME) Church.[31] Despite the schisms in the Union Bethel congregation, the cornerstone of a new building was laid in 1881.

During Stevenson's second year, other conflicts arose. The Bethel Literary and Historical Association began to take on a life of its own. At first all of its officers were church members, but as the debates began to draw a large and prestigious audience from outside the church, demands for a different leadership were heard. W. Calvin Chase editorialized in the *Bee:* "Observing [friends] of this association have for some time noticed the growing tendency to restrict and contract the high purposes of its founding to denominational man worship and glorification. The fact has been lost sight of that an intelligent general public and men and women outside of church denomination have made the Bethel Literary Association a success." Chase also objected that only those speakers whose views were in accordance with Stevenson's were recognized when they sought to join the discussion.[32] As John W. Cromwell noted, the character of the audience had changed from the "brothers and sisters of the 'amen corner'" to some of the most progressive and educated elements of Washington society who were not in sympathy with the current outlook of Union Bethel under its fund-raiser pastor.[33] The controversy further split the congregation and caused an identity crisis over what it meant to be an elite church.

Stevenson, according to several accounts, decided that since he could no longer control the Literary, he would disband it by forbidding use of church property for its meetings. Such was the influence of the progressive members of the elite, however, that the Bethel Literary endured and Stevenson's pastorate did not. By the end of his second year, Stevenson had alienated so many people in the congregation that even Bishop Payne wanted him removed. Stevenson still had a following among the more conservative members of Union Bethel, and they left the church with him to found the Central Methodist Church in 1882. Amidst great turmoil, James A. Handy succeeded Stevenson. Perhaps hoping for a fresh outlook, the church voted to change its name to the Metropolitan AME. The congregation spent most of the next decade readjusting to its new outlook. After the completion of the new building in 1886, the church began to resume its preeminent position among the black elite, becoming known as the "National Cathedral of African Methodism." As indications of its prominence, Frederick Douglass's funeral and Howard University's commencement exercises were held there.[34]

The second of Washington's most prestigious black churches, the Nineteenth Street Baptist Church, faced fewer disputes between progressive and conservative elements. Baptists were better protected from internal divisions because of the democratic structure of their organization. If a group of parishioners in a Baptist church desired to split from the congregation, they could easily form a new congregation without the need to apply for formal permission. This situation had it drawbacks. In cities as large as Washington, schismatic movements developed, and since the churches essentially appealed to the same community, hostilities often endured. In the 1870s, members of the Nineteenth Street Baptist Church splintered to form the Metropolitan, Vermont Avenue, and Berean Baptist churches, partly in protest against ministers, partly because the Baptist population of Washington was expanding rapidly and required other churches.[35] The expansion of the Baptist population was partly responsible for the survival of Nineteenth Street.

Most elite blacks, believing that Episcopal and Presbyterian churches were more highbrow, did not typically belong to Baptist churches, but the Nineteenth Street Church was an exception. It gained a reputation as an elite church with the appointment of the Reverend Walter H. Brooks, who took over the pastorate in 1882 and served there for over fifty years. Dr. Brooks was a progressive Baptist with a firm belief in an educated clergy and citizenry. As such he endeared himself and his church to black high society.

The large concentration of educated African Americans in Washington gave the city's black elite definite advantages. Mary Ann Shadd Cary called Washington "the Capital of the Country[,] the central point of national hopes and aspirations," and "the Mecca of the colored pilgrim seeking civil religious social and business enlightenment, and preferment or protection." The most promising institutions, according to Shadd Cary, were the schools: "The public colored schools of Washington steadily and determinedly brought to their present standard of excellence by colored men alone is the grain of salt to keep intact the civilization and enlightenment of this forty-thousand mass until the other appliances religious and political are wheeled into line by the growing intelligence and comprehension of the masses."[36]

Without a doubt, the District's black public schools became the best of their kind in the country. Families often moved to Washington to give their children the opportunity to attend them. Washington was in this respect unusual, since the best black schools in other southern cities tended to be denominational. Elite black education had a long tradition in Washington. In the early nineteenth century there was less opposition to education for blacks than in the years before the Civil War. Early students tended to be privileged, however. Children of prosperous free blacks and servants of prominent families or government officials attended private schools established by free blacks or benevolent whites. One of the earliest black schools in the District was the Union Seminary School, established by John F. Cook Sr., on H Street near 14th Street, NW. The school's curriculum included reading, composition, recitation, sculpture, physiology, and health. The building was partly destroyed by riots in the 1830s but was rebuilt, and after Cook's death in 1855 it was continued by his sons until the public schools opened.[37]

After an act of Congress created the public school system in 1864, the black schools of Washington and Georgetown were organized under a black board of trustees. In 1874 this board was consolidated with three others to create a nineteen-member board of trustees for all of the District schools. After Washington lost home rule in 1879, the District commissioners appointed the board members, and the black and white schools came under separate superintendents. George F. T. Cook, one of the sons of John F. Cook Sr., was appointed superintendent of colored schools, a position he held until the schools were reorganized in 1900. Both the black and white schools were directly responsible to the Board of Trustees, on which it was customary for three black men to serve; after 1895, women served also. The school system became an early magnet for black teachers, as salaries were relatively high, the segregated school system diminished the effects of discrimination, and the amenities of Washington black society provided an attractive way of life for teachers. By 1869, half of the teachers in the black schools were African American, and by 1901 the last white teacher would withdraw.[38]

The centerpiece of this system was the black Preparatory High School, established in 1870, two years before the establishment of a white public high school. From the beginning, the high school offered a classical curriculum and aimed to prepare children of the elite for a university education. Its aims ran counter to the prevailing white notion of the position of blacks in American society at the turn of the century.

Those students who wished to become teachers attended Myrtilla Miner Normal School, established first as a private school in 1851 as a "genteel school for missus of color." It was the first school of its kind in the country dedicated to teacher training. Myrtilla Miner was an abolitionist and feminist who instilled the value of education to racial uplift in her students. The school closed in 1860 but was reopened under government auspices in 1863 and became a part of Howard University in the 1870s. After operating briefly on an independent basis again, by the late 1880s it was absorbed into the District black school system.[39] In the 1880s many of the District's black teachers were graduates of Myrtilla Miner; by the turn of the century native-born teachers faced increasing competition from outside applicants.

Upon graduation from the high school, if children of the elite were not going into teaching, as most black elite women did, they had several choices. Many chose to go to northern universities such as Oberlin, Dartmouth, Harvard, and Yale, perhaps after a few years at a private preparatory school in the

Northeast. These students often faced discrimination from university administrations, but in general they managed to form friendships with other black students and in many cases with white students as well. These relationships formed the basis for networks across the country and could provide a foundation for later political connections. Some chose to attend one of the many black universities, such as Fisk, Wilberforce, or Atlanta. Howard University, in Washington, was one of the best black universities in the country. Although the administration of Howard was biracial and no black president served there until the 1920s, the Howard community provided a mostly congenial atmosphere for both students and professors. It was here that many blacks studied medicine, law, and education, as few professional schools admitted African Americans. Like the public school system, Howard attracted some of the leading black intellectuals of the time. Few women held other than administrative positions at Howard, however; to most men, "female intellectual" was a contradiction in terms. The university offered cultural and intellectual programs to the local black community and its professors made up a key part of the black elite.

Howard also helped the community financially. The university used the income from its shares in the Aetna Fire Insurance Company, worth about $20,000 in 1873, as security for loans for itself and for District institutions, primarily black churches. Beginning in the mid-1880s, Howard made a series of such loans, including $8,000 to Shiloh Baptist and $7,000 to the elite Plymouth Congregational.[40] Such loans cemented the relationship of the university and the black community, promoting united efforts toward racial uplift and establishing Howard as an important institution.

Yet the situation at Howard mirrored that in the public schools to some extent. The white-dominated board of trustees attempted on many occasions to force a manual training curriculum on Howard. Although the faculty generally united in opposition to the plan, some outspoken professors faced discrimination from the white president of the university. Perhaps in retaliation, professors in applied sciences with ties to Tuskegee faced discrimination from the black deans and other faculty members. Howard's black intellectuals were successful for the most part in holding off compromises in the curriculum, but paranoia about curriculum reform made Howard University resist modernizing its curriculum until long after other universities across the country had done so.

As education became increasingly available to elite blacks, more traditional upper-class occupations became open to them, but in the 1880s occupational choice was often limited. As a result, distinctions between elite and working-class occupations often depended on arbitrary characteristics. In the early nineteenth century free blacks had chosen occupations that had ties to distinctions created under slavery. For the most part, elite blacks entered occupations such as catering, restaurant service, or running a barbershop, which corresponded with the services once provided by house slaves. The social distinctions that had accompanied occupations during slavery lingered on.

As a border city, Washington held greater opportunities for economic advancement for African Americans throughout the Progressive Era than any other city in the South. The government provided clerkships, the school system and Howard University offered teaching positions, and the press required editors and printers, not to mention the fact that the size of the black community was large enough to support a limited professional class. The boom in the building trades to accommodate the influx of people during the Civil War provided opportunities for black contractors and architects.

Before the Civil War, the number of free blacks was so small that black businessmen had to serve whites as well as blacks to survive. Elite blacks often found more prestige in business enterprises that catered to whites exclusively. Nonetheless, changing objective conditions after the Civil War brought new attitudes. Reconstruction brought many business opportunities. An early and successful type of black business venture was providing places to stay for visiting elite relatives and race leaders. White hotels in Washington were not willing to allow blacks to register, and those that did were inferior. The most famous black hotelier was James A. Wormley. Like other early members of the elite, Wormley began as a steward and caterer in the family business. In 1871 he established the Wormley Hotel, one of the finest hotels, black or white, in the District. A brilliant businessman, intelligent and good looking, James Wormley was bound to be successful. Even before he established the hotel he had amassed a fortune of $87,000 from his family's catering and livery businesses.[41] Wormley provided service almost exclusively to whites, and prospered in the 1880s and 1890s before selling the hotel. He passed on his fortune and business acumen to his sons, who ran other ventures in the District.

In the same year the Wormley Hotel opened its doors, John Chamberlain opened a hostelry a half block from a prominent boardinghouse on Capitol Hill. A Washingtonian later recalled that Chamberlain's was to Washington what Delmonico's was to New York, complete with poker game. To Chamberlain's hostelry came prominent blacks and whites, including Mark Twain and Buffalo Bill Cody. Very often black politicos would send envoys to Chamberlain's "upon the very delicate mission of negotiating a quart bottle."[42] The sort of hotel and hostelry business that flourished during Reconstruction, however, depended on the patronage of both blacks and whites, a declining possibility by the 1890s. But even at the turn of the century some of the wealthiest blacks still owned businesses that catered to whites.[43]

After the Civil War, the establishment of black universities such as Howard and more liberal admissions policies at white universities made it possible for some members of the next generation of elites to prepare to enter the professions. During Reconstruction, the legal profession took on great importance for blacks, who saw it as a stepping-stone to politics. At this time a great many black men also trained for the ministry—a field that would remain open to blacks as long as there were black churches.[44]

The profession most in demand in the nineteenth century, however, was teaching. Denied entry to white schools, blacks realized that they needed men and women to train others of their race, and to prepare them for the few colleges that would accept blacks. Thus the Preparatory High School immediately hired its first graduating class to teach the other classes. Elite blacks were particularly concerned about providing their children with a good early education to prepare them for professional training and acceptance at one of the better universities.

While some elite blacks did enter professional occupations, not all of these professions brought upper-class status in the white community. Black teachers and ministers gained an inordinate amount of prestige in the nineteenth century in relation to their economic status, particularly after the Civil War, when both were in great demand by the masses of newly freed blacks in the South. To the black community, the teachers and ministers were the leaders of the race—symbols of the future. They were to uplift the rest of the race by imparting to other blacks the knowledge or wisdom their education had provided them. However, members of these professions were often too involved in the problems of day-to-day life to spearhead movements for social reform. Teachers in rural communities were often tied to the church and could not venture into areas of social reform that might undermine its influence. In urban areas, teachers became so overloaded with work that they had little time to participate in any uplift effort beyond their teaching. Thus, when the numbers of other black professionals available to lead the community increased at the turn of the century, teachers would relinquish their symbolic roles, perhaps even gratefully.[45]

Of all the professions in which elite blacks participated, the one unique to Washington was employment in the federal government. The civil service gave two things to a black employee: economic security and the prestige of white-collar employment. Elite blacks often sought government employment to bolster their income. Black professionals, many of whom could not fully support their families by their professional practices alone, found the civil service especially appealing. Others depended on presidential and other official appointments as their sole source of income, creating Washington's unique official subelite.

One such member of the black elite, John A. Simms Sr., spent his entire life in government service. In 1849 he worked as a messenger in the Navy Department. After a two-year stay in California, he returned to the Navy Department in 1853, and remained there until at least 1867. In that year he was appointed commissioner of elections, Second Precinct, First Ward. He served as commissioner of the Washington Asylum in 1869 and again in 1871. Simms was a steward in the Executive Mansion from 1877 until 1880, during the administration of Rutherford B. Hayes. From 1880 to 1882 he served as an Army private, assigned to the Ordnance Department. After his discharge he remained in that department as a messenger until his retirement in 1913. In the years between, he served as a member of several inauguration committees.[46] Civil service could become almost a family business. Simms's grandson, John A. Simms III, a Graphotype machine operator for the Pan American Union, would later serve as a personal messenger to J. W. Hoover in the Office of Public Buildings and Public Parks of the Nation's Capital.[47]

While some blacks were professional civil servants, others gained appointments through meritorious service or through influential connections. Blanche K. Bruce's confidential secretary for twenty-seven years, George C. Smith, was appointed to the Treasury Department shortly after Bruce's death. H. C. Harris, who trained as a jockey while a slave in Kentucky, settled in Washington in 1881. There he caught the attention of several important horse fanciers, and by 1898 he was an attaché at the McKinley White House, in charge of a string of horses.[48] As early as 1883, the *Bee* noted that most young men who were government employees tried to better themselves through education, especially in law, medicine, and theology.[49] Many a member of the Washington elite supported his studies at Howard University through government employment.

The prestige the black community accorded to federal employees was hardly commensurate with the nature of their employment. In 1882 W. Calvin Chase, always the watchdog against discriminatory practices, editorialized in the *Bee* against the abuse of black government messengers, clerks, and laborers. These employees, he wrote, were treated as personal flunkies and forced to do menial labor for chiefs of divisions—waiting on tables, cleaning houses, putting down carpets, shoveling coal. Many of these workers saw the government building where they were officially employed only on payday. Chase called these practices a new kind of slavery because the employees were afraid of losing their jobs if they spoke out. The following year Chase noted that few blacks served in high positions in the civil service outside the regular executive departments. Washington had only one black letter carrier, two black firemen, and five black policemen (but no black detectives), and if the new U.S. marshal, Clayton McMichael, prevailed, there would be no blacks left outside the executive departments.[50]

Not all government agencies were so harsh. In 1882 the *Bee* pointed out several that treated blacks fairly. Sterling P. Rounds, the public printer, was one official with a positive attitude toward blacks. He removed Democrats from under him and appointed men who treated blacks fairly, including one who "never discharged any man, white or black, for any cause, without first hearing both sides of the question." The *Bee* also noted that the Pension Office under Colonel W. W. Dudley was one place where blacks were treated as human.[51] But such praise was often showered on new appointees, perhaps in an effort to pressure them to avoid discrimination against blacks. In any case, federal employment, while bringing a steady income and social status in the black community, was certainly not an upper-class occupation in the traditional sense.

Frequently denied a sense of fulfillment in their employment, many elite black men turned to secret societies to foster a sense of importance and to find a congenial atmosphere apart from the rest of the black community. Groups such as the Masons and the Odd Fellows offered them the chance to belong to a restrictive organization in which they could relax without worrying about societal pressures. In the nineteenth century, membership in these organizations separated the "respectable" people from the "nonrespectable" ones.

Black fraternal organizations had existed since the eighteenth century. Part of their appeal was that they offered a private place for men to congregate that excluded nonmembers in much the way that white organizations excluded African Americans. Such a psychological advantage helped counteract the humiliation that members of the black elite experienced in society at large. Another important reason for membership was that the secret societies stressed manhood in their rituals and impressed upon their members a strong sense of masculinity. For black elite men this aspect was particularly attractive, since they faced symbolic emasculation from white society every day.[52]

Some fraternal orders were established to assist working-class blacks with burials and death benefits; black Freemasonry, in contrast, began as a movement among the elite and only in the late nineteenth century became less exclusive. Prince Hall of Boston, reputedly a free black, applied for a charter for a lodge of black Freemasons in Massachusetts. When the Grand Lodge of Massachusetts would not grant him a charter, Hall obtained one from the Grand Lodge of England in 1784 and thus established Prince Hall Masonry in the United States. Freemasonry embraced the Enlightenment ideas that influenced the American Revolution, most important of them the equality of all men. This ideology made Freemasonry attractive to free blacks who wanted to socialize as equals with elite whites. Freemasonry may have created ideological ties with the white elite, but unfortunately most white Masons were not willing to accept blacks as their equals. The rejection of black Masons by the white lodges did much to promote racial consciousness.

Segregated though it was, Freemasonry offered many benefits to elite blacks. Since economic distinctions between elite and working-class blacks were not clear, membership in any group that attempted to exclude persons who lacked refinement gave a boost to one's social status. In the beginning, black Masons were unwilling to offer insurance to its members simply because working-class fraternal orders usually did.

Freemasonry had traditionally been a means of connecting traveling artisans with a network of friends across the country, and in much the same way it became a way of connecting isolated black elites with their fellows in other cities. Freemasonry not only became a source of race consciousness but promoted the creation of a national black elite that could work together for common goals.[53]

The first black Masonic lodge in the District was established in 1846, and in 1848 three lodges joined to form the first black grand lodge of the District of Columbia. John F. Cook Sr. served as one of the lodge's earliest grand masters, and William H. Bruce served as deputy grand master of the District lodge.[54] Other prominent nineteenth-century leaders joined the Masons in their home states and continuted to be active after moving to Washington. All were active to some extent in national politics, and all were members of the same social set.

It is possible that for nineteenth-century black leaders, Freemasonry also provided access to political circles, or at least was a prerequisite to gaining political acceptance. In the revolutionary era almost all the Founding Fathers were Masons, and although most white politicians dropped out of the order, Prince Hall Masons appear to have kept the revolutionary spirit alive into Reconstruction.

Although elite blacks in the 1880s made many efforts to distinguish themselves from working-class blacks, they still recognized their unique cultural heritage. Both in the media and in their personal correspondence, elite blacks revealed a strong sense of racial pride, even when they were trying to distance themselves from less respectable representatives of their socially designated race. In 1882, when a southerner commented that the black race would deteriorate without whites to teach them, the *Bee* responded that since there would also be fewer mulatto children, the race would actually be stronger.[55] Such statements revealed that the elite did not necessarily see race in itself as a handicap. They believed that they could achieve the same goals as whites could if they had the opportunity to do so. If white society discriminated against African Americans, it did so through ignorance. The color of one's skin should be a source of pride rather than humiliation.

The *Bee* was fierce in its defense of blackness throughout the 1880s, particularly on the subject of skin bleaching. An 1883 editorial told of a Chinese girl in London with blotchy dark skin of a yellow cast who, instead of trying to change her complexion, chose clothing in colors to complement it. According to the *Bee*, she was a huge social success and appeared very sophisticated.[56] The black press often gave such morality lessons to express disapproval of blacks who attempted to become more "white." Chase reported that at one white church he saw at least three black women powdered up and pretending to be white. The *Bee* also criticized the teacher Anna J. Cooper for her casting in an improvised drama. Apparently a fair-skinned girl played the queen, and two dark-skinned girls played her ladies-in-waiting.[57] Chase's criticisms reveal that a distinct preference for lighter skin was common among the black elite, and ironically, the *Bee* itself regularly carried advertising for hair straighteners and skin bleaches.

This preference did not usually prevail in the matter of interracial marriage, however. Frederick Douglass's marriage to a white woman sparked a new debate on marriage between the races. The society column of the *Bee*, which in the 1880s consisted of a series of letters between "Clara" and "Louise," showed the issues involved in 1884. Louise reported to Clara that she had attended a service at the Fifteenth Street Presbyterian Church (where the couple had married), and many people snubbed Douglass and his new wife. Louise defended Douglass's marriage to a white woman, but believed that Helen Douglass was not their social equal: "While I have no objections to him marrying whom he pleased, I do object to him forcing his bride upon our society."[58]

Many of the District's black elite believed that Douglass had become a traitor to his race when he married a white woman. They saw the marriage as implying that white women were somehow more desirable than black women. Douglass's sons did not approve of the marriage either, but whether their attitude was prompted by Helen Douglass's race, her access to the family's money, or their loyalty to the memory of their mother is uncertain. What is clear is that many people in the black community believed Douglass was setting a poor example. Nonetheless, Douglass did have supporters in Washington, including Francis J. Grimké, who married the couple, and Blanche K. Bruce, Richard T. Greener, and the physician Charles B. Purvis, all of whom were his personal friends.[59]

The controversy surrounding Douglass's marriage to a white woman had as much to do with maintaining social standards, however, as with maintaining racial integrity. Most elite blacks in the 1880s still cherished their relationships with prominent whites as imparting prominence to themselves in proportion to the status of their white friends. While few would have wanted his sister to marry one of them, many believed that lighter skin was a mark of social distinction, and chose their partners and friends accordingly.

Nannie Helen Burroughs found that her dark skin and strongly African features in combination with her undistinguished family background worked to her social disadvantage. Washington black society snubbed her in the 1880s. Perhaps for that reason, Burroughs never sought to interact socially with the black elite on her return in 1909, after she had gained national prominence for her work in the Baptist church and in national club circles.[60]

Burroughs frequently criticized the elite for their snobbery, and socially she remained apart.

Having come of age during Reconstruction, when race relations were in flux, elite blacks in the 1880s expected to assimilate into white society because of their kinship and cultural ties as well as the sensibilities that marked them as acceptable in polite society. Some of them clung to this hope up to the turn of the century. In the nineteenth century, elite blacks still attended mixed churches, but this situation existed only as long as race relations were relaxed. In 1883 the *Bee* had noted that the mixed congregations at St. Augustine's Roman Catholic Church on 15th Street and the Congregational church at 10th and G Streets would be good places to visit for those who did not believe in the possibility of equality. "High moral character, a well regulated supply of intellect, strict integrity, and a reasonable *bank account* will knock the very bung out of the keg of prejudice."[61] Such positive statements generally focused on churches attended by the elite, but in mixed congregations, the rise of prejudice would challenge even elite participation.

Because they believed they would ultimately assimilate, elite blacks scorned separate institutions in the 1880s if it was possible that they could still gain entry into equivalent white groups. Black doctors in particular expected that they could gain admittance to the American Medical Association, for example. In 1884, frustrated by the low numbers of black doctors who had been accepted, a group of black and white doctors formed the Medico-Chirurgical Society of the District of Columbia to provide protection and encouragement for black physicians. But most elite blacks saw a separate organization as inherently inferior and did not support it. As a result, the Medico-Chirurgical Society suffered from lack of interest and ceased meeting after several years.[62] Faith in the possibility of ultimate assimilation is what kept the black elite from uniting with the rest of the black community.

Black social status was precarious at best in the 1880s. In Washington those families that had assumed leadership positions based their status largely on idiosyncratic distinctions. Primary among these distinctions was free status before Emancipation. Free black families had been able to take advantage of opportunities not available to other African Americans. However, the ability to earn an income had meant only that these families could buy property, educate their children, and establish a lifestyle that went beyond mere subsistence. Occupation was not a significant factor in the equation of social status in the 1880s. Members of Washington's early black social elite were overwhelmingly in service occupations—barbering, catering, livery service. Nor was high income a qualification, for even the richest blacks were middle-class by white standards. With economic opportunities so severely curtailed for blacks, the size of one's salary was less important than its reliability. For this reason, many minor clerks in the federal government assumed social status in the black community out of proportion to their income and the importance of their positions. Thus, by all definitions, black social status had little to do with economic status.

What defined the distinct group to which other blacks and even some whites attributed high social status in the 1880s? Entry to this group could be gained for a variety of reasons—family connections, education, skin color, special contributions to racial uplift. Washington's black social elite in the 1880s were peculiarly clannish, and most of the leading black families prided themselves on their ancestry, both black and white. They used their political and professional connections with the white community to bolster their own social status and to differentiate themselves from the rest of their race. Since elite blacks were de facto leaders of their community, looked to by the majority of their race for guidance and patronage, they saw themselves as in the vanguard of the movement toward social equality. Once they had been accepted by the white community as individuals and raised their own standard of living, they would be free to help uplift the rest of the race. In the meantime, members of this group saw themselves as models of what other members of their race could accomplish with the proper training.

TWO

The Family

In 1891, Frederick Douglass noted that "where there is no family there is no morality, no truth and no happiness."¹ That the institution of the family was important to the black elite there is little doubt. It was the first and primary influence that a child felt. It decided how that child would be raised and what course it would take. It provided protection against the pressures of society. For those with an old family background it created identity. When elite families combined, they reconfirmed their social status. And for the Washington black elite at the turn of the century, the family was an incubator for the leaders of the next generation.

The black elite family taught values that changed little between 1880 and 1920. Reinforced by those taught in the church, these values were the cornerstone of "respectability": thrift, hard work, self-respect, and righteousness. Yet the family also taught responsibility to the race. Parents were the example for children to follow, and if the parents became involved in racial uplift efforts, the children would probably do likewise. Even if the parents were simply paying lip service to the ideal of racial solidarity, the children took them at their word.

As objective conditions for African Americans changed at the turn of the century, racial solidarity became more important to elite blacks, and their children, schooled in responsibility to their race, played an important part in the transformation of the elite itself. Angelina Grimké knew that one way to regain her father's approval was to write plays and essays on the race issue. Roscoe Conkling Bruce, after graduating from Harvard, chose to teach at Tuskegee Institute, as his father would expect him to do. Ionia Rollin Whipper decided to forgo marriage in order to serve her race as a doctor, as her mother would have understood. The attitude of the parents clearly affected the paths the children chose to take.

The natural affection of the black elite for their children gave them what they saw as a personal opportunity to elevate the race by raising intelligent, educated sons and daughters who would in their turn continue the work their parents had begun. The closeness of these families may have been a defense mechanism in reaction to discrimination from the outside world, but it was undoubtedly legitimate. The warmth they created in the home environment provided a shelter, but it also nourished the growth of happy children and provided continuity and hope for the future. The majority of marriages were partnerships forged to further family goals as well as to perpetuate status. Divorce was not unheard of but it was rare, although separations were not uncommon. The black elite family in Washington was a line of defense against society, and its values and strategies ensured that family status would continue through succeeding generations.

During the Progressive Era, the African American family became a bulwark against the prejudices of society and was a shield against the harsher elements of Jim Crow.[2] Washington's black elite families sheltered their children from the humiliation of American segregation and provided a loving home environment. Robert Scurlock remembered a benevolent childhood. "There were parties and other activities. Our social life was spent apart from the city as a whole, but nothing about it was unpleasant. . . . We never felt the apparent dissatisfaction with life that became apparent in the 1950s and 1960s. Of course plenty of people were aware they were being discriminated against."[3] Yet parents also realized the importance of contact with the outside world, and sent their children to preparatory schools to prepare them for life as well as for college. In short, elite blacks used the family as an agent of socialization as well as education, preparing children to accept leadership roles in society.

It is difficult to discern how the family functioned on a daily basis. Few diaries are available to the public from this period in Washington, and most letters between family members were of necessity written only at times when they were separated. Consequently secondary sources regarding the black family have focused mainly on the working-class families that were the subjects of studies by charitable organizations. These studies are largely statistical in nature and do little to illuminate individual lives. In addition, the little research conducted into the lives of elite blacks at the turn of the century is rather outdated work that sees these families as extensions of the white middle-class ideal.

To compound the problem, most research into black families has either tried to show that the nuclear family pattern is the most prevalent among blacks, thus disputing the stereotype of the single-parent black family; or has, more recently, tried to justify "aberrant" family behavior patterns by relating them to familial values in African culture. This alternative agenda has lent a propagandistic bent to many of these studies that has made it difficult to create a methodology for the study of black elite families, or paradigms from which to view individual family behavior.[4]

Nonetheless, it is possible to make some generalizations about the function of elite families in the black community. Both Jessie Bernard and E. Franklin Frazier noted the division within black society between "respectable" and "nonrespectable" families. These divisions did not depend necessarily on income, but generally "respectable" families rose through hard work into the upper ranks of black society. Similarly, elite status did not necessarily depend on income, but generally status brought better incomes. Frazier, St. Clair Drake, and Horace Cayton noted that lower-income "respectable" families tended to become involved with church activities and were more stable. Similarly, attachment to certain churches in Washington at the turn of the century conveyed respectability to many families. Education was a primary concern for the "respectable" families, as it was for the District's black elite. Bernard notes that family stability and conventional moral behavior were key criteria for determining social status until World War I, when sufficient numbers had achieved such stability and other blacks had begun to achieve wealth through less legitimate means. After World War I, income was not the only criterion for arrival among the social elite, but lack of it barred entry. As a result, many of the old aristocratic family names faded from the social columns. This trend in the black community was mirrored by changes in white society, where the "gentlemanly tradition" was disappearing along with the traditional aristocracies.[5]

It was not impossible for someone of an unremarkable family to rise to prominence in the late nineteenth century, and the phenomenon became more common in the twentieth century. Most of Washington's elite families, however, had distinguished pedigrees. These families generally maintained their elite status by encouraging their children to follow in their footsteps or to pursue other suitable endeavors.

The Whippers exemplified Washington's elite black families. The South Carolina socialite and political activist Frances Rollin had married the controversial yet influential black politician William J. Whipper, with whom she had five children, three of whom survived infancy. Winifred, the oldest surviving child, became a teacher in the Washington school system but died young of tuberculosis. Leigh Whipper, after obtaining a law degree at Howard University, went on to become a well-known performer on the black vaudeville circuits, and later an actor and film celebrity. Ionia Rollin Whipper graduated from Howard Medical School in 1903, after teaching in the District schools for over ten years. She served as resident physician of the Collegiate Institute of West Virginia and physician of girls at Tuskegee Institute, and maintained a private practice for women in Washington. She also founded a home for unwed mothers. With such a prominent social reputation, Ionia bore herself with great dignity. Ionia's great-niece remembered her as a regal woman even in old age. "My great-aunt made her descent from the upper floor in a mist of powder and perfume. She would be magnificently dressed and coiffed, her hat poised at a stylish angle, gloves in hand, her pocket book containing the requisite white handkerchief, her ample bosom replete with pearls." Ionia's sister-in-law told her, "Your aunt was never dressed for any kind of housework."[6] Such images instilled in elite black children the proper way to behave.

The Rollin-Whipper dynasty was one of many family success stories in Washington. John Wesley Cromwell Sr., editor of the *People's Advocate*, the first black lawyer to appear before the Interstate Commerce Commission, principal of grammar schools in the District, and secretary and original member of the American Negro Academy, had seven children. Otelia Cromwell, born in 1874, was the first black graduate of Smith College, with a degree in education. She taught for thirty years in the District schools, got her master's degree at Columbia University in 1910, and received a Ph.D. from Yale in 1926. Her sister Mary E. Cromwell, born in 1876, earned her bachelor's degree at the University of Michigan and her master's at the University of Pennsylvania in 1917, then went on to teach mathematics at Dunbar High School. She was an officer and trustee of St. Anna's Home and was extremely active in charitable organizations in Washington. John Wesley Cromwell Jr., born in

1883, received his bachelor's degree from Dartmouth in 1906 and his master's degree from the same institution the following year. He taught mathematics, German, and bookkeeping in the District high schools for twenty-two years, and became the first black certified public accountant in 1921.[7]

The genealogies of these families make it clear that the parents educated their children to take full advantage of opportunities, and, when possible, to provide service to their race, either by opening new avenues to success, as did Leigh Whipper in the film industry, or by engaging directly in service to racial uplift, as did Mary Cromwell. Parents encouraged their children to enter the professions to ensure respectability in a changing society. That the children took their training to heart is evident in the choices they made.

The parents' ability to instill such devotion in their children is related to the way the families interacted. The closeness of Washington's elite black families is apparent throughout the documentary evidence, and seems to have been the key factor in maintaining both social status and a sense of responsibility to the race. The photographer Addison Scurlock and his wife, Mamie, kept fairly close control over their sons, Robert and George. The sons were expected to run errands and help their father in his studio or darkroom, but they were free to pursue sports and other favorite activities. Ultimately both sons entered their father's business after graduating from Howard University, thus ensuring their own social status.[8]

Geographical proximity or frequent visits to family members promoted family devotion. Blanche K. Bruce and his older brother, Henry C. Bruce, stayed close to each other in Washington, and Henry and his wife were on hand to help Josephine Bruce during Blanche's last hours. After Blanche K. Bruce's death in 1898, the *Colored American* reported that the entire Bruce family was suffering from illness as a result of mourning. Robert R. Church and his family often stayed as guests of his daughter Mary Church Terrell and her husband, Robert, in their Le Droit Park home. Since Robert Church usually went north for the summer, it was not uncommon for him to stay with his family in Washington on the way.[9] The extended family played an important part in creating a loving environment that instilled devotion.

At times the extended family took the place of the nuclear family when parents were estranged or when official duties kept them apart. Angelina Weld Grimké was born to Archibald and Sarah Stanley Grimké in 1880. Sarah was white, the daughter of a minister, who did not approve of his daughter's interracial marriage. Under pressure from her family, Sarah separated from

Archibald in 1883. She kept Angelina until the child was seven, then sent her to live with her father.[10] The Grimké family, however, was especially close. While Archibald was stationed in Santo Domingo as U.S. consul, Angelina stayed with her aunt Charlotte Forten and uncle Francis J. Grimké, the minister of the Fifteenth Street Presbyterian Church. Upon Archibald's return, the two lived in a separate apartment in the same house. Angelina and her father shared an extremely close relationship.

All of these families displayed strong emotional ties and a sense of responsibility for the care of one another that contributed to the stability of the black elite. When one aspect of the nuclear family disintegrated, the extended family stepped in to take over that role. It was this factor that perpetuated a strong black elite through many generations.

Usually a good family began with a good marriage, and for elite blacks this usually meant marriage within their own class. A marriage was a reason for celebration. A good marriage was even better. Ionia Rollin Whipper at first objected to her niece's romantic involvement with Hylan Garnet Lewis, but she could not object to Lewis's family, which included a school principal, a doctor, and the private secretary to an assistant secretary of war under Woodrow Wilson. Ultimately she was pleased with the match.[11] Weddings were lavish affairs reported fully in the social columns of the newspapers. The *Bee* devoted an entire column to the wedding of W. L. Lewis and Emma Cusberd at the Nineteenth Street Baptist Church, detailing all the presents. Of those attending the wedding only the Cooks and Murrays were of extraordinary prominence. When Dr. Furman J. Shadd married Alice Park at the Fifteenth Street Presbyterian Church, the entire guest list was composed of notables.[12] As with many society affairs, sometimes the reason for the affair was not as important as who showed up.

For elite blacks a good alliance between prominent families ensured status retention and reaffirmed friendships between elites both in and out of the city. In some circumstances it forged new bonds between families that strengthened the black elite network. Last but not least in the minds of the parents, if the spouse came from a good home, it was a reasonable guarantee that the marriage would be a happy one, or at least one that would not leave their son or daughter in the position of wanting anything.

Within black elite families the husband and wife occupied relatively equal positions. While some men still opposed women's rights, for the most part black elite men saw common cause between civil rights for blacks and equal rights for women. William Whipper, for example, seems to have chosen Frances Rollin to be his wife because she would be an asset to him personally and professionally. Frances Rollin Whipper helped her husband out of many financial troubles by agreeing to have his property put in her name.[13] Of course romance certainly played a role in the selection of a spouse, but the black elite, in the manner of most elites, stressed the importance of a good alliance between partners of equal social status as well as similar temperament.

One reason for this focus on alliances was that after Emancipation many members of the elite saw themselves as having a mission to lead the race. For activist elites, a marriage was a partnership designed to strengthen both partners by combining their efforts to improve the race. Of course not all elites were activists, but few black elite women were merely decorations. Even in the 1880s most had some form of education, and those who grew up during Reconstruction were filled with a sense of what could be accomplished with enough support. After 1900, increasing numbers of elite black women attended universities, as did their white counterparts. The black women, however, tended to train as teachers or nurses, the two fields fully open to them. As a result, before their marriages most elite black women in the twentieth century had performed some useful service for their race and were well versed in the politics of racial uplift. Without the support of husbands and fathers, however, none of this growth would have been possible.

Most couples devised their own methods of dividing family duties. In Norma Boyd's home her father was the breadwinner, but he turned his money over to his wife, who was a better money manager.[14] The Bruce family divided financial matters less neatly. Josephine Bruce bought her son's clothes, decorated his room, and advised him on financial matters, such as fees for his tutoring services. When a question arose about the rent that Roscoe was paying at school, it was Josephine Bruce who took care of matters. It was still Blanche Bruce, however, who wrote the checks to pay for Roscoe's tuition and expenses, and made sure he had enough money and dressed warmly.[15]

Robert and Mary Terrell were an ideal couple. They shared political beliefs, and Robert encouraged his wife to pursue a speaking career at a time when many men felt that married women should stay at home. When the *Washington Post* asked Robert Terrell to respond to a racist article in *Collier's Weekly,* his wife reported that "Berto and I put our heads together and tried to respond to every false statement—."[16] Mrs. Terrell's speaking engagements often took her out of town, but she had an agreement with her Lyceum employers that she would never be gone more than three weeks at a time. When her children were young, Mary Terrell's mother stayed with the family, so she was able to leave them with a free conscience. Upon her return, the family would all meet her at the station, and they would often spend the next day in some family activity, such as a picnic. During the week, Mrs. Terrell would sometimes go downtown to meet her husband and go shopping.[17]

Even the best marriages suffered tensions, however. On one occasion the Terrells fought about their maid, Eva. Eva had offended Mrs. Terrell, and Mr. Terrell's failure to side with his wife prompted Mary to think her husband did not love her. The fight lasted a week. At one point Mary wrote in her diary, "'I hate you' are words that should never be spoken by one who loves another." Matters remained unsettled. Mrs. Terrell crossed out "make up" at one point and then complained about Eva again, who "completely failed" to make mayonnaise. On another day, she told a friend that she did not have enough peace and calm to write her recollections of the South. The couple soon made a tentative peace, and the two spent the evening watching an eclipse of Mars together. Two weeks later, however, they again had a misunderstanding.[18]

Not all misunderstandings were as inconsequential as these. While Mary Terrell and her two daughters were staying in Oberlin, Ohio, Robert Terrell placed most of their belongings in storage and presumably took a smaller lodging to save money. He also canceled the fire insurance as an unnecessary expense; unfortunately, the storage area burned down, destroying some of their prized possessions. In her autobiography, Mrs. Terrell tactfully excused her husband, but she was still angry.[19] The issue behind the argument was finances, and their problem may exemplify the sort of financial choices that black elite families were forced to make. Here it was the decision to stop paying for fire insurance to maintain two households while the girls were at school. Unfortunately, the choice brought added problems to the family. Although Mary's father assisted the Terrells with purchasing property, he could not always support the couple. Financial difficulties only placed greater pressures on elite families trying to maintain a stable environment.

Interracial marriages faced the greatest tensions. Archibald Grimké married Sarah Stanley in 1879. From the beginning Sarah's family opposed the marriage, particularly since they did not meet Archibald before the wedding. Sarah's father, who had been active in the abolitionist cause, was especially vehement in his condemnation of the affair. "I would gladly give my life this moment—yes go with a bounding heart to the scaffold and hang till I am dead, if I could restore you as you were a few months ago. . . . It is what has been flung at me scores and perhaps hundreds of times in years past when I have advocated the rights of the colored race. . . . Toward them I cherish none but philanthropic feelings but to give them my beautiful & accomplished daughters for wives seems perfectly abhor[r]ent. . . . Death seems the only relief."[20]

The Grimkés' daughter, Angelina, was an infant when Sarah left Archibald and took the baby to live with her family in Michigan. Sarah's father had obviously modified his opinion by that time, for he urged her to reconcile with Archibald. The damage was already done, however, and the couple never reconciled. Angelina later wrote, "It was a terrible blow to my Father and for a while it looked as if he might lose his mind."[21] In 1887, Sarah sent Angelina to live with her father. Sarah died in 1898, probably by suicide, without seeing her daughter again.

Not all interracial marriages were unhappy, but few were without tensions. Charles B. Purvis married a white woman, and despite the *Bee*'s prediction that neither black nor white society would accept them, the couple led an active social life within the black community. Frederick Douglass's second wife, Helen, was a white woman he had met while he was recorder of deeds and she was a clerk in his office. They were married by Francis J. Grimké, but many people in the black community saw Douglass as betraying his race, and Frederick's sons resented their father's remarrying. After Douglass's death Francis Grimké continued to defend her, arguing that "she continued loyal to his memory, and was never ashamed anywhere, in any audience, to rise and own that she was his widow; nor did she cease until her death to wear on her breast a cameo likeness of Mr. Douglass. She was in every way a noble woman,—refined, educated,—a lady."[22]

Helen Douglass faced the greatest difficulties after her husband's death. He had willed her a $10,000 bond, but the bond had been sold before his death. She asked for the value of the bond from the estate, and eventually sued but lost. As a result, Helen could not pay the mortgage on their home in Anacostia. She borrowed the money to buy Cedar Hill and then spent the rest of her life trying to raise money to pay back her debt and to create a national monument for her husband.[23]

Family hostility to an unpopular marriage such as that of Frederick and Helen Douglass could isolate couples as much as break them apart. This enforced conformity to family wishes in cases of marriage usually ensured that sons and daughters would marry within the accepted group of respectable families that made up the national black elite.

When tensions in a marriage became too intense, separation was an option. Separation did not mean that all family ties were cut, or even that the marriage had ended. Four generations of Whipper women experienced their own variations of separation. Frances Rollin Whipper's mother, Margarette Rollin, separated from her husband and as a result was not able to gain free title to their property upon his death. Frances Rollin Whipper moved to Washington in the 1880s after William J. Whipper's career had suffered many setbacks, and after she had saved him from financial ruin by accepting the transfer of his properties to her name to avoid their seizure during bankruptcy proceedings. There she established a lively social life and held frequent salons. William Whipper came to Washington for several years, but ultimately returned to South Carolina. Still, when Frances knew her health was failing, she returned to South Carolina to spend her final days with her husband.

Frances's son Leigh Whipper met Virginia Wheeler while both were on the black Theater Owners Booking Association circuit in the early 1900s. Their romance was stormy, and the couple split shortly before Virginia discovered she was pregnant. The Whipper and Wheeler families extended helping hands to Virginia, and Leigh sent financial support occasionally. Their granddaughter later recalled, "My grandmother had never, to my knowledge, lived with my grandfather—I could hardly imagine them together—and she always kept any conversation about him to a bare minimum." Ultimately Virginia sent her daughter, Leighla, to live with Ionia Rollin Whipper, who formally adopted her.[24]

Leighla Whipper married Hylan Garnet Lewis in 1935 after a two-year courtship while the couple were at Howard University. A year after the birth of their daughter, Carole, Hylan accepted a grant for doctoral studies at the University of Chicago and moved there without his family. The separation placed a strain on the marriage, and Leighla discussed divorce with a lawyer. The family came together again in Alabama for two years, but the earlier separation had taken its toll and the couple ultimately divorced. Carole and Leighla divided their time between Virginia's home in New York and Ionia's in Washington, so once again the family was close at hand.[25]

Divorce was less common in older elite families than in those that had achieved elite status more recently. Nationally the divorce rate was on the rise at the turn of the century and there was a sharp decline in the birth rate.[26] Much of this change is attributable to the women's rights movement, which worked for less restrictive divorce laws and greater independence for women. Within the black community, however, attitudes toward women's rights were already liberal, and there was no evident increase in the black divorce rate. Divorce was certainly a topic of interest to the elite community, and the black press followed divorce proceedings closely.[27] Nevertheless, divorce did not appear to be a significant factor in the lives of the black elite, especially when the extended family stepped in to take the place of the missing spouse.

The unity that the extended family promoted was most obvious in times of crisis. Death brought families closer together both emotionally and physically. When Mary Church Terrell's mother died, the whole family felt the blow. The family came for the funeral, and neighbors and friends of the family came by to help at the house. Terrell traveled to Memphis shortly after the funeral to tell her father, who was also ill. Her brother Robert and stepmother, Anna, advised against telling Robert Church Sr., but finally he asked her directly, "Mollie, how is Lou?" After much urging Mary told her father the truth, and "he turned away without saying a word." Although the couple had been divorced longer than they had been married, Robert Church still cared deeply for his first wife. Even Mary's stepsister Annette referred to her as "Mama Lou."[28] The extended family in this case was almost as close as the nuclear one.

The primary purpose of a marriage was to create a family. Raising children was one way the elite could contribute to racial advancement on a personal level. By raising educated and dedicated youths, the elite could ensure continuation of the family status and provide leaders for the next generation. At the turn of the century white middle-class parents looked more and more to science to teach them proper parenting. No longer considered natural experts, mothers were to be trained in these skills. Children were to be weaned early. Parenting was still primarily the job of the mother, although the father was encouraged to participate in the process. This involvement became increasingly limited, however, with increased urbanization. The father went into town to work and saw his children only a few hours each day. In school and at home, children learned to be useful citizens and to be orderly and polite.[29]

The black elite absorbed some of these ideals in their daily lives but with subtle variations. They taught their children to be model citizens, for example, but to the black elite being a model citizen meant something other than what it meant to whites. Rather than teach docility, black parents taught their children to stand up for themselves without showing disrespect. Although the father went to work during the day and was away from the home, often he was intimately involved in the raising of his children. Mothers studied the latest scientific methods of raising children and applied them at home, but more important, they viewed these methods as a way to uplift other black women and spread these ideas through reform programs in black working-class neighborhoods. Elite blacks expected more from their children because they realized that more was at stake than simply raising children; they were raising leaders who would in turn raise the race.

This attitude brought with it a great sense of responsibility and added to the pressures that black elite families faced. In this situation it is not surprising that some parents felt overburdened. The Terrell family consisted of Robert and Mary; their daughter, Phyllis; and Mary Church Terrell's niece, Mary, whom they adopted in 1905. Each summer Mrs. Terrell and her daughters would vacation for a month in Harpers Ferry or Opequan, and Robert Terrell would join them there for a week. Seemingly the family relationship was a close one, but it was not without pressures. Mary Church Terrell loved her daughters, but she often was forced to choose between her reform activities and her motherly duties. Entries in her diary illustrate this conflict. "I spend a great deal of time with my little girl but do it cheerfully, for she needs it." Her diary also reveals a sense of martyrdom. She reported feeling bitter about spending so much time on a dress for Phyllis only to have it come out wrong, and seemed to begrudge the time spent on these duties.[30]

One other feature of Mrs. Terrell's relationship with her daughters revealed in her diaries is her favoritism for Phyllis. This favoritism is perhaps understandable, for she suffered several miscarriages before giving birth to Phyllis. The circumstances surrounding Mary's adoption are unclear. Phyllis receives the most mention in her mother's diary, both positive and negative. If Mary misbehaved, her mother often criticized her, but if Phyllis did something wrong, her mother was more inclined to blame herself rather than her daughter.[31]

Robert Terrell's role as a father seems peripheral but largely congenial. His daughters appeared to find him humorous and kind. For example, in an amusing picture of domesticity Mrs. Terrell records Phyllis's first haircut. Phyllis was very happy, although the barber appears to have done a poor job, and her mother "could scarcely keep the tears back when [she] saw the long thick braids sheared off." For his part, Mr. Terrell did not even notice the haircut, and his wife called him the most unobservant man she had ever seen.[32] Robert Terrell no doubt had other things on his mind—running a law firm, making real estate deals, covering the losses of the Capital Savings Bank, of which he had been an officer, and serving as municipal judge, all occupations that were necessary for the survival of the family. Still, the family participated in many group activities such as singing around the piano, and friends commented on the beautiful family scene they presented.[33] The family environment for the Terrell children was largely very loving. There were stresses from outside the family, but the home seems to have provided a cozy atmosphere.

Blanche and Josephine Bruce provided a similar environment for their son, Roscoe Conkling Bruce. As an only child, Roscoe did not have to face competition from siblings, and it is clear from the loving letters he exchanged with his parents while he was away at school that the Bruce home was a warm shelter. Roscoe wrote home in 1897: "There are moments when I feel like 'a dilly baby' lost in an unfriendly world far away from home. . . . I wish for a moment I could be with you and Mother at home. But my jail-sentence doesn't expire for ten weeks—ten, long, dreary weeks."[34] Whether or not it was because Roscoe was male, his relationship with his father appears to have been very close, and both mother and father took equal interest in their son's upbringing. Blanche Bruce wrote his son: "We miss you very much, but of course your absence at school is a necessity to your development and your life equipment."[35]

Roscoe was, in turn, a devoted son, who worried immensely when his father's appointment as register of the Treasury was held up in 1897. When the appointment came through, Roscoe confided to his father that he had considered leaving school to earn money to finish the course the following year.[36] The Bruces had an ideal relationship, with each responsive to the other's needs, and each sharing a sense of camaraderie and close emotional ties.

The home environment was the least settled aspect of life for the young Angelina Grimké, yet she maintained a strong sense of family ties. Archibald was absent for several years around the time Angelina entered her teens, and there is a rich record of correspondence between the two that clearly shows a young woman rebelling in adolescence. Yet the fact that Angelina carefully preserved every letter from her father, long or short, loving or harsh, testifies to the closeness of their relationship.

Angelina was, in essence, abandoned by her white mother at an early age. In the letter in which Sarah informed Archibald of her decision to give up Angelina, this dissociation is clear. "She needs that love and sympathy of one of her own *race* which I am sure her father still has for her, but which it is impossible for others to give. My own family, kind and anxious as they are to do right, do not, neither is it possible for them to give her the *love* she requires. . . . She is now getting old enough to see and feel the *thoughts* of others, which the difference in race & color naturally engender regarding her."[37] Sarah wrote to her daughter for the next year or so, but her letters soon stopped, and the two did not see each other again. The lack of a mother was always a theme in Angelina's life, and she often wondered how it would be to have a mother in whom she could confide.

For several years Angelina lived with her father in Boston, and upon his appointment as consul in Santo Domingo she moved to Washington to live with her uncle and aunt. It was here, the correspondence reveals, that Angelina began misbehaving. It is uncertain what this misbehavior entailed, but Archibald's response was clear enough. Charlotte had written to Archibald to tell him that ill health prevented her from continuing to care for her niece. Archibald replied that he was very disappointed in Angelina and her behavior since she had come to Washington. He was particularly upset because he had asked Angelina repeatedly to think less of herself and more of others. He wrote Angelina that Charlotte had "written me very frankly about yourself, and the evil influence which Washington is exerting upon you." Archibald decided to send her to boarding school, but postponed the decision after her behavior improved. In 1897, however, when Charlotte's ill health continued and Angelina's improvement did not, Angelina was sent to the first of a series of boarding schools in the Northeast.[38]

At school Angelina's erratic behavior continued. At one point she considered leaving school for Boston at midterm, and spent relatively large amounts of money on frivolous items such as evening dresses. Her father repeatedly exhorted her to exercise restraint. "I wish you to dress like a young school girl & not like a woman in society." Archibald gave his daughter an allowance of 50 cents a week. "That I think is quite sufficient for all your needs in this regard," he wrote her. "Please bear in mind dear, that your fond old papa is not rich." Angelina persisted in her spendthrift ways. "Will you never learn little girl to think of something else besides dress & having a good time generally?"³⁹

After two years of pleading, the last straw seems to have come in February 1899, when Angelina borrowed money from a friend and asked her father to help repay the loan. In one of Archibald's rare harsh letters to his daughter he replied in the negative. He would never be proud of her, he stated, since she only thought of herself, and suggested that she learn a trade so that she could make a living. For Angelina, the letter must have been a slap in the face.⁴⁰

Whether in response to her father's letter or through simple maturation, Angelina again became the dutiful daughter. By May, perhaps partly to regain the respect of her father, she was writing and publishing on race issues. By November, Archibald was so pleased with her progress that he was sending her extra money for items for school.⁴¹ The absence of both parents seems to have left Angelina uncertain as to her role in her family, and led her astray in her values. Nonetheless, there was no lack of love surrounding her, and ultimately it was the extended family's values that brought her back to a straight path. It was also through writing on racial issues that she achieved ultimate approval.

Providing children with a loving environment was one way in which elite blacks counteracted the effects of the larger society. If their children were to become the leaders of the next generation, they needed confidence in themselves and in their abilities, something that Jim Crow society was not likely to give them. Thus elite black families sheltered their offspring as much as possible in their formative years so as to nurture their natural talents. To ensure that their children would have respectable values, they set positive examples for them to follow, and relied on the extended family to help regulate their children's behavior. It was a strategy that apparently worked, for the children of Washington's black elite invariably went on to successes of their own that perpetuated family status.

Education was another important part of parental strategy for the black elite. Most families sent their children to the Washington segregated public schools, and many attended the prestigious M Street High School. But for the Terrells, at least, educating their daughters meant more than sending them to school. Mrs. Terrell helped Phyllis with her lessons and coached her as she practiced at the piano. She showed disappointment in Mary's failure to study her Latin and thought it indicated a lack of pride. In the summer of 1909, while on vacation, she encouraged her daughters to write compositions and do spelling exercises. Her concern about Phyllis's poor progress was especially marked. Phyllis had reached the seventh grade, but her reading skills were poor. "I feel like a criminal when I think how I allowed her to run wild nearly six weeks last summer without requiring her, forcing her to read every day as I am doing now—I have tried to use as little force as possible because I feared I would make her hate the sight of a book if I compelled her to read against her will." [42]

Archibald Grimké often wrote to his daughter about her school, comparing the District schools favorably with those in Boston. He advised her to read certain books and she wrote him reports of those she had read. Blanche K. Bruce counseled Roscoe on good study habits and made sure that he got the grades he deserved from his professors. He sometimes gave indirect advice by commenting on the poor study habits of other students. [43]

After high school, the children of many families attended preparatory schools before entering college. Sending children to these schools was a way to mature them, as with Angelina Grimké. But even for children who were well behaved it was seen as an important step. Roscoe Bruce's grandmother wrote to Josephine, "I was glad to hear that you had made up your mind to send Rock away to school. I think it will be the making of him to be away from Washington." [44] Roscoe, in turn, later wrote of his own son, "I do believe that the association with those fine, clear eyed, clean-souled New Englanders would be the only salvation of the poor child. He has brains and to spare; what he needs is contact with fine spirited men and boys." [45] The parents, then, viewed education as bringing opportunities of many kinds.

The choice of preparatory school was revealing. Mary and Phyllis Terrell, like their mother before them, attended Oberlin Preparatory School in Ohio. Mrs. Terrell decided that a multiracial atmosphere would be an important element in her children's upbringing. Angelina Grimké attended several preparatory schools in Massachusetts. Her father felt that a boarding school would require her to settle down and work hard. Eventually this strategy seems to have worked. Roscoe Bruce went to Phillips Exeter Academy in New Hampshire to prepare to attend Harvard. All three families chose to send their children to predominantly white schools, presumably to accustom them to dealing with the majority culture, as well as to enable them to make valuable contacts. Both Archibald Grimké and Robert Terrell maintained friendships with men they had met at school and college. The Bruces also understood the importance of personal contacts and advised Roscoe, "It is well to cultivate people, especially those who show such a desire."[46]

The difficulty with this situation was that the children faced discrimination at a fairly early age. Mrs. Terrell actually moved to Oberlin to be with her children and perhaps protect them from an increasingly hostile community. As a student in the 1880s she had encountered very little prejudice herself, but by 1913, when the girls were ready to attend college, she discovered that the dormitories were not open to blacks, and that school officials seemed disinclined to change the policy of segregation.[47] There is no record that Angelina Grimké suffered any discrimination at her schools, perhaps because of her family ties with New England abolitionists. Roscoe Bruce, however, appears to have suffered from rent discrimination. Nevertheless, in 1922, when the time came to send his own son to Exeter, he believed his son "would have no trouble of a racial character with those boys. They would never in the world *think* of him in that way."[48] This early exposure to segregated society, albeit in insular circumstances, was a way for parents to socialize their children both to their race and to their social status. These parents hoped to immunize their children against racial prejudice by exposing them early to a multiracial environment in which these prejudices would be limited. By sending their children to exclusive schools, they introduced them to a larger society and ensured connections with people of influence in the future.

The family was the most important institution for the black elite. Although the majority of elite families were stable, there were many variations. At any time the extended family could take on more importance than the nuclear one. It was less important that the nuclear family remain stable than that the family's values remain in place. These were the values that created elite status.

The networks created by marriages between members of elite families ensured continuation of economic and social status. Marriages themselves were partnerships designed to further pursuit of common goals. While generally most families aimed at bettering their own situations, as the marriage partners became increasingly sensitized to racial issues, they looked to lead their race. In this situation the way they raised their children was extremely important. They prepared their children not simply for life, but for life as African Americans. The parents also gave the children the means to become leaders in their community through education and introduction to influential people. They isolated the family from the harsher aspects of society until the children were prepared to handle them. Finally, they taught their children responsibility and decency, values that would stand them in good stead when they took over leadership roles.

While the values that the black elite families taught did not themselves change substantially over time, the relative importance of commitment to racial uplift changed in tandem with objective conditions for the black elite. In the 1880s, when these families expected ultimate assimilation, their devotion to uplifting the race was not as strong as their emphasis on personal civil rights and political power. In the twentieth century the children of the elite never knew a time when assimilation was a possibility and accepted word for word their parents' lectures on responsibility to the entire race. They had been trained to become the new leaders of the race, and to them part of being a leader was devotion to racial uplift.

THREE

Culture and Leisure

One of the key ways to identify members of a social elite is by their cultural and leisure activities. The social activities of elite groups tend to be exclusive, creating distance between the members of the elite and the rest of society. Membership in certain social clubs is often one of the ascribed, or subjective, characteristics of an elite, so one would expect such clubs to be the least likely areas in which to discover connections with the larger community. Yet Washington's black elite clubs indeed developed such ties at the turn of the century.

While exclusivity remained an enduring legacy in the social and cultural organizations of the black elite, the nature of these organizations underwent a transformation. Concerned only with creating social status in the 1880s, in the early 1900s these organizations began to embrace concepts of racial pride and racial solidarity. Excluded from white social institutions, elite blacks increased their pride in their racial heritage when they created their own. In activities designed to provide escape from daily struggles the black elite only became more aware of the need to uplift the race. Even in their leisure time, the elite blacks found the emphasis in their values shifting.

All forms of culture and recreation were readily available to black citizens of the District at the turn of the century, particularly to those with the means to enjoy them. Black residents attended their own plays, musicales, poetry readings, lectures, and special exhibitions. They prided themselves on their literary organizations and annual galas. But their social and cultural life was not without its bitter side. Segregated in many white theaters, black patrons often attempted to pass for nonblack in order to obtain better seats and to avoid any stigma. While traveling away from Washington they had constantly to search for hotels that would accommodate blacks. Excluded from Washington's premier social clubs, the elite formed its own. The simple experience of eating lunch downtown could become an ordeal, even for the District's leading black citizens. Nevertheless, while some private facilities, such as theaters and restaurants, were segregated, the public museums and libraries in Washington, unlike those in some other southern cities, were open to blacks.[1] Washington's black community reacted to cultural exclusion, as to exclusion in most other areas, by turning to themselves for the creation of cultural institutions. While occasionally they protested their exclusion either overtly or covertly, the black elite ultimately created a rich cultural life for themselves that brought respect and praise from African Americans nationwide, even if white society was largely unaware of it.

Social life among the black elite mirrored that among whites. They considered it important to observe social niceties in order to emphasize their superiority to the masses. There were many warnings in the press about public decorum, and certainly comments when common courtesy was lacking. Mary Church Terrell gave a revealing image of cultural mores in her 1904 description of Washington society: "If a matron or maid from a sister city visits Washington, her hostess will probably give a reception in her honor, so that the stranger may meet her Washington friends. Then there will be a succession of luncheons, dinners, card and theatre parties and small dances given for the stranger by the friends of her hostess. She will certainly enjoy one or more drives and the chances are that she will be taken in a conveyance owned by the friend who invites her."[2] The social columns of the *Bee* and *Colored American* support this description with repeated references to guests of residents charming the city and having parties held in their honor. Generally, who was staying with whom was a subject of frequent comment in these columns, even if the guest was a relative returned to town.[3]

Even when not entertaining out-of-town guests, Washington's prominent black citizens attended numerous cultural events and social gatherings year round. Outdoor activities were particularly popular during the hot summers. In the early 1880s, the *Bee* reported that Lincoln Park was a favorite place for children in the summer because of the abundance of shade trees and the fact that no tramps roamed the park to interfere with their play. At the turn of the century lawn parties became a fad, and the *Colored American* reported that the 11th Street tennis courts in Northwest Washington were attracting the smart set.[4]

Although many parks were segregated, there were plenty that welcomed blacks. It was commonly accepted that African Americans would gather in Rock Creek Park on the Monday after Easter in an annual celebration. On that day whites traditionally chose to go elsewhere. McMillan Park, next to the reservoir and Howard University, quickly became a black preserve. Amusement parks tended to be restricted to whites until 1921, when Suburban Gardens in Deanwood opened its gates to blacks. The park held little appeal for elite blacks, however, because it catered to less refined sensibilities.[5]

Theme parties were common. Mary Church Terrell attended a "picnic" in February 1908, at which everyone had to wear summer clothes. The party of four hundred people included Josephine and Clara Bruce. F. McCullough Settle and young Josiah Settle Jr. gave a party for Phyllis Terrell with a theme of pink rosebuds, at which the children participated in a grand march and sang "Rock-a-Bye Baby." Phyllis and Mary Terrell attended their first masquerade party in 1911: Phyllis as a Spanish dancer, Mary as an Italian peasant. Their choice of costumes was revealing, since they chose roles outside of the African American world. Their mother had made the same choice earlier when she dressed as a Native American.[6]

If the Terrells' way of life can be taken as typical of the lifestyle of the black elite, the social atmosphere of Washington was busy indeed. In November 1905 Mrs. Terrell recorded in her diary attendance at a concert, taking her daughter to see *The Mikado*, hearing a lecture by a man who had been kidnapped in Tangiers, and participating in euchre and whist parties with friends over Thanksgiving. In between these more formal engagements, she took her children to the zoo, did some gardening, and took care of one of her daughters when she fell sick.[7]

Home entertainments often required elaborate preparations. At a reception in their home for a legation from Liberia, the Terrells served deviled crabs and salad. The men gave speeches and leaned against the mantel, loosening it so that it had to be removed. On one occasion, Mrs. Terrell spent twelve hours making mayonnaise for her husband's stag party. Everything went well, although "there was too much refreshment of a liquid nature." The following day she served the leftover chicken salad at a ladies' entertainment, where "Mrs. Tyler and I talked about the shortcomings of our husbands who can do nothing about the house." She concluded that, while she enjoyed entertaining, it was very hard work.[8]

The Grimké brothers, Francis and Archibald, enjoyed a sophisticated cultural life in Washington as a result of their contacts with race leaders and academicians. Anna J. Cooper, for example, regularly held musical evenings at her home to which she inevitably invited the Grimkés. After Archibald returned to the District in 1898, he described its society life in a letter to Angelina. "There is, between you & me & the gatepost, no comparison between coloured society here and in Boston. I am feeling quite at home here now, getting to be quite a Washingtonese. Last Friday we went to a fine dinner, given in my honor by a gay widow who has plenty of money! Tonight we go to the Merriweather[s'] for an evening entertainment of some sort & last night we took tea and spent a most delightful evening at Mrs. Coopers where we enjoyed fine conversation & fine music."[9]

There were many alternatives both formal and informal to entertaining at home. Aside from trips to the zoo and nearby parks, the Terrells took daytime excursions to Deanwood and Takoma Park, and the two of them attended baseball games together. When motion pictures became available, the Terrells attended. They viewed an early film of a fight featuring a white boxer named Kelstrel against the black world champion, Jack Johnson. Mrs. Terrell enjoyed the fight immensely. "It was wonderful to see Johnson put Kelstrel out of commission after he had been knocked down himself." This from a woman who thought football a barbaric sport![10] The fight was more than sport, however; it was a chance for the black elite to express race pride by cheering on the black boxer. It was also one of the few outlets for frustration with segregated society. Each punch was a blow to white prejudices, and a black victory gave hope that ultimately the cause of civil rights for African Americans would also be victorious.

As privileged members of society, the Terrells were often among the first to enjoy the benefits of modern technology. A Mr. Walker took Mary Church Terrell for a drive in his automobile in 1908; it may not have been her first ride, but it was certainly remarkable enough to be recorded in her diary. By 1920, it was not uncommon for a member of the elite to own his own automobile.[11] The automobile was liberating. Although trolley cars in Washington were not segregated, despite repeated attempts to segregate them, experiences on them could be unpleasant.

In an extraordinary incident, when a white man refused to move as Mrs. Terrell tried to make her way through a streetcar with her suitcases, she said to him, "When I tell you to move, you move." The man retorted, "I won't be sassed by a nigger." Terrell slapped him in the face, but admitted in her diary that she had pulled her punch. When the man threatened to hit her, she told him to go ahead, but fortunately a white woman intervened to discourage him and another white woman defused the situation by talking to Terrell.[12] Mary Terrell was probably one of the few black women who would have stood up to or struck a white man. She believed she was entitled to the same respect accorded any other woman. If similar incidents occurred with any frequency on the streetcars, undoubtedly other members of the black elite were glad of the privacy of automobile travel.

In the 1880s, elite blacks still ate some meals at public restaurants, but dining out became increasingly uncomfortable after the turn of the century. The situation was particularly difficult for darker-skinned blacks with more prominently African features. Mrs. Terrell reported that once when she ate lunch at a restaurant in New York City, two black girls at a nearby table were ignored, and all the white waiters smiled when the girls finally left after waiting twenty minutes for service.[13] At the cafeteria under the House of Representatives in the 1880s, elite blacks had felt discrimination by black waiters who did not want to lose face. By the end of the nineteenth century, however, as the old elite occupations were replaced by those that accorded firmer social standing , the problem was no longer with black waiters but with white managers. Nevertheless, black restaurant patrons were not without their allies. When two black women attempted to eat at the House restaurant in 1898, they were told that the policy was to serve no blacks. The women left but went immediately to see Speaker of the House Thomas R. Reed, who promised to help them. When the owner again refused them service the next day, they called for Reed, who forced the owner to serve them and showed that he would not tolerate any color line.[14] The women typically did not attempt their own protest but sought the help of a white man, and thus were able to maintain their dignity. However, many were not willing to suffer the humiliation of being refused service or having to fight for a chance to eat at a certain restaurant. It was easier to go to a black-owned restaurant or simply to stay home.

Most of the elite escaped the sweltering Washington heat for several weeks in the summer. As the black elite nationwide had favorite vacation spots, this was often a chance for people to renew acquaintances with social equals from other cities, and to strengthen the networks that linked the nation's black leaders. For example, the Pinchbacks summered in Saratoga Springs, New York, where they were joined by the Churches of Memphis, Charles W. Anderson of New York, and the Ruffins of Boston.[15] Rosetta Lawson wrote to the *Colored American* of her summer in Asbury Park, New Jersey, describing the many excursions she and her friends planned to local places of interest. But "much of the time is whiled away in some of the numerous pavilions dotting the coast, watching the restless ocean and drinking in the cool, health-giving breezes, constantly wafted landward from the sea."[16]

Vacation was a chance for the black elite to escape the pressures of daily life in the company of peers. While vacationing in Opequan, Virginia, for a month, Mary Church Terrell wrote: "Mrs. Turner, Imogene Clarkston and I lie around in the hammocks and so do the Wormleys. We talk a great deal together and have jolly times."[17] Angelina Grimké summered in Jamestown, Rhode Island, where she enjoyed evenings at the Fairweather Yacht Club and days with her friends.[18] Mary Terrell and her daughters often vacationed without Robert, as witnessed by the many letters back and forth between them. Robert Terrell, however, usually joined them for a week during their stay. Such separations were not uncommon, as many government appointees and employees could not leave their positions for extended vacations. The *Bee* reported that "Mrs. Daniel Murray and sons will leave about the first of July to spend the summer in the mountains of Virginia."[19] Obviously, as assistant librarian at the Library of Congress, Daniel Murray could not spare the time to join his family.

Harpers Ferry, Virginia, where the Murrays owned a cottage, was another fashionable vacation spot. It offered good accommodations for blacks and was closer to home and less expensive than many coastal resorts. The Wormleys simply summered at their nearby farm to escape the bustle of the city. At Colton, Maryland, another waterfront location, Washington society members gathered to take advantage of the resort's exclusivity, as well as swimming, fishing, and other forms of recreation.[20]

Vacations were not all without troubles, however. The Terrells and Jane Wormley vacationed with the Jenifers in 1908 amidst a little domestic tension. Mrs. Jenifer collapsed in hysterics one evening, and was carried to her room declaring "she could not stand Mr. J's treatment of her any longer." Miss Wormley worried that the landlady would ask her to leave, but Mrs. Terrell promised to speak to Mrs. Jenifer.[21] This disturbing episode has a larger significance, for it shows that even on vacation the members of the elite were not able to relax completely. If the landlady was white, they needed to present a respectable front so that she would continue to accommodate blacks. If the landlady was black, they needed to keep up appearances for the sake of the other guests who chose the inn for its exclusivity.

To avoid unnecessary complications and save expenses, many of Washington's black aristocrats chose to purchase summer homes nearby. The Highland Beach community in Anne Arundel County, Maryland, offered great advantages to families such as the Terrells, Francises, Wormleys, and Curtises. Developed by Lewis H. Douglass, the area offered exclusivity in a vacation setting. Mrs. Terrell wrote to her brother that "in this beautiful country spot on the Chesapeake Bay . . . the beach is perfect. At times there is a fine supply of crabs."[22] Elsewhere she described Highland Beach more fully: "There is a charming spot on the Chesapeake Bay, which has been converted into a summer resort by one of the most progressive and useful colored men in Washington. Here some of the flower of the social flock of Washington and neighboring cities take their summer outings in pretty little cottages which they themselves own. Boating, fishing and crabbing are the order of the day, together with an occasional dance, to which a few of the sweltering friends of Washington are invited."[23] Highland Beach offered a hotel for people sojourning at the resort, but "the expenses are such as to maintain a superior atmosphere."[24]

Vacations were designed to be an escape from the daily pressures that the black elite faced, yet even on vacation there was always a need to maintain what the historian Willard Gatewood has called "the genteel performance."[25] Propriety was undoubtedly the watchword in black cultural and recreational activities, for it was in these activities that the black elite could prove their superiority to other blacks and their social equality with whites. The fact that the elite blacks faced discrimination despite their "genteel performance" persuaded them that they could no longer realistically hope for ultimate assimilation and strengthened their bonds with the rest of the black community.

For those who wanted to attend the theater there were several alternatives. After the 1890s, most theaters were segregated, and blacks had to sit in the balcony, often referred to in the white community as "nigger heaven." The stigma attached to sitting in such spaces was obvious. Black-owned theaters in the late nineteenth century did not appeal to the sophisticated tastes of the elite, who desired to dissociate themselves from the working-class blacks who frequented the establishments.[26]

Neither whites nor elite blacks wanted to attend the theater with "the mentally undeveloped Negro." Carter G. Woodson claimed that theaters were segregated because of disorderly conduct on the part of some blacks, who thought the "tragically serious settings on the stage" were ludicrous, and "when others were shedding tears would be giving forth outbursts of uproarious laughter." Segregation did not solve the problem, according to Woodson, because the "disturbing factor" was still present.[27]

Some elite blacks attempted to pass for white or foreign in order to attend theaters that excluded blacks. The historian Constance McLaughlin Green noted that in the 1920s passing was so common "that the National Theater employed a black doorman to spot and bounce intruders whose racial origins were undetectable by whites."[28] Mary Church Terrell described one strategy for passing. Her daughter, when attending the theater, would go in the company of a friend of darker complexion, saying that if her friend had the nerve, "I certainly had the nerve to go ahead, get her ticket, give it to the ticket taker, lock arms with her and walk in boldly with her if she would come along with me."[29] Her mother did not recall her having any difficulties with this approach.

But Terrell did recall a harrowing incident when she and five friends of varying complexions decided to see a team of black comedians at a segregated theater. The fairest woman entered with the darkest woman and the ruse seemed successful. However, the usher approached the darker woman before the curtain rose, presumably to ask her to leave. The quick-thinking and courageous woman assumed a foreign accent, and the usher apologized and left them alone. Blacks were well aware of the irony of the discrimination that denied light-skinned blacks access to the theater while allowing darker-skinned Mexicans, Indians, and southern Europeans the privilege. Many blacks preferred to stay home to avoid public embarrassment. The invention of radio allowed them the opportunity to hear many black performers who before had appeared only in Jim Crow theaters.[30]

The alternative to poor theater seats and passing for nonblack was the black-owned theater. During the nineteenth century such theaters had somewhat unsavory reputations, but by the 1910s black theater had begun to flourish, in parallel with the rise of race-conscious business in the black community. In part this development was a response to Jim Crow, but management techniques also played a role in it. The career of the Howard Theatre exemplifies the process by which black theaters gained better reputations. In 1909, white entrepreneurs had established the first Howard Theatre, but the community boycotted it and it was forced to close. Black businessmen later reopened the theater as the Minnehaha.[31] In 1910 three theaters were open to blacks: the Maceo, the Ford-Dabney, and the Hiawatha, all in the vicinity of the True Reformers' Hall. These establishments were well patronized but did not supply the demand of the 100,000 blacks in the District. White entrepreneurs established these "optional Jim Crow theaters," naming them after heroic whites who had helped blacks, such as General Oliver O. Howard, and hiring African American managers to convince the public that the theater was run by members of the black community.[32]

The second Howard Theatre, at 7th and T Street, owned by the same white entrepreneurs who had made the first attempt, invaded the heart of the black cultured community. The white owners were reluctant to reveal their identity and used a black manager as a front. Despite its location near Howard University, the white owners reportedly stated that "this theater is located in a community of a different class of Negroes from those of the True Reformer Community. As a whole they have less self-respect and are not as comfortably situated. I think the theater will take."[33] The theater was nevertheless the first to claim all-black management. Some saw it as a symbol of black pride, but to others it meant succumbing to Jim Crow. Many members of the elite preferred to go to downtown theaters, even if segregated, because they perceived them as more prestigious and did not want to mix with the working classes. The management of the Howard, however, began running some regular nights for the "classes" and others for the "masses." On "class" night higher ticket prices discouraged working-class patrons from attending. In addition, the quality of the performers improved, in part because of the frequent appearances of the Howard University Players.

Though off to a rocky start, by 1913 the Howard Theatre was widely praised by Washington's leading black citizens.[34] In 1914, Robert H. Terrell wrote to his daughter that "I do put in an evening every week nearly at the Howard. There have been some very good shows there recently, and this week is to be a banner." Terrell also mentioned another black theater, the Majestic, which featured prominent vaudeville acts and had "not begun to draw well yet," but was "a very pretty place."³⁵ Terrell's attendance at black-owned theaters may reflect his attempts to patronize black businesses in general, since Terrell was active in National Urban League activities. That he and others of his social circle did make these attempts was a sign of growing race pride among the black elite.

Frequent dances and other social events added gaiety to the life of the black elite. These dances, sponsored by fraternal organizations and social clubs, were usually held in dance halls such as the Lincoln Colonnade, which could accommodate 1,000 people. The hall was in the basement of Lincoln Theatre, and so was popular with people of all social statuses in the black community. One of the more popular dance halls for the black elite was Murray Palace Casino, owned by the same Murray brothers who ran a printing establishment. Located on U Street, the building was the only one of its kind owned, designed, and built entirely by African Americans. For larger events and celebrations, the black community used Convention Hall, with a capacity of 4,500, or the Coliseum, which was later converted into a bowling alley. More intimate affairs might be held at Jenifer's Hall, in the auditorium of the former Jenifer Business School, at the corner of N Street and New Jersey Avenue, NW, or the Scottish Rite Temple on 11th Street, which was available only to members. The dances all received prominent notice in the social columns of the black press, and could be the highlights of the social season, particularly during inauguration week.

Cabarets and billiard rooms, which generally catered to working-class tastes and had unsavory reputations as gathering places for criminal elements or for those who practiced ostentatious display, held less appeal for elite blacks. A Chinese-owned cabaret, the Phoenix Inn, located on U Street, did attract both black and white socialites with its more refined entertainment. The Phoenix's patrons sat in small booths with glass doors through which they could watch the show. A billiard parlor operated near Howard University by Theus Smith was one of the few to attract a civilized crowd, mostly students. The parlor offered six good tables and good ventilation, something not usually associated with this sort of establishment. The Idle Hour Billiard Parlor, at 1110 U Street, catered to the older generation of the black elite, also offering clean air and well-kept equipment.³⁶

To compensate for their exclusion from many of the city's social activities, the black community organized recreational activities exclusively for themselves. Church activities played a welcome role, as did the annual St. Luke's picnic in 1898, where "the younger set tripped the light fantastic and kept the swings moving; the older folks enjoyed the cool breezes and did full justice to the 'old fashioned country dinner.'"[37] In the same year, Captain L. J. Woollen purchased the steamer *River Queen* to take trips to Notley Hall in Oxon Hill, Maryland, and other points on the Potomac. African Americans enjoyed trips to the beach at Cedar Hill as well as other boat excursions. These trips were generally organized by church groups, but were popular among all social groups. In 1917 the black businessman J. O. Holmes bought the steamer *E. Madison Hall*. The boat was mobilized into government service during World War I, but after the war it did a tremendous business on the Potomac. The steamer could accommodate 800 passengers, had twenty staterooms, and took two or three trips a day down the Potomac to River View, a summer resort open to blacks. With a season running from May through September and with demand high, Holmes did exceedingly well.[38] The rise in the number of black-owned excursion enterprises, like that of black-owned theaters, reflected growing support for businesses built on a foundation of racial solidarity.

Sports were popular among the black elite, who enjoyed them both as spectators and as participants. Since there was no professional black baseball team in Washington, fans had to attend games at the American League baseball park. Here they were not segregated and waited in the same food and ticket lines as everyone else, a circumstance that perhaps accounted for the popularity of the sport among African Americans. Beginning in 1925, however, the ballpark began to refuse to sell tickets to black fans whose names they recognized. The practice continued despite protest in the press.

Golf and tennis were popular participation sports among the black elite. Originally the white golf courses set aside certain days of the week for blacks to play, but white golfers complained that they did not like being restricted to certain days only. The black players petitioned for a separate black golf course, but again encountered opposition from the white community. Ultimately the city agreed to build a nine-hole course for blacks in Potomac Park, near the Lincoln Memorial. The course was so beautifully kept that problems arose when white players tried to use it.

It was difficult for blacks outside the elite circle to play tennis, since the courts designated for use by African Americans were located far from most black neighborhoods. By the 1920s the city boasted five black tennis clubs, most of them affiliated with the schools or Howard University. The most prestigious was the James E. Walker Club, which held regular smokers to promote tennis and organized annual tournaments. The club was also instrumental in building new courts, first in Le Droit Park and later at 13th and T Streets, NW, near the Terrell home. The Howard University Club also held annual tournaments, at which silver loving cups donated by local businessmen were awarded to the winners.[39]

Exclusive social clubs were an important part of black elite life because they restored a sense of prestige to their members. In the 1880s black elite social clubs such as the Lotus Club focused largely on excluding those with darker skin or dividing social groups between longtime residents of the District and newcomers. While light skin did remain an important indicator of elite status well into the twentieth century, so many darker-skinned blacks were rising to the ranks of the elite that social clubs no longer made this distinction.

The divisions between old citizens and newcomers continued to some extent in the social clubs in the late nineteenth century, and organizations such as the Oldest Inhabitants Association sprang up in the twentieth century, yet these divisions also largely disappeared as newcomers became old citizens themselves. At the turn of the century the Capital City Club gave luncheons and held get-togethers in the cozy apartments and parlors opened to them. They held musical entertainments and at one meeting gave a spring parasol to every lady present. The Bachelors' Club, made up of "Washington's brightest social and intellectual young men"—a jovial group that included John S. Love, Gary Wormley, and M. O. Dumas—gave frequent receptions open to other members of the elite. Congressional employees formed the Capitol Pleasure Club and held picnics at Eureka Park in Anacostia.[40]

The most exclusive club after 1899 was the black Cosmos Club, later renamed the Monocan Club, which held four or more receptions annually, as well as balls on special occasions such as the president's inauguration. Its membership list included the cream of black society in Washington, both newcomers and old citizens. In 1901 a competitor to the Cosmos Club, the Citizens Committee, led by Daniel Murray and William Bruce Evans, vied for the privilege of organizing inaugural activities. The Citizens Committee was composed largely of the younger members of the elite, and seems to have been justified in its claim that it was the premier social group in the city. By 1905, however, the Monocan Club had regained that title and offered an elaborate inaugural celebration.[41] Men's social clubs tended to be a means of affirming elite status as well as providing opportunities to socialize, but in a society where half the population did not recognize that elite blacks had any status at all, this affirmation became psychologically important.

The women of the black elite tended to spend less time than the men in socializing in formal clubs. One reason for this difference was that women often spent most of their spare time involved in charitable and reform activities. A few women's social clubs did exist, however, including the Matron's Whist Club. Aside from playing cards, the women frequently entertained with elaborate meals. Most of the members were wives of prominent men.[42]

By the second decade of the twentieth century, social clubs began to put less emphasis on status than on racial solidarity. The transformation in objective conditions for blacks affected all aspects of their lives, and perhaps made the black elite more conscious of their responsibility to their race. In addition, the members of the black elite themselves had become more interested in promoting racial solidarity and racial uplift. With the decline of the aristocratic elite and the rise of the professional elite came a new dedication to serious concerns. Perhaps shamed by the activities of the women of their social circles, the men had become more involved with racial uplift activities and had little time for purely social diversions.

Even groups begun as social organizations began to take on race issues. The Mu-So-Lit Club, established in 1909, rivaled the Monocan Club in prestigious membership, but invited writers to present papers and guest lecturers to address the members. In 1913 the club launched a campaign to raise subscriptions for the NAACP; it immediately raised $53, and over $100 more was pledged.[43] Though the Mu-So-Lit Club had devolved to a purely social organization by the 1920s, it did have the effect of uniting the different generations of the elite, as well as the old citizens and newcomers. This was an important step toward uniting the black community in the District.

Not all black elite groups, however, were so directly concerned with race issues. Washington also boasted many clubs devoted to the fine arts. Even art could bring race pride, however. At the Atlanta Cotton States Exposition in 1895 several Washington artists received attention for their work. Daniel Freeman painted a symbolic work titled *30 Equals 453*, representing the idea that 30 years of emancipation for blacks had brought them to a point where they had become as civilized as whites, who had had 453 years of emancipation. In addition, Freeman showed portraits of Frederick Douglass, Blanche K. Bruce, and Abraham Lincoln. Most of the artwork at the exposition came from the Amateur Art Club of Washington. This group brought crayon sketches and photographs of black schools, churches, and hospitals in the District, and exhibited some fine needlework.[44]

The Washington Artists Association was established in 1917, with departments of literature, drama, aesthetic dance, painting, sculpture, and architecture. The organization comprised fewer artists than patrons; among its officers were the sociologist Kelly Miller; the clubwomen Mary Church Terrell, Mary P. Burrill, and Coralie Cook; and the actor and dentist C. Sumner Wormley.[45] Nonetheless, it created a firm foundation for fine arts in the Washington black community, as the patrons were not only helping individual artists but providing opportunities for the race to enter the aesthetic world.

Musical organizations proliferated in the District, some of them highly exclusive, others embracing the community. In the 1880s and 1890s the Carreno Club and Aeolian Mandolin and Guitar Club typified exclusive elite musical groups. The Aeolian Club, which was composed of graduates and students of the M Street High School, was established in the late 1890s and held regular meetings and musical presentations. Members of the black elite from both Washington and elsewhere attended the group's musicales.[46]

The greatest musical organizations in black Washington, however, were not these rather snobbish groups created in the 1880s and 1890s but those with a dedication to the improvement of the race through education: the Treble Clef Club and the Samuel Coleridge-Taylor Choral Society. The Treble Clef Club was founded in 1897 by Mamie F. Hilyer, Harriet Gibbs, and other elite women who desired to have a black formal organization dedicated to performing classical music. The group gave regular recitals and did much to promote interest in classical music among the black elite.[47] The group became interested in the works of black composers, particularly those of the English composer Samuel Coleridge-Taylor, whose masterpiece, *Hiawatha*, had captured the imagination of Europe. In 1901, Mamie F. Hilyer and her husband, Andrew, visited England, where Mrs. Hilyer had the good fortune to meet the composer. Upon her return to Washington, she proposed to some of her musical friends that they create a group to perform Coleridge-Taylor's works.[48]

In 1902 the Samuel Coleridge-Taylor Choral Society, composed of both male and female singers and musicians, proposed to offer *Hiawatha* while Colcridge-Taylor was visiting America, and invited the composer to conduct the performance. The event was not without significance to racial uplift, as the society believed that "such achievement . . . would mark an epoch in the progress of the American Negro toward higher ideals of civilization and culture."[49]

Coleridge-Taylor did not have time to conduct the performance in 1903, but the Choral Society, before a large audience at the Metropolitan AME Church, enjoyed great success. The group boasted seventy-two sopranos, fifty-five altos, thirty-four tenors, and thirty-eight bassos, and its membership resembled a *Who's Who* of the Washington black elite. The group presented *Hiawatha* and other Coleridge-Taylor works on several occasions, the crowning glory being the performance of *Hiawatha* in 1904, when the composer came to conduct it. The group continued for many years, running excursion trips and in 1913 giving a testimonial upon Coleridge-Taylor's death.[50]

The Choral Society's importance to Washington went beyond the simple diffusing of culture to the masses, its stated purpose. The organization was indeed a vehicle for racial uplift. It educated the public about black composers and stimulated racial pride. By showing that blacks created more than plantation songs, the group educated the white public as well, some of whom attended the performances, and most of whom read the reviews in the Washington press. The significance was not lost on the black community. One audience member wrote to Andrew F. Hilyer after the first performance of *Hiawatha*: "I am more than glad that 'Hiawaitha' [*sic*] was a success. All of the success means so much for the race. . . . You have lifted the *whole* race just so many degrees. . . . Of course 'To God be the glory' but thanks and praise and blessings be unto you who have lifted us that much near[er] to God."[51]

While the artistic and musical organizations of the black elite indirectly benefited all members of the race by opening up the fine arts to them, it was the literary societies that most directly addressed race issues. The black elite recognized literary societies as important cultural institutions. They also realized that discussion of issues of importance to the race could be made more palatable to white society if it were conducted under the guise of a genteel literary or debating society. The *Leader* noted that "the various colored literaries throughout the country should devote their time as much as possible to the discussion of living issues, and the best course to pursue in order to accomplish something tangible for the good of all."[52] Black ministers such as Daniel Alexander Payne and Henry McNeal Turner saw church-sponsored literary societies as a means to keep the attention of the younger educated generation of African Americans. In addition, they hoped, these societies could attract new church members if they were properly managed. Turner believed that the most important goal was "infusing human beings with pride and confidence in themselves and their race."[53] The black literary societies of the nineteenth and early twentieth centuries were the first cultural organizations to address the issue of race pride and solidarity directly.

The evolution of Washington's literary societies reflected the shift in the emphasis of elite values. The evolution began primarily with the establishment of the Bethel Literary and Historical Association in 1881. At first the seventy-five members planned to meet biweekly. The group soon grew larger, however, and began to meet weekly. With ever larger audiences, the character of the Bethel Literary became more sophisticated and members demanded less domination by the church.

From the start, the topics discussed revealed a definite agenda. In its first season the Bethel devoted three sessions to discussing Egyptian history, one to Ethiopian history, one to a history of the Zulus and racial connection with them, and one to "eminent men of the Negro race." Lewis H. Douglass published a letter in the *People's Advocate* praising the Bethel Literary as "promising to accomplish very much more for the enlightenment of the people than the social literary organizations for which our city had been noted."[54]

At first there was no audience discussion of the papers presented, but Bishop Payne encouraged teachers to visit museums and to travel in the summer to follow up on the topics, and gradually the discussion livened up. Under the guidance of its unofficial advisory board and President Robert J. Smith, the quality of papers improved along with the discussion. All of this activity was monitored by the Advisory Board. "Many a paper which might have lowered the high standard [to] which our efforts were aimed was declined with thanks, and many a discussion which would have stirred smouldering embers or latent combustibles to dreadful explosions [was] averted by their discretionary actions."[55] The conflict that arose over the leadership and direction of the organization soon after it was founded caused the division of the Union Bethel AME Church into conservative and progressive elements. The progressive elements, who favored an educated congregation over an emotional one, won the day and regrouped as the Metropolitan AME Church. Despite the efforts of the conservatives, the fate of the Bethel Literary was secure.

The Bethel Literary and Historical Association became the center of black intellectual life in the capital. In the 1880s, the organization debated "The Black Woman in the South," "The Negro in Science," "Crispus Attucks," "The Race Problem in the United States," "Separate Schools," and "The Duty of the People of the United States to the Colored Soldier," among other topics. Debate was often heated but always interesting to the race.

In the fourth season, 1885–86, as racial discrimination increased, the tone of the discussions changed from radical Republican to conservative and independent. About the same time, African Americans in Washington also stopped pursuing legal efforts to end discrimination in public accommodations and sought new ways to contest Jim Crow. Discussions at the Bethel Literary centered mainly on travelogues and other topics unrelated to race. This situation prevailed for the next seven years, during which time participation and interest in the Bethel Literary dropped off. Community leaders no longer had confidence in the efficacy of overt protest for civil rights, and disillusionment with the possibility of assimilation seems to have created little inclination to discuss the state of racial affairs.

In the organization's eleventh season, however, a renaissance occurred. Topics for the season were printed in advance. Half of the papers were on scientific topics but the other half concerned racial topics, including "The Dialect Story and Its Evil Influences," "An Analysis of Color Prejudice," and a symposium on African American business. By 1893, the Bethel Literary again focused almost exclusively on racial issues. The season that year closed with two papers, "What Has the Bethel Literary Done for the Race?" and "What May It Do?" By 1896, the organization had evolved into a debating society par excellence that spawned imitations in the District and nationwide. The *Colored American* reported that in 1898 the average attendance at meetings had been 150, and as many as 800 had attended the larger meetings.[56]

Three factors accounted for the success of the Bethel Literary. First, it provided an outlet for frustrations through discussion of racial topics. Second, it operated at an intellectual level that appealed to the educated and largely professional black elite that was assuming a leadership role in the community. Third, and possibly most important, the Bethel Literary boosted racial pride in a nonconfrontational manner. Discussing historical issues was an acceptable elite behavior for both blacks and whites, and the lyceum format was quite fashionable in the late nineteenth century. Washington's elite blacks were able to maintain their "genteel performance" while strengthening pride in their heritage.

Ironically, by studying their past in an elite setting, Bethel members rediscovered their kinship with all African Americans and felt an increased sense of responsibility toward their race. In their history they also discovered powerful moral lessons for future generations. By showing that their distant ancestors had once been great, they gave reason to hope that the race would rise again. By teaching the struggles of their more immediate ancestors, they showed the virtues of hard work, selflessness, and determination.

By the turn of the century, the Bethel Literary was already a firmly established institution among the race leaders of Washington and arguably throughout the country. It was, therefore, a natural forum for debate between proponents of Booker T. Washington and W. E. B. Du Bois in 1903. Robert H. Terrell, William Bruce Evans, Whitefield McKinlay, Jesse Lawson, and Richard W. Thompson, who led Booker T. Washington's advocates, all owed positions or favors to Washington's influence. The debate began in earnest after William H. Ferris of New Haven, an ally of William Monroe Trotter of the *Boston Guardian* and therefore aligned with W. E. B. Du Bois and the Boston Radicals, gave a scathing criticism of Booker T. Washington before the Bethel Literary in January 1903. Friends of Washington promised to respond to Ferris's charges at a later meeting. Richard W. Thompson, a columnist for the *Colored American,* gave a paper at the Second Baptist Lyceum at the end of January but appears to have failed to hold his ground against Ferris, who was present at the meeting.[57]

The meeting was a prelude to a debate at the Bethel Literary at which Jesse Lawson presented a paper in favor of Washington's views. The *Colored American,* a pro-Tuskegee newspaper, reported that the discussion was notable for the show of antagonism to Booker T. Washington's industrial ideal. Jesse Lawson proclaimed the meeting a Washington affair, but the editor, Edward E. Cooper, reported that "other than his [Lawson's] word for it there was very little reliable evidence of the fact."[58] Nevertheless, the meeting was important enough that Washington's lieutenants in the District felt the need to report to him on it in great detail. In addition to assuring the Wizard of Tuskegee that the strength of the Washington supporters' arguments outweighed their numerical strength, the reports noted which Washington supporters were absent from the meeting or failed to rise to his defense.[59] Clearly the Bethel Literary had great influence on African American leaders nationwide.

In later years, the Bethel Literary continued its involvement in the racial issues of the day. In 1912 the organization cosponsored a mass meeting with the NAACP, and in 1919 W. E. B. Du Bois spoke before the group on "the Negro and the Great War."[60] The Bethel Literary and Historical Association both reflected and sparked interest in the study of black history among black leaders in Washington. Kelly Miller, who as a college student cut his teeth at the Bethel Literary by thoroughly trouncing a paper by the Reverend Benjamin T. Tanner, was just one of the many African American intellectuals who came to the meetings. The Bethel Literary had influence that spread beyond its members into the community.

While the exclusive social clubs and vacation spots provided means for the black elite to create social distance and to escape the pressures of the larger society, the segregation of the theaters and racial discussions of the literary societies drew the black elite closer to the working classes. Yet even in their social clubs elite blacks began to tire of purely social diversions by the early twentieth century, and the discrimination that the black elite sometimes faced on vacation served as a reminder that social status depended on race in American society.

By forcing blacks into their own community, whites spurred the creation of black cultural institutions that knitted the black community more closely together. In imitating white conventions such as literary societies, the elite were able to forge a sense of racial awareness through the study of African and African American history. By following white elite standards, elite blacks were able to agitate for racial uplift under the guise of refinement without openly challenging white hegemony. The elite social clubs and vacation resorts did allow the members of the black elite a chance to reinforce networks of influence and distance themselves from the working classes, yet even there the black elite began to recognize that they had more in common with other blacks than with the white elite.

The cultural and leisure activities of the black elite provided a strong impetus for its transformation. Activities designed to reinforce social status distinct from that of the black working classes ultimately reinforced the ideals of racial solidarity. Membership in a particular cultural organization or social club still qualified one for entry into the elite at the turn of the century. It is important to note, however, that the nature and activities of these organizations had changed to become more racially conscious. Social status, even in the most exclusive aspects of black elite life, was becoming more dependent on awareness of racial issues and efforts to uplift the race.

FOUR

The Church

The development of the black elite church between 1880 and 1920 reflected the transformation of the elite themselves. After distancing themselves from the mass congregations in the 1880s, in the 1890s the elite churches began to create institutions to gain independence from white control or supervision. In the 1900s, as church leadership in racial uplift efforts began to give way to larger community leadership, black elite churches attempted to enlarge their appeal through reform efforts, but the churches became followers rather than leaders.

Mirrored in these changes within the elite churches were all the aspects of the evolution of the black elite itself. The self-conscious distancing of the 1880s mirrored the attempts of the black elite to establish a distinct, if precarious, social status. The building of independent black churches mirrored the building of institutions within the black community designed to obviate the need for white support. The declining leadership of the church in racial uplift efforts mirrored the rise of the new professional elite and the rising interest in secular racial uplift that permeated the black community. In short, the black elite churches of Washington, D.C., provide a microcosm for the study of the transformation of the black elite.

By the 1890s and early 1900s, elite black churches such as the Metropolitan AME, the Fifteenth Street Presbyterian, and the Nineteenth Street Baptist had succeeded in differentiating themselves from the emotional churches of the working classes and had begun to assume leadership roles within the community. As belief in the possibility of assimilation declined and racial prejudice within the white church increased, black elite churches began the fight for autonomy. Creating independent institutions and parallel church hierarchies, the black churches declared independence from white control. It was during the 1890s that the elite churches were at their strongest, having prepared for leadership roles by electing educated and progressive ministers who in turn had educated the members of the elite congregations as to their role in society.

In the 1890s the move to reform the larger society led naturally to reforms aimed at combating racial discrimination. Under the Reverend Walter H. Brooks, Nineteenth Street Baptist entered a new phase of conflict for the black church and similarly for the black elite. As racism and segregation increased in American society in the 1890s, the white church began to absorb some of these ideas. Black ministers found themselves forced to defend organized Christianity against charges of hypocrisy to an elite that was beginning to realize that assimilation would not come any time soon.

The black elite had begun to advocate racial solidarity, realizing that this was the only way to escape dependence on whites. The black church led the way in creating parallel black institutions that would relieve this dependence. Brooks was particularly vocal in the disputes between the black Baptist church and its white counterparts in the late 1880s and 1890s.

The main organizations for Baptists in the country were the Northern and Southern Baptist Conventions, which were controlled by white Baptists. Most black Baptist churches were affiliated with the Northern Baptist Convention. The Convention ran the foreign missionary efforts, the American Baptist Home Mission Society (ABHMS), and distributed denominational literature through the American Baptist Publication Society. During the 1880s, blacks began to agitate for the appointment of black faculty at schools for blacks run by the ABHMS. In addition, black ministers and churchwomen who were active in the movement for education complained that the American Baptist Publication Society would not accept works by black theologians, and that the only Sunday school literature available for black churches was written by whites. Walter H. Brooks was among those black ministers who protested the Convention's policies.

Brooks had already made a name for himself as an advocate for education before his arrival in Washington. In 1881 he had written a widely read article advocating the expansion of the curriculum in the black Baptist colleges beyond the current theological courses; he wanted to see them include the sort of courses being offered by Howard and Fisk universities. He particularly emphasized the importance of education for black women. In response to his and others' pleas, northern white Baptists established Hartshorn Memorial College in Richmond, Virginia, for the education of black women.

In Washington, Brooks led a group of black ministers in protesting the administration of the white president of the Baptist-affiliated Wayland Seminary, G. M. P. King. They accused King of arbitrary corporal punishment and abuse of black female students at Wayland. Despite their formal protest, the ABHMS did not remove King. The lack of resolution led to black demands for separation from white Baptists in much the way the AME church had separated from the Methodists in the early nineteenth century.[1]

Separation from white supervision had, in fact, already begun at the national level. In 1880 a group of black Baptists had formed the Baptist Foreign Mission Convention in response to efforts to exclude blacks from missionary work in Africa. In 1886, concerned by conciliatory policies between the Northern and Southern Baptist Conventions, a group of mainly southern black Baptists formed the American National Baptist Convention, intended as a way to discuss common issues of the race. In 1892 the National Baptist Educational Convention was founded to oversee black educational efforts. Washington elite Baptists, under Brooks, welcomed all these developments as part of the emerging independence of the black community.[2]

Further separation of the black Baptists came after debates over publication of black authors in the American Baptist Publication Society's materials. In 1889, Brooks, William J. Simmons, and Emmanuel K. Love offered articles for publication and, under pressure from black churches, the Publication Society agreed to publish them in the journal *Baptist Teacher*. When southern white Baptists objected, the society reneged on its promise, offering to publish the articles as pamphlets instead. Unhappy with this offer, blacks organized the National Baptist Publishing Board. Now that they could publish their own materials, black Baptists were able to restore self-confidence and ensure that material by black authors could be used in their Sunday schools to instill racial pride and counter discriminatory theology.[3]

In 1895, all these groups merged to form the National Baptist Convention, U.S.A., which could claim to be the only national Baptist convention in the country, and with close to two million members at the turn of the century was arguably the largest convention of any religion. There was no "cathedral of black Baptists," as the National Convention could claim many strong religious leaders, and Baptist power was concentrated mainly in southern and rural areas. Under Walter H. Brooks, however, the Nineteenth Street Baptist Church was one of the nation's leading Baptist congregations and wielded considerable influence.

By the turn of the century, black elite churches had established distinct identities with a strong reputation for race leadership. What elite blacks had sought for themselves in the 1880s, they now sought for the rest of the race. The elite church led the movement for education for blacks and for the building up of independent institutions.

The ideal of a progressive elite church, dedicated to racial uplift, was the Fifteenth Street Presbyterian Church under Francis J. Grimké. The church had been organized in 1841 by none other than John F. Cook, and early ministers had included such notables as Benjamin Tanner, William B. Evans, and Henry Highland Garnet. In 1878 Francis J. Grimké took over ministerial duties, and with the exception of a three-year hiatus in Jacksonville, Florida, in the 1880s, he served as minister for nearly fifty years. Although black Presbyterians never established a hierarchy separate from their white counterparts, ministers such as Grimké kept the issue of racism constantly before the church synods. According to one contemporary historian, Grimké's arrival at the Fifteenth Street Presbyterian heralded "a great spiritual awakening as the result of his forceful preaching."[4]

Judging from the official church session minutes, this statement was accurate. During his first year, many new people joined the congregation, most of whom had recognizable elite status. Nor were these newcomers inactive in the church. Four years after joining, James H. Meriwether was elected elder; two years later, Furman J. Shadd became a trustee. The church weeded out members who had not participated actively yet were still on the rolls. By 1890, it was clear that the Fifteenth Street Presbyterian Church had become an elite, activist church.[5] Grimké regularly preached special sermons on racial topics during inauguration week because many representatives of the race from all over the country came to his church then and he could reach a larger audience.[6]

Grimké typified the new generation of ministers. He was well educated, he quoted poetry and scientific theory in his sermons, and, having grown up during Reconstruction, he felt confident of the abilities of his race and the capacity of the white race to recognize those abilities. As a result, he did not hesitate to remind white churches of their duty to the black race, and while his tone remained essentially polite, he did not hesitate to speak out against injustice.

Grimké believed that the church should be the center of moral and spiritual life and the source of information on what was good. Members should inspire goodness and fulfill this ideal in their personal characters and lives. The minister himself should be above reproach. His chief purpose was to teach and preach and therefore he should be thoroughly prepared both intellectually and spiritually.[7]

In an 1892 sermon, Grimké agreed with other progressive members of the elite that too many churches were too emotional, too frivolous, and too concerned with collecting money for the sake of money. He felt that ministers should try to eliminate these elements, which left the race open to ridicule by whites. "The moral plane upon which the masses of our people move is confessedly not very high," Grimké wrote, "and in view of their past antecedents could not be expected to be high. But if they had the proper kind of instruction from the pulpit, there is every reason to believe that they would stand much higher today than they do."[8]

Grimké felt that a minister should not be influenced by public sentiment and should do and say what he believed was right, pleasing God rather than man. Ultimately it was this belief that led him to become more vocal in his protests against racial discrimination. In the 1890s, although Grimké generally preached against race hatred, he did so in terms of biblical allegories. He compared the persecution of Jesus to the persecution of African Americans. He protested lynchings in the South by discussing the trial of Jesus to emphasize that there was a time to speak out against injustice. Grimké argued that Pontius Pilate was too much of a coward to challenge Jesus' accusers, because they were too popular. In the same way, he said, white northerners often did not mingle socially with the blacks they professed to care for because it was not a popular stance to take.[9]

In 1900 Grimké gave a series of sermons on the condition of the race that showed his increasing feelings of frustration. He described the divisions among African Americans that hampered protest and the negative attitudes that the press, the white churches, and the government held toward the black community. He outlined the hypocrisy in such attitudes and even issued veiled threats of violence if the situation did not change: "Do not misunderstand me. I am not counseling violence: I am not saying it is a wise thing for the Negro to resort to violence; but I am saying that sometimes violence is the means which God uses to arouse the sleeping conscience, and pierce the rhinoceros hide of indifference. I trust that it may not be necessary, but if it must come, then, I for one say, let it come, and the sooner it comes the better. The Negro will not be responsible for it."[10] Tensions had reached a new height by the turn of the century, and ministers such as Grimké were no longer willing to be passive recipients of race hatred.

Yet, while Grimké was willing to speak out on the issues, he could propose few spiritual solutions to his congregation. In his sermons "Signs of a Brighter Future" and "God and Prayer as Factors in the Struggle" he noted with pride that the race had moved beyond simply collecting material goods and had begun to stand up for its rights. However, the biggest reasons he could give for hope were, first, that God existed and so injustice could not prevail, and second, that prayer was a powerful force that could help right wrongs.[11] For a sophisticated audience such as that at the Fifteenth Street Presbyterian Church, the thought was consoling but offered little practical advice.

In the years that followed, Grimké changed the focus of his attacks on prejudice and its causes but not the solutions he offered. In 1903 he expressed the belief that the problem was that many whites did not truly accept God in their lives. In 1910 he demanded that the white church recognize the hypocrisy involved in its silence on the race issue and begin to teach racial harmony. In 1919 he stated that the white race should accept full responsibility for the race problem and should change its attitude toward blacks.[12] Grimké's rhetoric became more overtly hostile to whites as conditions remained oppressive, but he was speaking to an audience that did not need to be converted.

While the black church was orienting the elite to its responsibilities, other changes were taking place. American society was embracing the scientific method and religion was losing its authority. Racial prejudice within American churches caused disillusionment among elite blacks. Finally, as the black elite took advantage of educational opportunities, a new leadership class developed centered on black professionals other than ministers, and on businessmen who had the economic means and practical knowledge necessary to sponsor movements for racial uplift outside the church.

The black ministers responded to public disillusionment by trying to involve the church more in community reforms and sponsoring activities that would attract younger people to the church. Their activities paralleled the rise of the Social Gospel movement. If the white ministers were worried that labor struggles and poverty were hampering the development of a Christian nation, the black ministers worried that racial tensions were even more detrimental to its development. The Social Gospel movement held great appeal for black ministers. Its emphasis on community reform effort as opposed to individualistic reform translated easily into racial solidarity.

Elite black churchwomen also desired to involve the church more in reform activities. At the turn of the century they saw not only rising racism but the dawn of the woman's era, a time when women, working across racial lines and within their own communities, would lead the country into the twentieth century. Problems created by industrialization and urbanization were also problems that women could deal with through "municipal housekeeping," extending what they saw as women's unique abilities to nurture the bodies, minds, and spirits of their children to solve the problems the masses of their people faced. In particular, as Christian women they felt their qualifications to uplift the race morally were unmatched. Women within the churches were fundamental in fund-raising and organizing the reform activities that they and their ministers proposed.

Nevertheless, elite black churches began to reflect the values of their congregations more than shape them. In one of the ironies of the Social Gospel movement, even white ministers who advocated active participation in reform of societal ills seldom became activists themselves.[13] Although the church remained a rallying point for many racial uplift efforts, increasingly the minister became the supporter of those efforts rather than the leader. Nonetheless, involvement in racial uplift became an important qualification for entrance to the black elite in part because the intellectual ministers who gave elite churches their social status led their congregations in that direction.

In 1889, when Francis J. Grimké returned from three years spent in Florida for his health, he set about a vigorous reorganization of his church. Influenced by the growing Social Gospel emphasis on righting social wrongs in an institutional manner rather than helping individuals, Grimké hoped to help his race in the same way that white ministers emphasized helping those who suffered from the effects of industrialization and urbanization. He established nine standing committees to deal with church affairs in a more systematic manner. Some of the committees dealt with traditional church functions, but Grimké also introduced committees on temperance, missionary work with the poor, and "Systematic Beneficience."[14] These new committees showed

Grimké's commitment to extend the traditional role of the church to address the problems of a modern society.

Temperance was not a new passion for Grimké; it paralleled the growth of temperance sentiment in the country as a whole. In 1885, under Grimké's pastorate, the session had resolved to use unfermented grape juice for communion. Grimké believed that "a more horrible picture [cannot] be presented of the possible fate of the man who permits himself to come under the power of the intoxicating bowl, of this awful rum curse." Alcohol enslaved men, destroyed their will, and took away their manhood.[15] He expected his committee to hold public meetings, circulate tracts, personally try to get people to sign the temperance pledge as he himself had done, and endeavor to secure the adoption of temperance principles in the church's families. Grimké also organized children of the church into "bands of Hope" to promote temperance in the next generation.[16]

The other new committees that Grimké created in 1889 also reflected larger changes in society. The committee on the poor aimed at missionary work "to reach by Christian efforts, the lowest and most degraded classes of our people, and to aid such as may be in need of food and clothing, and also to look after the poor of the church."[17] The church had traditionally taken care of its poorer members, but what was new was the outreach to the larger community and the formation of a committee to deal systematically with charity work. In the early 1880s, the Fifteenth Street Presbyterian Church had regularly given individual charity to members in need, but with the pruning of the church rolls under Grimké, the Fifteenth Street congregation had few poor members remaining.[18] These changes spurred the growth of community outreach and reflected the elite's confidence in their ability to police their own morals.

At the Metropolitan AME Church, which in 1880 had 1,009 members, individual charity persisted longer. In the early 1880s several individuals repeatedly received charity from the church. At least three people continued to receive direct charity for the remainder of the decade. Generally the church dispensed charity to women without much debate, although it hesitated when men asked for help. Typically it gave money readily to help defray funeral expenses or in times of illness. In 1894 the Board of Trustees approved a motion to change the name of the Poor Fund to the Relief Fund after having made several attempts to make general distributions to the poor rather than donations to specific individuals. In the years following, fund-raising at the

Metropolitan AME Church became more systematic, and the church appears to have donated mainly to established groups such as the Home for Friendless Girls. By 1901 this tendency had perhaps gone a little too far, as the assistant superintendent was authorized to get rid of an "objectionable beggar" who had been loitering in the entrance of the church at regular service time.[19]

Francis J. Grimké's Committee on Systematic Beneficience was designed to interest people in the boards of the church, to secure regular subscriptions to at least one of them, and to ensure their payments.[20] This committee perhaps influenced attempts at the Metropolitan AME to increase its own fund-raising efforts. In the 1880s the Metropolitan AME had relied mainly on events such as lotteries to raise funds. For one such lottery in 1885, the first prize had been a barber's chair; the second prize, originally hoped to be shoemaker's irons, was a barber's looking glass. Although these lotteries continued, the prizes reflected more sophisticated tastes in later years. In addition, the church began offering prizes for fund-raising efforts themselves. In 1895 the Board of Trustees offered a gold watch to the person who solicited the most contributions. Second prize was a clock, and other prizes included "an elegant china tea set."[21]

In the same year, the Metropolitan AME adopted the subscription method of fund-raising that Francis J. Grimké had initiated at the Fifteenth Street Presbyterian Church. A committee circulated among church members, soliciting subscriptions to be paid on a monthly basis. Each committee member was responsible for collecting the payments. More significant, the board voted to print subscription booklets to be circulated among white people in the city in the hope of obtaining donations.[22]

The subscription method of fund-raising was popular, but unfortunately, while contributions from subscriptions increased, the more traditional contributions, such as basket collections and public offerings, declined. Most money still came from the class collections. In 1900 the contributions of the Financial Board of the AME Church to the Metropolitan AME Church began to decline, but rallies and subscriptions made up for the loss. In 1901 the Board of Trustees reported that "the departments and organizations of the church have added permanency to their method and habit of work, thus fixing this church as a strong influence for the general uplift of the community." Despite the new permanence of the committee, subscriptions declined. In 1902 they totaled $1,091, in 1903 only $713. The Financial Board's contributions ceased altogether.[23] Ironically, the Metropolitan AME, with some of Washington's wealthiest black citizens as members, was hampered in its charitable activities by a lack of funds, partly because of declining interest in church activities.

Increasingly the black elite churches tried to counter this apathy by becoming more involved in the social welfare movement. The churches had always been social centers for blacks in the nineteenth century, as few had money to build recreation centers or theaters. In addition, the black church had always been an educational center, and encouraged education for practical purposes. Nevertheless, a certain conservative contingent of the church had resisted involvement in worldly affairs on a large scale, believing that man should be more contemplative and disengaged from the world. When the YMCA and YWCA opened, they were seen as competitors to the church, and many ministers refused to support them.

With the decline in interest in religion in favor of practical reform at the turn of the century in American society, these conservative elements bowed to the pressure. Elite blacks tended to have a more progressive outlook on reform, and thus were more likely to lose interest in the churches' activities when they did not keep up with the times. It was inevitable, therefore, that elite black churches would become strong advocates of social welfare as the members of their congregations began to sponsor reform activities outside the church.

Of the elite churches, the Baptists were probably the most active in social welfare work. In 1908 the Nineteenth Street Baptist Church sponsored a health clinic with a free dispensary, staffed by doctors, nurses, and dentists. The Woman's Convention of the National Baptist Convention opened the Social Settlement Centre in Washington, operating it in conjunction with the National Training School for Women and Girls, Howard University, Associated Charities, and the District Juvenile Court. The Centre was part of the settlement house movement in Washington and in the nation as a whole, which, under the guidance of some of the city's leading blacks, had accomplished a great deal for the cause of racial uplift. Among the Social Settlement workers' programs to feed and clothe the poor was a soup station operated in the bitterly cold winter of 1915. The Centre also provided a medical clinic with volunteer doctors, offered classes for children and adults, and sponsored recreational activities such as baseball games. To complete the picture, the

Social Settlement Centre provided legal counsel for juveniles in court. This church effort paralleled the growth of other settlement houses in Washington, to be discussed in a later chapter.

Another Baptist minister, the Reverend John Milton Waldron, who took over Shiloh Baptist Church in 1907 and greatly increased its prestige, established day-care centers and committees to oversee improvements in alley dwellings. Waldron came to Washington from the Bethel Institutional Church in Jacksonville, Florida, where he had been instrumental in creating a kindergarten, life insurance company, and night school, among other community services.

None of these activities would have been possible without the tireless efforts of the Baptist women in both congregations. Churchwomen had long seen social welfare projects as the key to racial uplift, and had taken these projects to be women's unique contribution to the race and to black spirituality. Evelyn Brooks Higginbotham's study of black Baptist women shows that they believed that Christian education was the solution to problematic race relations and necessary for racial uplift. Through cooperative reform efforts with white northern Baptist women, black women were to act as intermediaries between whites and blacks. These women argued that the churches should aid blacks to form good character rather than focusing on reforming bad characteristics. The church should provide job services and recreational activities rather than sermonizing on the evils of idleness and crime.[24]

After 1909, one of the leading members of the Nineteenth Street congregation was Nannie Helen Burroughs. Born in Virginia, Burroughs moved with her parents to Washington in the mid-1880s and attended the black public schools, including the black high school in its pre–M Street location. Burroughs was active in church programs from an early age and honed her oratorical skills there and in her high school literary society. Denied a position teaching domestic science, allegedly because of her dark skin and lack of social connections, Burroughs cultivated a friendship with Booker T. Washington and sought work in Philadelphia and later in Louisville, Kentucky. Burroughs was instrumental in the formation of the Woman's Convention of the National Baptist Convention in 1900. She served as corresponding secretary from 1900 to 1948, and in this capacity traveled the country lecturing on racial and women's issues. She was a vocal opponent of racial discrimination in all forms and a strong advocate of woman suffrage. In 1909, Burroughs returned to Washington to head the National Training School for Women and Girls, established by the Woman's Convention to further education for black women. The school provided girls with industrial training, with emphasis on domestic service, but also offered courses in nontraditional fields such as printing and shoe repair. Burroughs placed importance on teaching "Bible, bath, and broom," reinforcing Christian teachings with practical lessons.[25] It was the efforts of churchwomen such as Burroughs in elite congregations that helped push the church into greater reform activism.

As the spirit of the Social Gospel took hold, race pride soared. Elite blacks became less willing to accept discriminatory treatment from white churches. St. Augustine's Church, a predominantly black, mostly elite Catholic congregation, had always been liberal, but even in the 1880s there were signs of discontent. In January 1889 the first of three African American Catholic conferences was held at St. Augustine's, at which black Catholics asked for increased recognition by their white counterparts. Among other things, they asked for entrance into labor unions, industrial schools, hospitals, and asylums, and public condemnation of discriminatory housing practices.[26] The color line eventually penetrated even the Catholic church in the twentieth century. In 1918 Mary Church Terrell reported that a committee of black Catholics was investigating charges that black nuns were relegated to the balcony at the Church of the Immaculate Conception in Anacostia. She also reported a rumor that blacks were allowed only in the basement of St. Theresa's Church, unless they were taking communion.[27]

As race relations worsened, some white ministers even condoned lynching and preached race inferiority as instituted by God. Such hypocrisy led to a general disillusionment with Christianity among the black elite. In 1891 Frederick Douglass wrote that "the Christianity of this country as exhibited in the Church is not the Christianity of Christ. It is a man-degrading and Negro-hating Christianity . . . and in its presence today, the Negro is robbed, lynched and murdered without rebuke or remonstrance from these Christian pulpits."[28] Such criticism was not isolated, and led to disaffection from religion in general. A white minister, Charles R. Winthrop, wrote to Francis J. Grimké that the presence of this evil in the church had done much harm to faith. "The younger generation of the Negro has not the faith of their fathers. . . . I talk often with young Negroes—many of them college and university graduates—and it is hard to persuade many of them that they can hope for much from Christianity."[29]

The rise of white Christian fundamentalism in the second decade of the twentieth century contributed to this disillusionment. Alice M. Dunbar found it "increasingly hard to hold to the church! It seems so hollow. I find myself listening with a sneer to Billy Sunday and other Caucasian divines as they proclaim the Fatherhood of God and the Brotherhood of man." Mary Church Terrell called Billy Sunday "the worst Jim Crow Artist I ever saw." Anna J. Cooper found it hard to warm up to fundamentalist preachers who said nothing about lynching or the reduction of African Americans to a state of peonage.[30] It was hard to stay involved with a church that did not recognize the rights of the race.

By the 1920s, the black church faced criticism for doing too little. People complained that the churches carried too much debt, and were always demanding more money without paying it off. They were supposed to advance the race but they accomplished little unless they received money from whites, and acceptance of such donations dealt a blow to the independence of the black church. Even when ministers promoted black businesses, people assumed they were accepting kickbacks. The paradox, as with the issue of social welfare, was that ministers were supposed to be involved in worldly affairs while remaining withdrawn from them. The younger professional generation of elite blacks tended to become alienated by out-of-date programs in urban areas that offered other opportunities for social activities.[31]

Disillusionment with established churches made denomination a subordinate factor for many of Washington's black elite. Norma Boyd recalled that although her family had been Baptist before moving to Washington, they joined the Catholic church upon their arrival, partly because it was conveniently near their home. When they moved in later years, they changed denomination again, first to Episcopalian, then to Unitarian. Frederick Douglass reported that he used to be sectarian, but after becoming disillusioned with Christianity, he was happy to recognize the true spirit of God wherever it existed.[32]

In 1896 a group of Washington's black elite joined together in the basement of the Terrell home to form the University Park Temple, which united with Lincoln Park Temple in 1901. The founders included Blanche K. Bruce and John Mercer Langston. The church was nominally Congregational, and grew as an offshoot of Plymouth Congregational Church, which had split from Union Bethel AME in 1880. Josephine Bruce wrote to her son as she was about to take official membership that she hoped "the new work will deserve and receive the blessing of God."[33] The Plymouth Congregational Church, however, was founded in protest against the conservative policies of Union Bethel AME, and it is likely that its members drifted more easily into other churches. Ten years later, one of University Park Temple's founders, Mary Church Terrell, was no longer attending its services.

The Terrells, like many elite blacks, had a practical approach to church attendance. Certainly no one could accuse them of lack of faith, but they often either attended different churches for specific reasons, such as to hear a notable minister give a special sermon, or stayed home to attend to their affairs. In May 1909 the Terrells attended the First Congregational Church to hear a sermon on drudgery, and afterward they discussed it together. In September, Mrs. Terrell reported that "Berto and I have decided to attend other churches sometimes." In October the family went to hear a minister at another church who had known Mrs. Terrell as a child. In the same month Mrs. Terrell attended the Church of the Epiphany, possibly a mixed Episcopal church. She enjoyed the walk but related nothing of the sermon. On the day after Christmas that year the family attended both Congregational and Lutheran services.[34]

It was not uncommon for the Terrells to stay home on a Sunday, for reasons as varied as catching up on reading the papers, going to the zoo, or watching an eclipse. When the Terrells' daughter Mary attended church on Mother's Day, she could persuade no one in the family to go with her. "Papa had more fun over my going," she wrote to her mother. "He said he had Billie [the family dog] out walking but had to hurry and bring him back so as he could see his mistress go to church for once in his life."[35] Mary Terrell was not the only member of the black elite whose faith was sporadic. Francis J. Grimké urged P. B. S. Pinchback to accept Jesus before he died, particularly when Pinchback was growing old and feeble. Pinchback acknowledged Grimké's concern as "timely and pertinent," but did not profess a sudden call to religion.[36]

Although the mainstream religions suffered as an indirect result of racial prejudice, few of Washington's black elite moved to splinter organizations. The one exception was the involvement of a few in the Baha'i movement. Based on the principle of the oneness of mankind and the equality of men and women, Baha'i offered an attractive alternative to Christianity. Founded in Iran in 1844, the religion spread to the United States in the early 1890s. With its emphasis on eliminating all prejudices, the Baha'i movement soon drew the attention of the black elite.

Harriet Gibbs Marshall, founder of the Washington Conservatory of Music, was one of the earlier converts when Abdu'l Baha, the charismatic leader of the sect, visited the United States in 1912. Coralie Cook, wife of George W. Cook, was also a strong believer in Baha'i. The Cooks became members in 1913 but had heard of the movement as early as 1910. Other sympathizers with the movement included the Howard University professor Louis G. Gregory, the civil servant Thomas H. R. Clarke, and the attorney Charles F. Adams. Abdu'l Baha visited Washington during his tour and spoke before the Bethel Literary and Historical Association and at Howard University. Though the religion attracted a few faithful, eventually it suffered a fate similar to that of the mainstream churches. As Carter G. Woodson noted, "others who represented this faith in this city had difficulty with race prejudice. It was not very easy to take the Negro all the way."[37]

Religion remained important spiritually to the black elite in the twentieth century, but it played an increasingly smaller role in day-to-day life. Elite churches adapted their programs to address the social welfare interests of their congregations, but they were not always able to compete with secular organizations. As the elite became increasingly educated and professional, they expected more from the churches than they were able to give. The professionals became the community leaders that the ministers had once been, although the church still played an important role in shaping the values of these leaders. Gradually racial uplift took on a more secular aspect, and in some ways it displaced religion. Booker T. Washington sought "to imbue these young men who are going forth as leaders of their people with the feeling that the great task of uplifting the race, though it may be for others merely a work of humanity, for them, and every other member of the Negro race, is a work of religion."[38] Nonetheless, individual members of the black elite, particularly women involved in reform activities, found active participation in the church to bring both spiritual and secular benefits.

The black elite church both reflected and reinforced elite ideals. In the 1880s it searched for an identity to differentiate itself from the masses, as did its elite members. In the 1890s it took the lead in protesting discrimination, establishing independent institutions, and shaking off white control. In the twentieth century it became involved in social welfare reform in order to retain the interest of members who had become active in racial uplift. Although the church lost much influence to the secularization of society, ultimately it was the church that shaped the values of elite blacks and led them to embrace secular reform.

The church remained an important institution despite internal divisions, external prejudice, and financial difficulties. Its development mirrored that of the black elite community. Membership in certain churches remained an ascribed characteristic for entrance to the black elite. By providing social status while promoting racial pride and uplift, the black elite church created leaders with a greater commitment to their community and their race.

FIVE

Primary and Secondary Education

The experiences that members of the black elite underwent while providing for the education of their children did much to hasten the realization that without an independent power base they could never hope to protest discrimination effectively. Washington's black schools were unique in that they began as an independent system long before the black community had begun to create its own parallel institutions; but just as the movement for independent institutions gathered momentum at the turn of the century, the black schools came under white control. Education was becoming a fundamental qualification for entrance to the black elite, so it was doubly hard to accept white attempts to educate blacks for a lower social position. The frustration that elite blacks faced in their efforts to provide a basic classical education for their children and ensure stable jobs for the sisters, daughters, and aunts who taught in the schools only strengthened their conviction that complete independence from white control was necessary if racial uplift was to succeed. The black schools became hotbeds of controversy because they were of such importance to elite status, and they taught the elite that protest without independent control was doomed to failure.

The schools in the District of Columbia were important to the black elite for two main reasons. First, they provided a basic education for elite children that would set them on the road to acquiring social status of their own. A good early education was a necessary step to entering the professions, and a professional occupation was becoming increasingly important for social status. Second, the teaching profession was one of the few fields fully open to blacks, and thus black teachers had tremendous prestige within their community. Washington, moreover, had one of the few segregated school systems in which black teachers were paid almost as much as whites, and in which blacks sat side by side with whites on the school board. Until 1900, African Americans had almost total control over their own schools in the District, and in the twentieth century they still had a good deal of influence in the appointment of teachers.

Ironically, although the members of the elite had common educational goals, the schools became the fiercest battleground among them. The debate over industrial education was at the root of many disputes over the school curriculum. Those who owed allegiance to Booker T. Washington's patronage powers felt obliged to support an industrial curriculum. Those who aligned with the radical perspective bitterly opposed any attempts to "dumb down" the curriculum. As parents, almost all members of the elite favored a curriculum that would gain their children access to higher education. The white population of Washington, for their part, found the prospect of black college graduates disturbing. Teaching appointments and assignments followed the lines of battle. Cliques formed within the ranks of teachers along Washington/Du Bois lines, which, depending on their philosophy, could either support or sabotage the school administration. The white school administrators tended to support the teachers and officials who followed Booker T. Washington, although they were eager to take advantage of any division within the black community as a way to regain control over the black schools.

After Congress reorganized the school board in 1900, the deciding factors in school appointments and policy were the white superintendent of schools and the white-dominated school board, which generally supported a curriculum that would train blacks for subservient positions in society. By withholding funds from the black schools and opposing radical candidates for teaching and administrative positions, white school officials attempted to assert complete control over the black schools in Washington.

Despite the attractiveness of black schools in the District in comparison with other southern black school systems, objective conditions were still poor. From the beginning the schools suffered from overcrowding. The thirst for learning was strong in the black population, as is evidenced by the fact that between 1870 and 1910, the black illiteracy rate dropped from 80 percent to 30 percent. The resultant increase in school enrollments meant cramped conditions in the classrooms. By 1885 the Board of Trustees was renting additional schoolrooms to accommodate the overflow and was clamoring for more schools, both black and white. The shortage of space was particularly acute in the black elementary schools. Since most blacks attended only the first four grades, they spent half of their school life in overcrowded, unpleasant conditions. The overcrowding had forced the schools to schedule two half-day sessions to maximize space. Between 1874 and 1886 the enrollment in the black schools had doubled. Conditions did not improve. The half-day system continued, and many of the buildings suffered from dampness, lack of light, and poor ventilation. Class sizes averaged about fifty students.[1]

One way that whites could curb the relative independence of black schools was by withholding appropriations. Discrimination in appropriations made it increasingly difficult for the black schools to function effectively. In 1892 the Board of Trustees reported that for the first time, thanks to generous appropriations by Congress, physical accommodations were good in all districts except for the seventh and eighth. Of course the seventh and eighth districts encompassed the black schools under George F. T. Cook. From 1887 to 1891, Congress gave liberally to the schools to help build better facilities. Unfortunately, the black schools received little of these funds, although they did gain a proportionate share of the regular school budget. Black and white teachers' salaries were nearly equal and black and white supervising principals both earned $2,000 annually. Since there were only two-thirds as many black schools as white schools, however, the black superintendent made $2,250 a year while the white superintendent made $3,300. At the lower levels of the school administration, a white clerk made $1,200, a black clerk $800. A black messenger earned $200 annually, a white messenger $300.[2]

When congressional appropriations declined after 1892, it was the black schools that suffered the most because they had received little in the way of renovation in times of plenty. The oldest of the schools, Stevens and Bowen, were finally torn down and rebuilt in the late 1890s, but by that time even the newer schools were showing signs of age. In addition, half-day sessions continued in the lower schools, making the quality of elementary education for blacks substantially lower than that for whites. As a result, by the time many black students reached high school, they were behind the white students in basic education and found the high school course more difficult.

At the high school level, objective conditions were not much better. Facilities were substandard even at M Street High School, the jewel in the crown of the black school system. While Central High School had a huge stadium, Dunbar was forced to hold athletic events in a nearby baseball park until 1927, when it finally got a stadium of its own. This situation was made harder for black schools by the fact that they could not rent many of the parks that were available to white schools. M Street's library was inadequate to the needs of its students.[3] Washington's public libraries were open to both races, but the many black students who had to work or take care of their families had no time to visit them.

The main problem for the high school, however, was always overcrowding. In temporary quarters until 1891, the M Street School had already outgrown its new building by 1895. The building was designed to accommodate 444 students but its enrollment was 618. Such overcrowding was harmful to order and deprived students of such amenities as study halls and small classes.[4]

Accounts of overcrowding peppered the Board of Education's reports in the next twenty years. In 1909 the board reported that M Street had thirty-one full-time and three part-time teachers but only twenty-one classrooms, including laboratories. Teachers held recitations in laboratories, and it was common for two teachers to hold different classes in the same room at the same time. Students spent their study halls in the assembly hall, in which the choir was usually practicing. By this time M Street housed 700 students.[5]

In 1915 the principal reported that "the chemistry department is hampered more and more by the lack of proper space for work and by the frequent repairs needed in its worn-out plumbing system. . . . Under the circumstances it is a wonder that any good work can be accomplished."[6]

In 1917 Dunbar opened its doors. The new building boasted two large gymnasiums, dressing rooms with showers, a kitchen equipped to produce hot meals, a $4,000 printing plant, and an auditorium with a capacity of 1,500, a pipe organ, and facilities to show films. The library had room for 4,337 volumes. But by 1920, school authorities already complained of overly large classes and a lack of teachers. Some classes contained as many as forty students, and the number of volumes in the library never matched its capacity.[7]

Poor physical conditions were not the only problems facing M Street students. The principals often shuffled class schedules for no reason but disorganization. One teacher, James Wright, noted that the schedule forced one student to take a subject he had not planned to take because it was the only one available. Midway through the course, after he had bought the textbook, more schedule changes forced the student to drop the subject in favor of the required course, which was now available. Problems of space and scheduling prevented many business students from taking the recommended hours of shorthand each week, and two students were not able to take shorthand at all. Some second-year students took fourth-year classes and then had to go back and make up the work they had missed earlier. One entire senior class had to complete one year of English in a semester or stay in school for an additional semester, because they had had to drop English the year before when the program did not allow for it.[8]

While the faculty and administration were bedeviled by divisions and disorganization, material conditions for teachers were far from perfect either. Most teachers were single women, since married women were not allowed to teach in the day schools and salaries were not high enough to support a male head of household. For that matter, they were not high enough to support a single woman living alone. While Washington's black teachers were among the highest paid in the country, their economic status never matched their social status, which required them to maintain a dignified image. As a result, most taught night school also, and many worked as waitresses or chambermaids during the summer to maintain an income that would allow them to meet social standards.[9]

A group of M Street teachers petitioned the congressional Committee on Schools for the District of Columbia in 1900, and provided a revealing account of teachers' budgets. The petition itemized annual expenses, including room and board and items as frivolous as one winter suit, one summer suit, three suits each of winter and summer underwear, one dozen pairs of socks, two pairs of shoes, and streetcar fare, for a total of $963.35. This list made no provision for retirement or sickness, which at $25 a month would bring the total to $1,263.35. Teachers in the District schools were required to pay for their own substitutes when they were sick. At the time of the petition, ten teachers made between $500 and $750 and two received salaries of $400 and $475. The petitioners were seeking to equalize the salaries of black and white teachers, but the average annual salary of black teachers was only $75 less than that of whites.[10] Underpaid and at the mercy of capricious assignments and supervisors, the teachers would have been hard pressed to perform at their best on the job.

Appropriations and salaries were not the only matters of controversy in the schools. Teaching appointments had begun to take on an aspect of personal vendetta even in the early 1880s. The *Bee* assailed the tyranny of the board in 1883, alleging that "this way of bulldozing teachers and threatening their dismissal has become a favorite theme of certain trustees." When Charles B. Purvis, James H. Smith, and John H. Brooks were appointed to the Board of Trustees later that year, the *Bee* hoped these petty tyrannies would cease. The *National Leader* reported in the late 1880s, however, that personal feelings and prejudices were still influencing teaching appointments.[11] Josephine Willson Bruce summed up the problem neatly in a letter to her son in 1897: "The fuss in the schools keeps a-going, but as long as some are in while those out want the places, just so long will there be strife." She also reported a typical incident in which two black trustees had been summarily removed, "the first intimation to them being the names of their successors appearing in the morning papers."[12] By the late 1890s, W. Calvin Chase was hinting in the columns of the *Bee* about the need to shake up the system. "There are some principals in the public schools, who will be taught lessons in what their duties are."[13]

Whites took advantage of divisions within the black community to tighten their control over the black schools. In 1900, after more complaints of disorganization and a congressional investigation, the Board of Commissioners for the District of Columbia reorganized the school system, in part in an attempt to limit black control. The reorganization created a nine-member board of education appointed by the president of the United States; three members were customarily black. The greatest change was at the top: while white and black schools each had their own superintendent, these men were now designated assistant superintendents and served under a white superintendent who reported to the board. From 1900 until 1906, in addition, the black high schools came under the supervision of the white director of high schools. This reorganization was a blow to black independence.

The issue gained national attention when the board made it known that it would prefer not to appoint George F. T. Cook to the new position of assistant superintendent of colored schools. One of the possible candidates mentioned for the position was W. E. B. Du Bois, who was also considering a formal offer to teach at Tuskegee Institute and an informal offer to join the Howard University faculty. Du Bois wrote to Booker T. Washington that he thought he would not get on well at Howard and was not sure that he could be of use at

Tuskegee. He asked for Washington's recommendation for the assistant superintendency.[14] Washington had a great deal of interest and influence in the District schools. He recognized their importance as located among the largest concentration of the leaders of the race, and also as incubators for the next generation of race leaders. In addition, by 1900 Washington had established himself as the controller of black political patronage, so when any appointive position that required special talent became available, Washington received a flood of letters asking for his support or requesting a list of suitable candidates. In later years Washington maintained his interest in the schools as a way of rewarding his friends and punishing his enemies, particularly as the District became known as a hotbed of opposition to his policies.

Ultimately, Washington did give Du Bois a letter of recommendation but advised him not to use it, as he claimed it would put Du Bois in the position of seeking a post he was not certain of obtaining. Within the District a movement developed to nominate Robert H. Terrell, then principal of M Street High School, though it was known that the District commissioner of education, John Wesley Ross, wanted an outsider. Ross privately told W. Calvin Chase that if Booker T. Washington would support Terrell, so would he, but since Washington had already endorsed Du Bois, albeit reluctantly, this suggestion was no longer practical.[15]

In the last analysis it was the white superintendent who appointed the assistant superintendent, and the superintendent was appointed by the Board of Education, not the District commissioner. The superintendent chose a Tuskegee ally, Winfield Scott Montgomery, a Dartmouth graduate who was an officer of the Capital Savings Bank.[16] Montgomery was now in the unenviable position of having to placate a white superintendent of schools and a predominantly white board of education as well as to answer to the black community. In addition, it was not clear if the director of high schools reported directly to the board, to the white superintendent, or to the assistant superintendents. The M Street High School, which most of the children of the black elite attended, became a storm center in this struggle for control of the schools.

M Street High School was the pride of the District's black citizens. Among its graduates were many of the District's most prominent citizens. A sizable number of race leaders, including Robert H. Terrell and Roscoe Conkling Bruce, were early products of M Street. Other graduates included Benjamin O. Davis, Nannie Helen Burroughs, Walter H. Loving, Nellie Quander, Rayford

Logan, and Charles Houston. Ursuline V. Brooks, class of 1886, looking back after thirty years, concluded that "I would say we were taught that our lives were to be lives of service and uplift to our race and our country."[17] For the most part, the students who entered the M Street school were not ordinary children; they were, as many saw it, the future of the race. They came from privileged backgrounds, and, increasingly after 1900, from educated families. The parents of these students demanded excellence.

The teachers were as exceptional as the students. Initially the Board of Trustees sought qualified black college graduates all over the country, attracting, among others, the young Mary Church and Anna J. Cooper, fresh from Oberlin. By 1905, however, an abundance of young women and men trained at Myrtilla Miner Normal School were available to teach. Eventually there were many more applicants than openings, so the quality of teachers was ensured. Indeed, the number of college and normal school graduates teaching at M Street exceeded those teaching in the white high schools. The school's talented faculty included at various times Angelina Weld Grimké, Hugh M. Browne, and Carter G. Woodson. M Street students went on to Harvard, Oberlin, Princeton, Amherst, Dartmouth, and Radcliffe. The list of brilliant students and teachers affiliated with M Street and their accomplishments for the race, however, tends to obscure the realities of school conditions.

A review of the official records and correspondence seems to wipe away any ideas of a school united in an effort to better its students and prepare them for race leadership. Conflicts over appointments and educational philosophy far outweighed discussion of the students. The scarcity of teaching jobs led to conflicts within the black community over school appointments. Gradually the Board of Education began to favor those candidates graduated from the District school system, and as the sons and daughters of prominent Washington citizens completed their training at Myrtilla Miner Normal School, personal favoritism played an increasing role in appointments. Mary Church Terrell, the first black female trustee—she was appointed to the Board of Trustees in 1895 and served again from 1906 to 1911—recorded in her diary vicious school board debates over promotion of teachers and countless occasions when friends attempted to enlist her influence in support of the candidates they favored. After Armstrong Manual Training School opened in 1902, designed to promote the ideal of industrial education for blacks, many teachers assigned there sought transfers to M Street. Personal animosities wreaked havoc with teaching assignments. Terrell wrote, "Dr. B. E.

[W. Bruce Evans, principal of Armstrong] persecutes everybody who offends him."[18]

One of the teachers who offended Evans was James C. Wright, who taught typing in the business school. Although officially the business school was part of M Street, after 1894 it was moved to a separate building and for a brief period was under the supervision of the principal of Armstrong. Wright saw two reasons for Evans's opposition. First, Evans wanted to make room for the appointment of his nephew. Second, when Wright and other members of the business school faculty proposed that it be returned to M Street, Evans grew angry at the threatened loss of power. In addition, in 1905 Evans had applied for the position of supervising principal, and in his absence Wright had served as acting principal of Armstrong and applied for a permanent appointment. Evans attempted to have Wright dismissed in a way that would make the dismissal seem justified. He assigned Wright to teach ancient history, English, and European history, subjects in which Wright had no training. Understandably Wright protested to the Board of Education that the "primary interest of the pupils [was being] disregarded." Under his assignment for the year, Wright had to teach as many as six classes, each with up to twenty-eight students. In addition, Wright was still responsible for maintaining the school's typewriters and performing clerical duties for the school administration. The effects of the arbitrary assignment were immediately noticeable to both teachers and students. "The injustice done both pupils & teacher . . . has been brought to the attention of Head Teacher both verbally and in writing, but without relief. . . . A constant decrease in number of pupils enrolled may be noted."[19]

Nor were arbitrary assignments limited to Armstrong. Transfer of personnel between M Street and Armstrong was common. Officials reputedly made transfers to "break up factions in the M Street High School." In addition, "a frequent shuffle of classes could shift vacancies from one field to another, thus justifying the appointment of a certain candidate."[20] Promotions likewise depended on personalities, on which side of the Washington/Du Bois fence the teacher fell, and whether or not the white board members considered the candidate dangerous. A former teacher at M Street recalled that announcements of vacancies for supervising principals "were circulated among teachers in later years, when advanced degrees were required, but few would file an application since it was generally believed that personality and cooperation were the determining factors."[21] Without independent control of the black schools, particularly the high school, black teachers and administrators became more dependent on the caprices of white officials.

The overall curriculum of the M Street School was always a point of controversy in both the black and white communities, and became the cause for dismissal of Anna J. Cooper, one of the school's most active principals. A graduate of Oberlin in the same class as Mary Church Terrell, Cooper came to teach Latin at M Street in 1887. She became principal in 1902 and served until 1906. She strove to make M Street a classical high school on a par with the best such high schools in the country. Earlier graduates had had to attend preparatory schools before entering college, but under Cooper's program, students were accepted directly from high school into some of the most prestigious New England colleges. Cooper succeeded in obtaining scholarships for many of her students.

Opponents criticized Cooper for trying to keep the curriculum equal to that of the white schools. Traditionally the curriculum had been very nearly the same, and in 1899 the M Street students scored higher on standardized tests in English and general subjects than their white counterparts at Eastern and Western High Schools. One of the big problems for white administrators was that Cooper had invited Du Bois to address the school in the winter of 1902–3. Du Bois spoke of the tendency of the white community to restrict the curricula of black high schools. As M Street was at this time under the white director of high schools, Percy M. Hughes, Cooper seemed to be challenging white control. Seeking to curb her influence and allay whites' fears of college-educated blacks, Hughes claimed that M Street students were ineligible for college scholarships, and when Cooper continued to recommend students for scholarships, Hughes charged her with insubordination.[22]

Hughes claimed that M Street students did not seem prepared for English and algebra upon entering the school, and recommended changes in the curriculum to remedy this situation. In 1904 he acknowledged attacks from the black community, but nonetheless recommended an increase in manual training, particularly for M Street students, who needed to learn the "dignity of labor." They would be "better educated men and women and therefore better fitted to win out in life's battle if properly trained in the use of tools as well as books."[23]

Hughes also wrote a devastating critique of M Street and Cooper to the superintendent of schools: "The general work in the school is weak, a fact which is due, in many cases to poor standards and incompetent pupil-material. Even when efforts have been made to raise the standard of work and improve the pupil-material, these efforts have been *weakened or blocked* by the principal in her desire to run the school on the principle of making things easier for the pupils.... An *esprit de corps* is utterly lacking among the faculty, a fact which is due, in my opinion, to the failure of the principal to deal tactfully with the teachers, thereby preventing a spirit of cooperation, a vital element in the work of the school." Hughes charged Cooper with running the school "at her own discretion," against the wishes of the superintendent and himself. In addition, he claimed, the school was lacking in discipline and efficient management.[24]

The House Committee on the District of Columbia investigated the schools, and Hughes repeated his recommendations, saying that "the course of study in the M Street High School, while purporting to be the same as in the white high school has, in fact, never covered the same ground." The Board of Education had declared that all high schools should use the same texts and follow the same curricula and standards, but in Hughes's judgment, "based upon knowledge of the facts, . . . the M Street High School is not ready for this step."[25] In fact, Cooper herself had recommended to a colleague that M Street go at its own pace in Latin, "taking such time as is necessary," regardless of what the white schools were doing. She also rejected the purchase of another book that second-year students in the white schools were using, because time was too short.[26] Hughes's actions represented a clear example of how white officials were able to distort facts to prove that blacks were not worthy of control of their own schools. Since Hughes had direct control over M Street, moreover, there was little the black community could do to stop him.

This reality did not stop the black elite from protesting Hughes's actions, however. The *Bee* was outraged by Hughes's report, calling him incompetent and obviously prejudiced. In late January 1905 a member of the Board of Education moved that the report be stricken from the minutes, and the motion was carried. Chase editorialized: "The schools of the District are embarrassed altogether too much by a set of cantankerous employe[e]s who are more industrious about creating discord and strife than about the duties which they are paid to perform. The consequence is that the children of the schools suffer from a lack of proper teaching and supervision and imbibe lessons in insubordination which the schools are not established to teach."[27] Chase chastised W. S. Montgomery for not asserting more power in his position as assistant superintendent of colored schools. Unfortunately, that was the problem: Montgomery did not have more power to assert.

Disagreements over the curriculum were not the only problems at M Street. The *Bee* noted in June that M Street was so demoralized that insubordination was endemic and there was no submission to central authority. Rumors abounded of widespread drinking and smoking among the students, and two teachers were dismissed for alleged improper moral conduct. When formal charges of improper supervision of students were made, Cooper reported that the incidents of drinking and smoking were isolated, and had been dealt with in a proper manner. Hearings on the charges continued throughout the summer, during which time the personnel of the Board of Education changed. A group of black ministers, including Walter H. Brooks, W. V. Tunnell, Sterling N. Brown, and Francis J. Grimké, protested what they perceived as unfair persecution of Anna J. Cooper.[28] The *Bee*, one of Cooper's most loyal supporters, wrote that "no one will dare say that she would be guilty of anything that would reflect in any way on the honesty and integrity of the lady."[29] The board employed such "questionable tactics" during the hearings as forcing Cooper's supporters to wait in a hallway until after midnight to state their case before the board. An unfounded rumor circulated that Mrs. Cooper was involved romantically with her foster son, John L. Love Jr., who taught English and history at M Street. Through it all the board maintained that it had no personal objection to Cooper.

In late October of that year, the board finally came to a conclusion on the formal charges. Their report exonerated Cooper but chastised her for her loose discipline. The report set the precedent that the white director of high schools had greater authority than the black assistant superintendent, and that the Board of Education had a right to monitor the curricula of the black schools.[30] Although Cooper retained her position, the result of the controversy was a devastating blow to the black community. At a time when elite blacks depended on the schools to give their children an education that would ensure their future social status, the schools had become almost wholly dependent on white administrators who opposed black aspirations for higher education.

After the M Street controversy and disorganization in the school system overall, members of Congress began in December 1905 to introduce bills to reorganize the school system. Most agreed on the need to increase teachers' salaries and to provide a pension plan for school employees. Some bills introduced would have made the salary scale for black teachers lower than that for whites. The bills also reflected a desire to hold open meetings of the Board of Education to avoid tactics such as those used against Anna J. Cooper. None of the bills introduced, however, proposed restoring the black schools to independent control, a matter of some importance to the black community. While not all whites who introduced the plans for reorganization had bad intentions, none even considered that blacks were entitled to control of their schools. The key would be the personnel of the new board of education. The final reorganization bill provided that the Supreme Court should appoint the Board of Education, but did not specify that the board should have black representation.[31]

When the new black appointees to the Board of Education were announced, there was quite a stir in the black community. The Supreme Court had decided to appoint John F. Cook Jr., Mary Church Terrell, and Oliver M. Atwood, a retired physician who had graduated from the University of Michigan and Howard University Medical School. The *Bee* expected Mrs. Terrell to protect teachers from bossy supervising principals, but in general saw the appointments as a sign that the government did not care what African Americans wanted.[32] The real significance of the appointments was that both Terrell and Atwood publicly sided with Tuskegee and thus the white board members felt confident in their ability to dictate school policy without sharp contradictions from the black board members.

The reorganization of the board reopened the question of who would be named assistant superintendent of colored schools. The new superintendent, William E. Chancellor, was besieged by nominations and petitions for the post. Once again Du Bois was a candidate, but this time there was a difference. Between 1900 and 1906 Du Bois had completely broken with Tuskegee over educational philosophy and, more important, over the issue of patronage. He had publicly criticized Booker T. Washington in his 1903 work *The Souls of Black Folk*. Du Bois had garnered many allies in the District, no small number of whom were former supporters of Tuskegee. Some of these former supporters had allied with Tuskegee for fear of losing out on patronage opportunities, and had never truly agreed with Booker T. Washington's public stance. Others had gradually lost patience with Washington's conservative philosophy as conditions failed to improve for blacks. And there were those, like Mary Church Terrell, Ralph W. Tyler, and W. Calvin Chase, who straddled the fence, taking advantage of the best of both sides while retaining some measure of independent action.

In 1906, however, the battle lines were clearly drawn. The Tuskegee lieutenant James A. Cobb reported that "Du Bois is turning heaven and earth to be appointed assistant superintendent." Cobb felt that W. S. Montgomery's position was tenuous at best and the Du Boisians were trying to oust him. Robert H. Terrell and his wife were working day and night to prevent Du Bois from winning. Washington offered as an alternative candidate the native Washingtonian Roscoe Conkling Bruce. Bruce had been at Tuskegee, where he had headed the Academic Department for the past few years, but was bristling under Tuskegee directives to downplay academics in favor of industrial education. Bruce hoped to return to Washington and put his Harvard degree in education to use while still supporting Tuskegee and the industrial ideal.[33] Washington wished publicly to remain apart from the politics of the District schools, but as usual, privately he was manipulating a position for his protégé. In September he wrote to Chancellor endorsing Bruce for a supervising principalship, and Bruce received the position the same month.[34]

Montgomery retained the assistant superintendency, but only barely. Ironically, Hughes became the new assistant superintendent of white schools, a position that represented a promotion for him but placed him on the same level as Montgomery. With the promotion, Montgomery no longer had to fear that Hughes could try to control the black schools. In addition, Montgomery took advantage of the abolition of the position of director of high schools to raise the ratings of some of the teachers whom Hughes had rated as poor.[35] But Montgomery was asserting only temporary independence.

After the reorganization, confusion reigned supreme, and the new board of education took full advantage of it. The board took the position that it was within its power not to reappoint those teachers and administrators who had received poor ratings under the old school system. The board refused to reappoint fifty teachers and four principals, including, not surprisingly, Anna J. Cooper and her foster son, John L. Love Jr. The board held examinations for applicants for the principalship under the new rules of appointment, but the four former principals could not take the examinations without admitting that they had been legally dismissed from their positions. As the board had not officially dismissed them but had simply not reappointed them, their legal position was uncertain.

Ultimately most of the teachers were reappointed, but in September the board voted to officially dismiss the white principal of Central High School, Anna J. Cooper, John L. Love Jr., and one other black teacher. The board offered both Cooper and the former white high school principal a principalship of a primary school, but neither accepted.[36] To replace Cooper at

M Street the board appointed W. T. S. Jackson, a man with circuitous ties to Tuskegee and little inclination to rock the boat.

The black community placed much of the blame for the dismissals on Superintendent Chancellor, who chose this opportune time to depart on a tour of the South to investigate racial conditions in the schools. Safely out of town, Chancellor wrote a letter to the press saying that he thought that all the teachers should have been reappointed. The *Evening Star* complained that Chancellor had acted without any knowledge of local affairs. "No teacher, in his view, could exist except through the grace of the superintendent." Further indignation surfaced when it was discovered that Chancellor had reappointed the teachers, but only for a term of one year, rather than until retirement or dismissal, as the law required.[37]

A group of black ministers, including Francis J. Grimké and J. Milton Waldron, organized indignation meetings on behalf of Cooper, who, with the other dismissed teachers and principals, hired an attorney to plead their case. Cooper went so far as to show up at school on the first day as if she were still the principal, but left when confronted by police officers dispatched to keep her out.[38] But forces beyond Cooper's control doomed her case. The *Evening Star*, which had quite objectively and in great detail covered Cooper's case along with that of the white principal dismissed, stopped discussing Cooper but continued to cover the rest. One probable reason was the outbreak of the Atlanta race riot, which inflamed prejudices and may have made it impolitic for the *Evening Star* to support a black school administrator against a predominantly white board.

The second factor in Cooper's downfall was W. Calvin Chase. The *Bee* operated on a shoestring budget and Chase was continuously soliciting funds, but in 1906 his financial trouble was more serious than usual. Luckily for the continued existence of the *Bee*, he found a new source of funds. Unfortunately for the *Bee*'s editorial policy and for Anna J. Cooper, this source was Booker T. Washington. In 1906, Melvin Jack Chisum, a rather sordid character who specialized in espionage and held secret meetings with Booker T. Washington on park benches, obtained a job at the *Bee* and proceeded to persuade Chase to change his editorial policy by offering to arrange bribes from Tuskegee. In February 1906, for example, Chisum requested that Booker T. Washington send a $10 contribution in appreciation of several editorials Chase had printed favoring Tuskegee affairs. Chase also asked for $15 to reproduce a Washington speech with a picture from a conference at

Hampton Institute. After Chase had printed the speech, Chisum reported that "the Bee will be a surprise to everybody that knows it the forthcoming week and the war is on between his highness bub [William Monroe] Trotter and bub Chase."[39]

But Chase was an unreliable ally, and Chisum reported that he was jealous of Washington's influence with Theodore Roosevelt and would do anything to undermine it. Nevertheless, Chase accepted material for publication from Tuskegee throughout 1906 in return for money, and by October Chisum reported, "I have *Chase* in leash."[40] By the end of September the bribes seem to have been taking a stronger hold on the *Bee*'s editorial policy in the case of Anna J. Cooper. Chase began praising the actions of Superintendent Chancellor even in Cooper's case. Chase stated that while he had sympathized at first, Cooper had now gone beyond reason and the *Bee* could no longer support her. By November, in fact, Chase was practically gushing over Booker T. Washington and his allies in the District. "Tuskegee is a monument to the colored man in the South. . . . The Bee will continue to support Mr. Washington when he is right, just as it would any other American citizen. Mr. Washington is doing things that no other American can do." In December the *Bee* put out a special Tuskegee edition.[41]

Cooper, a strong advocate of classical education for blacks and an opponent of Booker T. Washington, was as great a threat to the Tuskegee ideal as to white supremacy. A victim of both, she fell between the cracks. As she told her fellow Oberlin alumni in 1909, "the dominant forces of our country are not yet tolerant of the higher steps for colored youth; so that while our course of study was for the time being saved, *my head was lost in the fray,* and I moved west."[42] Cooper moved to Jefferson City, Missouri, to teach Latin and Greek at Lincoln Institute.

For Anna J. Cooper the controversy was not over, however. After she returned to Washington to teach Latin in 1910, the board again held up her appointment. Eventually it came through, but Cooper faced similar controversies when she came up for promotions in later years. In a 1932 survey of black college graduates she remarked, "Said principal suffers to this day the punishment of the damned from both the white masters & the colored understrappers. . . . For human selfishness will always arise as the domineering *thumb* to override & keep down every finger weak enough to give up the struggle."[43]

The controversy surrounding the dismissal of Anna J. Cooper had repercussions in the ratings of teachers who had supported her. Angelina Weld Grimké was appointed in 1902 to teach physical culture and English at Armstrong. Since the Grimkés and Cooper were friends, Grimké suffered persecution at the hands of Armstrong's principal, William Bruce Evans. After several undeserved poor ratings, Grimké secured a transfer to M Street, where, according to her supervisor, she showed careful preparation and ability.[44]

The hostility among the teachers and school administration could scarcely have escaped the attention of the students, even had the inappropriate assignments not left them with unprepared teachers while taking away those best suited for their positions. Divisions among the M Street faculty continued, however, as Jackson recommended two teachers for removal and forced out six others "who had done their whole duty under Mrs. Cooper."[45]

With the shake-up in the schools, a change in the office of the assistant superintendent of colored schools was inevitable. Montgomery had dared to challenge authority when he changed Hughes's ratings of teachers in early 1906. In September, a misunderstanding between Montgomery and Chancellor further destabilized Montgomery's position. Without obtaining the approval of Superintendent Chancellor, Montgomery substituted names of his own choosing for those of three candidates for positions at the night school on a list to be presented to the board. Montgomery and Mary Church Terrell had discussed the changes before he made them and both had attempted to clear them with Chancellor before the board met, but neither had been able to gain an audience with the superintendent; and Assistant Superintendent Percy M. Hughes had insisted that any appointments to the night school had to be presented at that month's meeting. Montgomery had valid reasons for the substitutions but Chancellor was outraged, particularly about the disappearance of the name of William Bruce Evans, whom he wanted to appoint as principal of the night school, and the substitution of that of Clarence Wormley, who earned only a small salary and had a family to support. Chancellor demanded an investigation into the affair, accused Montgomery of insubordination, and generally overreacted. Montgomery had only tried to assert the power that was rightfully his, but the outcome showed that even black administrators had little voice in appointments.

The black community saw the incident as a racial attack on Montgomery and the black board members. Chancellor attempted to counteract these beliefs by attending a Bethel Literary meeting in November and congratulating the presenter of a paper on the importance of higher education for blacks. Since he had earlier written an article disparaging higher education for blacks, which had subsequently been printed as a pamphlet, the black community found his change of attitude difficult to credit.[46]

Chancellor replaced Montgomery in 1907 with Roscoe Conkling Bruce, the candidate most palatable to Tuskegee and also to the white board members. Bruce was faced with the same difficult task that had defeated Montgomery: placating the white community while keeping the confidence of the black community. With hostility against Tuskegee at a high point in Washington, and with more members of the elite joining the radical side each year, it was certain from the beginning that Bruce could not inspire confidence among the black elite. He was able to keep his position only because of the influence of Tuskegee and because he had the confidence of the white community. His tenure was plagued by personal animosities and scandals that radicalized the black elite and caused bitter disputes. Yet Bruce was not wholly committed to the Tuskegee ideal, and ultimately maintained the educational standards, particularly at M Street, that the Washington community expected.

In Montgomery's last report as assistant superintendent, he warned the board that the curricula of the black schools, particularly M Street, should not be allowed to deteriorate, since it was the task of M Street to furnish exceptional leaders.[47] In his first report, Bruce ignored this warning. He did admonish the teachers at Armstrong to apply more rigorous standards to the manual training subjects, but as for M Street, "Let them remember . . . that too great rigor is almost as disastrous in its effects upon the pupil's life and effort as too great laxity."[48] Bruce advised the teachers to teach what the students needed rather than drive them from the schools if they could not meet the standards. In addition, Bruce proposed a pension plan to retire old teachers who were no longer efficient in the intermediate grades. Obviously he was proposing changes that would not meet a warm reception in the black community.

Nevertheless, Bruce was an untiring advocate of improved education for blacks in the District. He regularly protested unequal appropriations, requested more equipment and space, and suggested reforms in the system to improve efficiency.[49] Bruce temporarily silenced critics of Tuskegee in his second report by writing that "M Street is, and must always remain, a high school of the literary type—a people's college. . . . From the M Street High School must continue to come bodies of young men and women with a basic literary education, destined for leadership by professional service—our teachers, our physicians, our clergymen."[50] Nonetheless, he had already outlined his opinion of classical education the previous year and the damage had been done.

Bruce's first clash over personnel came shortly after he assumed office in 1907. When Mary Syphax Gibson was up for reappointment, Bruce refused to approve her on the ground that she had tried to bribe W. Calvin Chase of the *Bee* to use his influence to secure the position. According to Bruce, Gibson had boasted that she had received an appointment to the night school thanks to Chase's influence and a fee of $50. Chase responded with an attack on Bruce in the *Bee*. Gibson admitted that the $50 she had paid Chase had been for his legal advice and services in obtaining an appointment. Furthermore, she said, Bruce had earlier opposed her promotion to librarian when he was acting as supervising principal, and the dispute was based on personal animosity. Seizing on a chance to discredit Bruce and his management of the black schools, in October Chancellor urged the Board of Education to investigate the incident. William Bruce Evans testified that he had appointed Gibson solely on her merits. Bruce blamed Chancellor for manufacturing a scandal, and the *Bee* labeled Bruce a servant of the Board of Education and a tool of Chancellor. At this point in the fracas, Booker T. Washington wrote to Chase asking him to tone down his criticism of Bruce, and Chase did so for two weeks.[51]

The debate surrounding the investigation exposed Superintendent Chancellor's petty nature to the Board of Education. The board had come to realize that Chancellor was quick to spread gossip to discredit his enemies, and did not mind causing a scandal if it promoted his own cause. In November 1907, formal charges of inefficiency were brought against Chancellor. In January 1908 he was dismissed from the superintendency by unanimous vote and replaced by A. T. Stuart, who had formerly held the position. Thus Bruce's first scandal led to a small victory.[52]

Chase resumed his attacks on Bruce after two weeks had passed, and it was only through the intercession of Mary Church Terrell that Bruce was able to retain his position. By attacking a member of the prominent Syphax family, however, Bruce had already alienated many of Washington's aristocratic society leaders, and by appearing to be the tool of the white community, he alienated many more. In addition, the white members of the board felt obliged to support Bruce rather than admit they had made a mistake in hiring him.[53]

Mrs. Terrell soon came to regret her support of Bruce. For most of 1908, aside from complaining that Bruce never kept appointments, she coexisted peacefully with him. Beginning in late 1908, however, Bruce began to favor appointments of candidates that Terrell did not support. On at least one occasion Bruce appointed a candidate after agreeing with Terrell to recommend someone else. Terrell and Bruce disagreed over administrative philosophy; when disputes arose, Terrell sided with the teachers and Bruce with the supervising principal.[54]

The situation was reversed in 1909, when a scandal arose involving a supervising principal who had cashed the paycheck of a teacher who had died in order to pay the substitute who replaced her. Bruce attacked the supervising principal, but Terrell defended him and gained the backing of the other black board members. Bruce backed down in the face of this opposition.[55]

The incident showed the difficult position that both Bruce and the black members of the board faced. Bruce could not afford to alienate the white administration, but he had to appear to have the confidence of the black population. As long as the black members of the board were divided, it was easy for Bruce to gain the support of at least one member, but when the black members united on an issue, Bruce was essentially powerless. Thus it was in his interest to have a divided community if he wished to achieve his goals, yet it was not in his interest to antagonize the black community if he wanted to keep its confidence in the long run and retain his position. The black board members also needed to keep the confidence of the community, but since they were on an equal footing with the other board members, they could afford to antagonize them. Yet too much antagonism could lead to the appointment of new board members who were less likely to cause trouble. Terrell's long tenure on the board was due to the fact that she was skilled at treading the line between independence and obsequiousness.

In late July 1909, a group of residents held a mass meeting to protest Bruce's reappointment and filed charges of inefficiency and improper conduct. In addition they protested Bruce's handling of M Street, where teachers had rebelled against some of Bruce's more objectionable reforms. The board dismissed the charges after teachers expressed their willingness to put aside personal differences to advance the school's welfare, but the cloud surrounding Bruce's administration grew darker. Each time the board dismissed charges against Bruce, it was committing itself to support him the next time for fear of looking foolish. Each time charges were filed against Bruce, his opposition in the black community grew in size and intensity. Bruce became a topic of derision in the *Bee* (when Chase was not getting payments from Tuskegee), and in general could be counted on as a subject of local gossip.[56]

In 1911 the black members of the board united in opposition to Bruce's reappointment. Terrell was no longer on the board and none of the three black members, Richard R. Horner, Caroline Harris, and William V. Tunnell, had any sympathy for Tuskegee. They opposed Bruce's appointment on a technicality: since there was a new superintendent, they argued, Bruce should be officially reappointed rather than continued automatically. Booker T. Washington wrote in support of Bruce, and the Tuskegee allies put pressure on the board to disregard the black members' efforts. The attorney for the Board of Education declared that Bruce could remain in office unless officially dismissed by the new superintendent. The board voted 5 to 3 to clear Bruce of further charges. All black board members voted against Bruce, but they were thwarted by the largely white administration. Once again Bruce was in the position of siding against the black community.[57]

Bruce, in charge of all appointments to the black schools from 1907 to 1921, repeatedly became the focus of protest by school board members, parents, and teachers. He was also the target of at least one investigative committee for each superintendent of schools under which he served. At one point during his administration, Bruce was threatened with two lawsuits by teachers who claimed that he had kept them from their jobs unlawfully. An article described the chaos resulting in the schools: "In the meantime, at the orders of and on the responsibility of someone, classes are being broken up and students moved around like mere toy soldiers on a board to hide the claims of the teachers threatening suit. In addition to this it appears that about a dozen people about the town, supported by a certain group of 'bread and butter, hat-in-hand, me-too, teachers' are endeavoring, at the suggestion of someone, to make it seem that the present regime has a representative and numerous backing in this city."[58]

After Booker T. Washington's death in 1915, the Tuskegee machine fell apart and could provide little protection to men like Bruce. In addition, the leaders of the black community, frustrated by continuing segregation, disillusioned by the treatment of blacks during the Great War, and jaded by the race riot of 1919, were no longer willing to appease the white community. Now they demanded educational equality. Though they could not have complete control over their schools, they could bring public pressure to bear in the matter of appointments. It became increasingly difficult for Bruce to keep his position.

In 1919, when parents discovered that a photographer had been allowed to take nude pictures of some of the Dunbar students, mass protest meetings of concerned citizens condemned Bruce for permitting such an outrage. The investigation, which also heard charges against him of moral laxity and excessive drinking, ultimately exonerated Bruce, and again he managed to keep his position. Not only was Bruce's case an issue affecting the black schools, but, as a Senate select committee concluded in 1920, the Board of Education used it as a weapon against the superintendent of schools. "Rightly or wrongly," the Senate committee stated, "Mr. Bruce does not have the confidence of a large section of the teaching force and has not had it for a good many years."[59]

Superintendent F. W. Ballou proposed three options to Bruce. He could either request an indefinite leave of absence and sue his defamers for libel, create his own grass-roots movement to counteract his opposition, or simply ask for a leave of absence and do nothing. Bruce did none of the above. In May 1921 Ballou reported to the Board of Education that he did not think Bruce capable of continuing in his duties, thus forcing Bruce's hand. He asked for an indefinite leave of absence and was replaced by Garnet C. Wilkinson, the principal of M Street.[60]

The controversies surrounding the tenures of Anna J. Cooper and Roscoe Conkling Bruce were ultimately struggles for control over the black schools. White administrators did not think blacks capable of administering their own affairs, and they found the idea of black students' preparing for higher education particularly alarming. They seized every opportunity to take power from black school officials and attempted to prescribe an industrial curriculum at every opportunity. They took advantage of the dispute within the black community over the merits of industrial education to seize yet more control. They gladly supported candidates proposed by Booker T. Washington, assuming they would not challenge their authority. By supporting Tuskegee they only further antagonized the part of the black elite who objected to Washington's control of patronage. The resolution of the controversy surrounding Cooper ensured that whites would be able to control the curriculum in black schools. The controversial tenure of Bruce ensured that he and the black school board members would disagree on school appointments, so that decisions would rest largely in the hands of the white superintendent or the white board members. As the black elite lost control of what had been a relatively independent black institution, it became clear that independence was the key to achieving its goals.

With all the problems that Washington's black schools faced, their record for producing successful graduates was one of the best in the country. To a large extent, M Street's success can be explained by coincidence. With the children of some of the nation's leading African Americans attending the school, its record was bound to be good. Leading citizens tend to make leaders of their children, since they have the means to send them to good schools, can give them connections that will benefit their careers, and provide examples of what it is possible to achieve. It is interesting to remember in this respect that some members of the District elite chose to send their children elsewhere for an education. Despite her long service on the school board, Mary Church Terrell sent her daughters to preparatory school at Oberlin, ostensibly to expose them to communication with people who were not of their own race. Archibald Grimké sent Angelina to boarding school in Boston to counteract "the evil influence which Washington is exerting upon you. . . . We all agree that Washington is not the sort of a city to develop the best in you, and that a change is necessary."[61] However, enough prominent citizens enrolled children at M Street to ensure that the quality of education was maintained.

The other demographic factor in the equation was the teachers. We know that the M Street faculty was exceptionally well qualified to teach and able to provide inspiration and knowledge to their students. Since there were few other professional opportunities for African Americans, many talented people entered teaching. Teachers often took courses at universities over the summer to improve their professional standing and knowledge of their subjects. After 1914 an official Teacher's Institute offered regular lectures on such subjects as "Modern Methods of Teaching History and Government" and "Moral Instruction Through the Teaching of Literature."[62]

James Wright reported that all students, whether in the business school or not, were allowed and encouraged to come and practice typing as much as they could and wanted to. Robert N. Mattingly constantly experimented with new methods of teaching mathematics, including varying the sequence of topics and basing problems on real conditions of modern life. Classes used the latest textbooks and methods whenever possible. Hugh M. Browne, physics teacher, supplied lab equipment with his own personal funds. Mary L. Europe and Mary Church Terrell led a campaign to get a phonograph for the use of the music class. Martha B. Briggs was another teacher who inspired a generation with her "missionary spirit," wrote John W. Cromwell Sr., and her student teachers "went forth from her presence stronger souls full of sympathy to magnify the teacher's vocation and to inspire the learner."[63] Arthur U. Craig, probably the first African American to receive a degree in electrical engineering, taught in the District high schools for seventeen years and was active in organizing playgrounds for the students. Carter G. Woodson inspired at least two of his students, Rayford W. Logan and William Montague Cobb, to pursue the study of black history. Students admired Woodson's "quiet, unsmiling dignity" as well as his strict attention to discipline.[64]

It was as if all the frustrations that the teachers faced in every aspect of their lives outside the classroom made them more determined to use what power they could within the classroom. Through their lessons and through personal example, they instilled in their students a sense of pride and responsibility. Many graduates of M Street looked back on their years there as the most formative of their lives. In 1940 Charles R. Drew wrote to his former athletics teacher at Dunbar, Edwin B. Henderson, to congratulate him on his recent book on black athletes: "I doubt if anyone has really told you how big a part you have played in the lives of a lot of the men you wrote of in your book. . . . I owe you and a few other men like you for setting most of the standards that I have felt were worthwhile, the things I have lived by and for and wherever possible have attempted to pass on."[65] The historian Kenneth R. Janken has noted that for elite teenagers in Washington, the "optimism inherent in an M Street education" outweighed the humiliations of a segregated society, from which M Street students were largely screened.[66]

Race pride was clearly one way to combat difficult conditions both physical and emotional. Teachers emphasized the special history of African Americans to their students, and discussed race issues when appropriate. Angelina Grimké, for example, assigned her classes a series of autobiographical essays on various topics—"My First Love Affair," "Am I Selfish or Generous?"— and included as a topic "When, For the First Time, I Was Made To Feel My Color."[67] African Americans had long realized that education was one of the most important aspects of racial uplift, but, as Frederick Douglass noted at the dedication of M Street in 1891, "booklearning is not the only thing taught in our schools."[68]

In the twentieth century, school officials were increasingly aware of the importance of racial pride and the effects of an education that excluded the heritage of African Americans. W. S. Montgomery asked the Board of Education to appoint a librarian for the black schools, "to take a hand in inculcating right habits of study, and in making students acquainted with the embalmed intellectual achievements of the race." As supervising principal, Roscoe Conkling Bruce reported that from the fifth grade on, students studied representative men, but that all those men were white, when there was every opportunity to study black men and women as well. In eighth grade the students gave "especial attention to the life and labor of the slaves and of the free negroes by means of type studies drawn largely from F. L. Olmstead's travels."[69]

In 1915 Bruce highlighted teachers' efforts to use the African American heritage as a resource and to make it more accessible to others. A principal of Armstrong, for example, had his students render black folk songs. Although some people objected to them as a relic of slavery, eventually the songs won the community's approval. The principal of one elementary school prepared a book of African fables and had it privately printed. Bruce noted that even white students had adopted this book in some cities.

In the teaching of American history, Bruce remarked in the same report, more reference could be made to the place of African Americans, and he noted that two teachers, Carter G. Woodson and John W. Cromwell Sr., had written black history texts to be used as supplements to the regular history text. In the past school year, Bruce noted, teachers had attempted to concentrate on using African American resources. In their morning talks, primary teachers had noted the birthdays of prominent African Americans, such as Phillis Wheatley, Benjamin Banneker, and Alexander Crummell. Bruce agreed that examples of noble white men could be inspiring, but argued that black examples were closer to the experience of black students, and so more worthwhile. "Can it be that all the generals, all the statesmen, all the men of letters were white men? Is there not a danger that our colored children and youth will be overwhelmed with what I may call the prestige of the white man . . . and their own initiative impaired[?] . . . Our schools must not shut their eyes to the very educational material best fitted to develop in our children race pride, self-confidence, a spirit of brave and noble emulation."[70]

Teachers committed themselves to uplifting the race through their students. They attended seminars on teaching black history. They attempted to find sources for teaching African American culture, including pictures of prominent blacks. They wrote articles on the importance of instilling youth with racial pride.[71]

Robert C. Weaver recalled "at least a half a dozen outstanding teachers who not only exposed me to the subject matter and instilled an appreciation for high standards of achievement, but also inspired me as human beings."[72] A member of the class of 1898 stated: "We hope from our numbers to supply the great middle and upper classes of society. We desire to be the vanguard and support of the army against ignorance, superstition and vice; and are confident that to secure the ends desired by our instruction 'we must not merely make our way; we must constantly stand guard.'"[73] Clearly, inculcating race pride was also a way to instill leadership qualities. John C. Payne Jr. wrote from Dartmouth: "I have found that the preparation I received at Dunbar, particularly in Latin and English, has placed me on a footing with men from any high school as well as from a majority of preparatory schools."[74]

The children of the black elite gained an extraordinary education in the Washington schools. Faced with abominable physical facilities, overworked and underpaid teachers, and continuous controversy, somehow the graduates of the District school system came through with only the fondest memories. The quality of the students and the dedication of the teachers created a unique situation in which the students learned not only racial pride but an awareness of their responsibility to the race.

The struggle for control of the black schools was necessarily a desperate battle for the District's black elite. It involved the future status of the next generation as well as the livelihoods of the current generation of teachers and administrators. Conflict was inevitable in a system that gave most of the power to white officials who were determined to keep blacks in a subservient position. These conflicts intensified as blacks became more frustrated by racial discrimination and more disgusted by incidents designed to reflect poorly on the ability of African Americans to manage their own affairs. Tensions within the black community caused by the scarcity of jobs and the divisions over patronage only made matters worse. But the struggle convinced the black elite of two things: first, without independent control over their institutions, African Americans could not hope to protest injustice effectively; and second, race pride was a powerful weapon in the struggle to counter the effects of discrimination.

SIX

Howard University and Higher Education

The lessons that the black elite learned from their ordeal with the black public schools were reinforced by their experiences with higher education. Students learned the value of racial solidarity through their organizational activities. Howard University's faculty learned that value through their struggles to maintain control of their institution and passed it on to their students and to the larger community. The battle for control of Howard University itself showed the black elite that discrimination could be resisted through a combination of racial solidarity and independent control. The graduates and faculty of Howard University thus played important roles in the transformation of Washington's black elite.

For the elite, higher education was an important part of social status. Without a college degree it was impossible to enter the professions or gain a position that would ensure relative financial stability with a minimum of risk. Since a professional occupation in itself conferred status, this education became extremely important, and it allowed some working-class blacks to join the ranks of the elite. Universities also brought together men and women of the same social status from different regions of the country. In predominantly white universities, black students bonded with others of their race to counteract the effects of discrimination and came to appreciate racial unity for other reasons. At predominantly black colleges such as Fisk and Howard, students developed a sense of racial unity and learned their responsibilities as future leaders of their race. Professors at these schools incorporated ideals of racial uplift and solidarity into their teachings, making them an integral part of professional training. In both situations, African Americans met like-minded companions and formed lasting friendships that extended the network of the national black elite beyond college.

Despite the high quality of education in Washington's black schools, the Washington elite followed the examples of their counterparts elsewhere. A degree from a predominantly white school was ultimately preferable to any other, and by 1900 increasing numbers of white schools were accepting African American students. Among the black Washingtonians who had already attended Ivy League schools were Archibald Grimké, Robert H. Terrell, and Roscoe Conkling Bruce, all of whom received degrees from Harvard; Otelia Cromwell, the first black woman to attend Smith College; and a multitude of M Street and Dunbar graduates who went on to Dartmouth, Yale, and Princeton. Many members of the Howard faculty had attended Oberlin College in Ohio, as had some of the District's black elite residents. Although often segregated in living and eating quarters, most members of Washington's black elite who went to Ivy League schools created lasting friendships with both black and white students that would further their own influence in years to come.

Attendance at other predominantly white private and state universities became less pleasant as time passed, especially during the second decade of the twentieth century, when segregation had gained a firm foothold in the nation. It was at this time that many older members of the elite were sending their children to the colleges they themselves had attended, expecting their children to have the same experiences they had had in the 1880s. Mary Church Terrell enrolled her daughters at Oberlin only to discover that the school would not allow them to live in the dormitory with the white girls. Terrell noted that segregation would never have been considered at the school when she was a student in the 1880s, and was shocked to see the taint of discrimination at her own alma mater. Oberlin denied that it was practicing discrimination, but Terrell appealed to the NAACP to investigate. Since her daughters could not get a room in a dormitory, Terrell moved to Oberlin to rent a house with them. As segregation became more widespread, even Harvard limited the access of black students to its dormitories and student dining halls.[1]

In 1913, the same year the Terrells moved to Oberlin, Rayford W. Logan matriculated at the University of Pittsburgh, where he and the other three black students kept largely to themselves and had few acquaintances among the white students. At Pittsburgh the white students and professors did not accept the black students as equals, although Logan learned that he could compete intellectually with the white students on an equal basis.[2]

Segregation was not the only factor that discouraged black students from attending white schools. The cost of a northern education could be exorbitant, particularly for those without a sponsor. Elite families could generally afford to pay tuition for their children, but not without sacrifices. It was for this reason that many black college graduates assisted other black students financially. Most black college students worked for their tuition in part-time and summer jobs. Thomas Wyatt Turner worked his way through school by sweeping, washing dishes, and carrying groceries for a rich Jewish family in Washington. Others worked as waiters at summer resorts or in white fraternity houses. Roscoe Conkling Bruce suggested he might take a job at a Washington newspaper during the summer to help defray his expenses at college. With a sense of guilt, Bruce told his father, "It would be foolish for an immense hulk of a fellow like me to be idle for three months."[3]

Since a degree bestowed instant social status on African Americans at the turn of the century, students' college experiences helped shape the values of the next generation of community leaders. In the late nineteenth century, racial solidarity at predominantly white universities was nearly impossible because so few African Americans attended them. Black students at these colleges concentrated on making connections with members of the white community and trying to assimilate into white society. By the beginning of the twentieth century, however, enough African Americans were enrolled in white colleges to establish black student organizations.

The development of the black Greek-letter societies reflected this change. The first black fraternities developed on predominantly white campuses and from the start focused their attention on matters of race. Black students faced growing social discrimination as well as economic discrimination in renting housing. In addition, the younger generation of black college students had learned from their parents and from their earlier education that race pride was an important part of black elite identity and that future race leaders would need contacts with influential members of their own race as much as with whites. The black fraternal movement thus initially developed from a need for mutual support rather than a desire to make social distinctions, and helped the younger generation of elite blacks to make the transformation to race leaders.

The first black fraternity, Alpha Phi Alpha, was formed at Cornell University in New York during the 1905–6 school year. The founders envisioned the organization as a social study group or literary group, modeled on similar white university associations and literary societies in the black community. After the black students had met for several months, they realized that a fraternity would be better able to address their needs and might bring the group more social recognition. The fraternity was successful and by 1907 had founded a second chapter at Howard University.[4]

Kappa Alpha Psi, founded at Indiana University in 1911, arose from similar circumstances. Two of the founders had met previously while attending Howard University, and they were shocked to discover how little their presence, and that of eight other African American students at Indiana University, was acknowledged by the college community, and how infrequently the black students encountered one another. They began by renting a house in which members could study undisturbed, where they could invite family and friends from the black community, and where they paid less rent as a group than they would have had to pay as individuals.[5]

The development of these two fraternities laid a framework for other black Greek-letter societies, which emphasized racial solidarity almost as much as social status. Beginning in 1911, members of Alpha Phi Alpha addressed issues of racial prejudice and informally campaigned to encourage African Americans to pursue higher education. In 1914 the fraternity began publication of the *Sphinx,* published in Washington, and called for the brothers to develop a greater purpose than to "meet, eat, sleep, resolve and adjourn." Despite many resolutions, the organization was slow to follow up on its plans, and it was not until 1920 that the group organized a formal campaign for black higher education. A founder of Kappa Alpha Psi stated in 1914 that one of the fraternity's main functions consisted in "stimulating a desire among Negro people for college training and inducing Negro youths to enter and successfully pursue college courses."[6] But this fraternity, too, could accomplish little of concrete value until the 1920s, when the fraternities had become established institutions.

Nonetheless, the early fraternities set the tone for the black Greek organizations. The groups were to promote racial solidarity, and should include service to the black community as part of their mission. Membership in black fraternities and sororities at the turn of the century provided the younger generation of elite blacks with a social and racial consciousness that would become a part of their social definition in the larger society. The students' experiences at black colleges shaped the later development of fraternities, particularly at Howard University. When the black Greek movement spread to Howard University, it emphasized class distinctions more than it had done earlier, but retained its commitment to racial service.

Kappa Alpha Psi did not establish a chapter at Howard University until 1920. Alpha Phi Alpha enjoyed a monopoly of fraternal activity on campus until 1911, when Omega Psi Phi was organized. At black universities students faced fewer problems of discrimination and experienced de facto racial solidarity. Students were more concerned, therefore, with social issues and matters of general administration of the university than with immediate economic issues. Copying the examples of Alpha Phi Alpha and Kappa Alpha Psi, later black Greek fraternities encouraged service to the black community, but the fraternities that developed at Howard University tended to center on different social groups.

The founding of Omega Psi Phi at Howard in 1911 marked the first division of fraternal organizations along lines of social status. The founders desired to gather student leaders at Howard together under one umbrella and create a first-rate group both socially and scholastically. The first Omega house was the property of the Terrell family and Robert R. Church Sr., located at 326 T Street, in one of the more exclusive black neighborhoods. The group's outlook was clearly elite but it was not uninfluenced by the ideologies of the first black fraternities. Omega was instrumental in rallying the Howard community to press for the creation of a black officer's training camp in 1917. Its members placed great emphasis on pride in their racial heritage, and in the 1920s, under the influence of Carter G. Woodson, an honorary member, they dedicated their efforts to promoting the study of black history and literature.[7] That Omega maintained an interest in race pride and service to the community, albeit from an elite standpoint, shows the transformation that had taken place within the black elite. At the same time that their fathers were reinforcing their social activities with efforts for racial uplift in the larger community, the sons were pursuing similar activities at the college level.

Although as selective organizations both the white and black fraternities and sororities provided a means of identifying social status, these distinctions were less clearly made in the black student community. A poor southern African American, for example, could, through benefit of philanthropy, attend schools to prepare him for university. Once he had received a college degree and perhaps professional training, he would probably qualify for high social status in any community. Should a selective black organization then exclude him on the basis of his unremarkable background when he was on his way to a position of social importance in later life? After the fraternities had become accepted institutions, they provided one more way for the black elite to distinguish themselves from the black working classes in a way that ensured continued exclusivity. Yet involvement in fraternal activities still imprinted the larger lesson of racial solidarity on members.

Black sorority members tended to be more involved in the black community than members of black fraternities, but they still concentrated their efforts on collegiate matters. As the sons took their cues from their fathers, so the daughters of the black elite emulated their mothers. Sororities were envisioned as service organizations as much as social clubs. Just as black clubwomen and churchwomen were leading the way in social welfare reform and racial uplift, so the early black sororities hoped to promote community service at the college level. Since the first black sororities developed at Howard University, their members already felt a sense of racial solidarity because of their exposure to Howard's atmosphere. What they hoped to achieve was experience in educational reform activities and the formation of a network of like-minded women who would ultimately form the core of national reform circles.

Black sororities did not spread beyond Howard until 1924. Modeled on Alpha Phi Alpha fraternity, Alpha Kappa Alpha was the first to be established, in 1908. Nellie Quander, one of the founders, listed the sorority's goals in its constitution: to promote scholarship and ethics, "keeping alive [members'] interest in college life and progressive movement emanating therefrom, for the avowed purpose of improving the social status of our race, raising moral standards, and increasing educational efficiency."[8]

Most of the sorority's founders were students in the College of Liberal Arts and went on to prominent positions in the black community. Lucy Diggs Slowe, who later became Howard's dean of women, was one of the original members, as was Margaret Flagg, an M Street graduate who later taught in the Baltimore schools. Many of the founders represented some of the most prominent black families in the District. Sarah Meriwether, an M Street graduate and daughter of the educator James Meriwether, later did graduate work at the University of Chicago and was active in the NAACP in West Virginia. Julia Evangeline Brooks became a noted clubwoman in the District and elsewhere, and Nellie Quander taught in the District schools and worked for the YWCA and the Women's War Work Council.[9]

By 1910, most of the founders of the sorority had graduated from Howard but were still officers in the organization. Once established, the sororities transcended the college community, since they were ultimately aimed toward community service. This ambiguity of its domain led the sorority to organize an alumnae chapter, a move that other black sororities imitated and that tied the sororities to the community as much as to the university. Within the organization a split developed that led to the creation of a second sorority, Delta Sigma Theta, in 1912. Rivalry between the two sororities took the form of competition for scholastic honors, among other things, and both sororities began efforts to help their local community. Although neither sorority was any more successful than the fraternities at achieving concrete goals before the 1920s, Delta members marched en masse in a 1913 parade for woman suffrage, and both maintained an interest in service to their race.[10]

Increasing prejudice in white schools led blacks to choose predominantly black schools, thus furthering racial solidarity. Howard University, referred to as "the Capstone of Negro Education," was the first choice for most of Washington's black elite. The school offered more to the black student than an environment free of prejudice, however. The *Howard University Record* advertised that the school had "a body of students who are preparing for leadership and authority among a race which stands so greatly in need of wise guidance and direction." William V. Tunnell, a Howard professor and former member of the Board of Education, commented that "Howard University is itself doing a great deal to populate the city."[11] Howard offered a secure environment for African Americans, devoted entirely to higher education and racial advancement. While the professional schools at Howard were sometimes the only ones available to black students, the university seemed an increasingly attractive alternative to the growing segregation in other universities.

The student experience at Howard was rich, if at times a little trying. Thomas Wyatt Turner, who would later return to join the faculty as a professor of botany, remembered that his information about Howard "was a sort of vague word-of-mouth description that pictured it as a grand place where the colored boy or girl could be trained for any profession or trade; where he or she would meet among his teachers, leading Negroes of the country and the finest of the whites." Turner attended Howard from 1894 to 1901, first at the preparatory school and then at the College of Arts and Sciences. He recalled that there were no professional advisers to recommend a course of study, but that individual professors and administrators provided plenty of inspiration to succeed. Registrar George W. Cook, in particular, "was extremely paternal in his admonitions and greatly encouraged me in my determination to enter Howard."[12] Cook, also remembered fondly for the times he provided his own money to bail out members of the football team at the police station, was just one of the members of the Howard faculty who added a personal touch to their teaching. Kelly Miller often visited students in their dormitories for intellectual discussions, and placed "constant insistence upon the relationship of scholarship to public problems."[13]

Howard University became an important center for the training of race leaders in the twentieth century. As discrimination at white colleges increased and as the quality of a Howard education improved, Howard University became a far more attractive option to the black elite. Some younger elite blacks even began to see a Howard education as advantageous for its ability to cultivate the qualities necessary to establish social status. Poor facilities made it difficult for Howard to rise to the level of many predominantly white universities academically; but the quality of the faculty and course offerings at the school improved over time, mirroring changes occurring in black society.

In part Howard improved in parallel with the improvement of other schools in the country as they increased their emphasis on the social sciences and modern languages and raised their requirements for both faculty and students. In part it improved because District elite blacks recognized the importance of having a first-class institution of higher learning in their community to which they could send their sons and daughters.

The curriculum at Howard improved spectacularly between 1880 and 1920. In the late nineteenth century Howard University actually consisted of four major divisions: the Academy, a preparatory high school; the professional schools, which operated semi-independently; the Teachers College, which emphasized the social sciences; and the College of Arts and Sciences. Between 1885 and 1895 the College and the Academy operated almost as one, although there were two deans. Many of the courses offered by the College differed scarcely at all from those offered by the Academy, and professors found themselves teaching remedial English to many students. In short, although the school bestowed bachelor's degrees on its graduates, it was hardly an institution with an outstanding reputation for scholarship, or one to which the black elite would consider sending their children for an undergraduate education.

The Teachers College and the College of Arts and Sciences operated in competition with each other, a situation that did little to promote unity among the faculty. The College of Arts and Sciences offered a classical curriculum, while the Teachers College taught more practical subjects. In 1907 the administration combined the two to create the College of Liberal Arts, which existed until the next major reorganization in 1919. It was only after 1919 that all secondary work was abolished at Howard and the school could truly be classified as a university.

Graduate programs were even less well organized than the undergraduate course. The Graduate School was established in 1867, at which time the university was authorized to grant an advanced degree to anyone who had completed one year of graduate study and submitted a thesis. In addition, on the recommendation of the faculty, any graduate of Howard who had been engaged in literary, professional, or scientific pursuits for three years after graduation could also receive the higher degree. Until 1889, the latter criterion was really the only one used; after that date, the Graduate School required a thesis for a graduate degree. The Medical School still granted honorary M.A. degrees to its faculty, however, and the Law School granted the M.A. to anyone who remained in residence at the school for a third year.

Between 1898 and World War I, few applied for the advanced degree because the requirements were gradually increased. This period was one of increasing standardization for the professions nationwide, so the development of more rigorous requirements at Howard simply followed the general trend. After the faculty petitioned the administration in 1904, the requirements for the M.A. were increased to one year's residence; a homogeneous course of study in any department, with at least a half year of advanced courses in the College of Arts and Sciences; and an examination and a dissertation on an approved subject. The Teachers College also required evidence of effective teaching skills, scholarship, and a capacity for leadership. In 1911 the school designated specific faculty members to direct graduate work and created a committee to supervise the Graduate School. In 1919, Carter G. Woodson again reorganized the graduate work to run more efficiently. Like the undergraduate program, the Graduate School left much room for improvement. Nonetheless, the increased professionalization of the Howard faculty and the standardization of its curriculum ensured that Howard maintained the same level of dedication to scholarship and higher education as that found at predominantly white colleges, and that it would keep up with educational reforms in the rest of the country.

As with the public schools, lack of adequate funding limited Howard's progress. Howard depended largely on congressional appropriations and philanthropy for its income, rather than on tuition, as did many white schools. One effect of this lack of funding was a lack of good research facilities. The library was largely built up with personal donations, such as the Cromwell Collection, donated by John Wesley Cromwell in 1900. Many donations were not so appropriate for an undergraduate library, however. Most books were either too specialized or too juvenile. In the library's early years it was open only two hours a day, and it had no full-time librarian. According to the librarian's annual report for 1889, only ninety-six books had been checked out of the library in the past year, and those by only twenty-two students.[14]

From 1900 to 1916 the overall modernization of the curriculum spurred library use as professors required more collateral readings, but since the Library of Congress and the Washington public libraries were open to blacks, the Howard University Library still grew slowly. In 1904 the librarian reported that new students were given instruction in use of the card catalog and reference books, which had increased their use. Nevertheless, a 1905 study revealed that over 60 percent of all books checked out of the library were works of fiction. The opening of the Carnegie Library in 1910 made books more accessible, and in 1916 a fully trained librarian, Edward C. Williams, formerly principal of the M Street High School, was appointed to upgrade the catalog. Once again, it was not until the secondary work was abolished at Howard that the library truly began to improve.[15]

Dependent on personal contributions such as that of Andrew Carnegie to build a new library, Howard administrators were also largely dependent on the personal agendas of the contributors and the Board of Trustees, which oversaw the budget. The situation paralleled that of the public schools to some extent. Howard was a boon to black academics, but it could also become a burden. A black college bestowed little prestige on scholars in the eyes of the white community. Since Howard suffered financial difficulties, it could not offer its professors the salaries they deserved or the facilities that a first-rate institution could provide. And since Howard was a black university under white administration until the 1920s, it had to battle as relentlessly as the public schools to keep its curriculum in line with the vision of its faculty. The university underwent drastic reforms at the hands of its white presidents and integrated Board of Trustees, and each change was scrutinized for any hint that it would lessen the reputation of Howard as a place of higher learning. As a result, the university was slow to modernize its curriculum, fearing attempts to industrialize the institution. With limited facilities, struggles between the faculty and administration, and even protest by the students, it was difficult for Howard to overcome its problems.

The administration and the faculty often found themselves at odds over the direction the university should take. This friction came about in part because the faculty believed that the largely white administration was attempting to change Howard from an institution of higher learning to an industrial school like Tuskegee or Hampton. The founders of Howard University had envisioned the institution as a school of agriculture and industry, but those programs had never proved particularly successful. From the beginning, the Howard faculty had a vision of Howard as a first-class university on the classical education model. Unlike the teachers in the public schools, the faculty could not be easily replaced, a fact they used to their advantage when they designed the curriculum.

Lack of sympathy among the faculty for the industrial course proved deadly for the program. Professors complained that industrial training interfered with regular classwork and so offered industrial courses only in the late afternoons and on Saturdays. Thomas W. Turner, a student at the Academy in the late 1890s, observed that while he had been as enthusiastic about manual training as he was about academic subjects before coming to Howard, the facilities at the university dampened his enthusiasm. "The set-up for these subjects was inadequate and unattractive," he recalled, and "the teaching, at least in the printing division, seemed aimless and with no other purpose than to keep the student busy." [16]

The struggle to control the curriculum came to a climax under the administration of Wilbur P. Thirkield (1906–12). Thirkield was an advocate of industrial education on the Hampton-Tuskegee model, and the black community firmly believed that it was his intention to "industrialize" Howard. His administration began at the height of the conflict between Booker T. Washington and W. E. B. Du Bois, when many of the District's black elite had already defected from Tuskegee or were beginning to chafe under Washington's control. As we have seen, the controversy over the issue in the black public schools had led to the dismissal of Anna J. Cooper from M Street High School when she persisted in supporting a classical curriculum, and Roscoe Conkling Bruce, a Tuskegee ally, had taken over as assistant superintendent of colored schools. The black elite were extremely sensitive to any perceived attempt to lower educational standards in the black schools, and they were particularly concerned about the situation at Howard University. To many people, Thirkield's appointment was just another attempt by the white community to keep blacks from improving themselves. Having already learned from the public school controversy that successful racial uplift efforts depended on independent control of black institutions, the black elite worried that Howard would lose what independence it had maintained, just as the black public schools had done.

Thirkield did not immediately antagonize the faculty. He was a good fundraiser, and he genuinely wanted to develop Howard into a sort of Tuskegee for urban blacks, emphasizing improved facilities and building up the sciences. Beginning in 1907, however, Thirkield embarked on a massive reform of the university that divided the faculty and the black community as a whole. The dean of the College of Arts and Sciences had resigned, and Thirkield attempted to have Edward L. Parks appointed in his place. Kelly Miller was elected nonetheless, so Thirkield then tried to minimize Miller's power by appointing Parks to five other positions and combining the College of Arts and Sciences and the Teachers College into the College of Liberal Arts. By giving Parks more responsibilities, Thirkield hoped to limit the influence of the deans, Kelly Miller and Lewis B. Moore, another powerful figure at Howard.

The ultimate blow for the black elite at Howard and in the larger community was the appointment to the Board of Trustees in 1907 of Jesse Moorland and James H. N. Waring, both Tuskegee allies; the white manager of Baldwin Locomotive Steam Works; and the Wizard of Tuskegee himself, Booker T. Washington. Thirkield sought support from the board to build a new industrial plant and better facilities for the applied sciences, and with these appointments ensured favorable treatment of his proposals.[17]

The new appointments to the board sparked outrage in the black community. P. S. Twister, the Washington correspondent for the *Chicago Conservator*, editorialized that "we have come face to face with the question: Shall

Howard University be made a second-rate industrial school, or shall it stand as a great National University for the 'Education of Youth in the Liberal Arts and Sciences'?"[18] The District's black elite saw Washington's appointment as just another example of Tuskegee manipulation. The faculty worried that the curriculum would become what they had fought against since the university was founded.

In fact, Booker T. Washington did not abuse his power as a trustee of Howard. He saw his appointment as a chance to put to rest the common assumption that he was opposed to the idea of higher education, and in fact performed significant service to the university. It was largely through Washington's influence that Thirkield succeeded in obtaining a Carnegie library for Howard. In 1915, when a southern congressman removed the Howard appropriation from the District appropriation bill, it was Washington who interceded with the White House to put pressure on Democrats in the Senate to restore the appropriation. He did manage, however, to block a movement led by Kelly Miller and Trustee John R. Francis to appoint Du Bois to the faculty in 1909. In addition, in 1912, when an opportunity arose to nominate Howard's first black president, Washington waited too long to support any black candidate, and when the board nominated another white clergyman for the position, he did not challenge the nomination.[19]

That Howard successfully resisted Thirkield's efforts at industrialization was due mostly to its faculty and some officials in the administration. The Tuskegee contingent on the Board of Trustees was balanced by such men as Francis J. Grimké, who served from 1880 to 1925, Charles B. Purvis (1908–26), William A. Sinclair (1913–25), William V. Tunnell (1898–1908), and John R. Francis (1908–13), all of whom emphasized building up Howard's reputation as an academically oriented university. Despite the efforts of Thirkield and other presidents to deemphasize the role of the deans, Kelly Miller, dean of the College of Liberal Arts from 1907 to 1919; Lewis B. Moore, dean of education from 1899 to 1919; Benjamin M. Leighton, dean of the Law School from 1882 to 1921; and George G. Cummings, dean of the Preparatory Department from 1885 to 1915, retained a great deal of influence in university affairs.

Added to this list was George W. Cook, the man who was most closely associated in the public mind with Howard University. Cook graduated from Howard with a B.A. in 1881 and was awarded an M.A. in 1886. In 1890 he received a bachelor of laws degree, and he earned a master of laws in 1903.

While gaining his degrees, Cook also taught on the Howard faculty. From 1881 to 1889 he was a tutor in math in the Normal Department and served as head of the department from 1889 to 1899, when he was appointed head of the English Department. Between 1899 and 1928, Cook served as dean of the English and Commerce departments, and from 1909 to 1919 he was also the secretary and business manager of Howard University. He was as active in the community as he was at Howard, being appointed to the Board of Charities in 1904 and serving as superintendent of a school for delinquent children in Blue Plains in the District. His wife, Coralie Franklin Cook, was active in community work, and taught elocution for several years in the English Department.[20]

Cook was a mentor and father figure to generations of Howard students, and his practical administration of Howard's financial affairs had much to do with keeping the institution true to the vision of an academic university, in part because the equipment required for industrial and applied science programs was often considered too expensive. For example, in 1914, when Thomas W. Turner, by then a botany professor, applied to Cook for a greenhouse to study the germination of seeds, Cook rejected the expense as unjustified. "When a school has a garden it goes about as far as is necessary for teaching the germination of plants," he wrote Turner.[21]

That the Howard faculty and black administrators were able to maintain control of their institution despite whites' attempts to interfere only reinforced the black elite's conviction that black institutions must be independent. One of the main reasons they had been able to maintain control was that there were few divisions within the faculty for the white administrators to exploit. The absence of strong support for the Tuskegee ideal among the faculty kept the faculty united. This situation further convinced the black elite that racial unity was the key to success. Despite Booker T. Washington's restraint as trustee, the Howard faculty believed his influence was as divisive as that of white administrators, and their opposition to the Tuskegee ideal solidified. Part of that ideal had always been accommodation, and thus the faculty members committed themselves to leading open protest against discrimination at the same time that they were defending the classical curriculum.

Bit by bit Howard developed into a modern university with excellent scholars on the faculty and a comprehensive curriculum. In the process it attracted a new generation of academicians, trained in the latest educational methods, whose experiences had already convinced them of the futility of gradual assimilationist approaches to racial uplift. They felt a keen sense of racial solidarity, which they imparted to their students. Their efforts to modernize Howard brought them into conflict with the white administration and drove them toward more radical approaches to racial uplift. They envisioned Howard as being in complete opposition to the Tuskegee ideal of industrial education. Tuskegee, in their eyes, educated African Americans to accept their subordinate status; Howard would educate its students to challenge that status.

The course of the History Department exemplified the changes and improvements that took place in the Howard curriculum in the first two decades of the twentieth century. History was not considered a serious subject except in conjunction with Latin or Greek studies until the late 1880s. Howard did not appoint a full-time history professor until 1906. Beginning in the 1890s, a movement to modernize the classical curriculum got its start at Howard with the appointment of Charles C. Cook.

Cook was the grandson of John Francis Cook Sr. and the brother of the social activist Elizabeth Appo Cook. Born in 1870, Charles Cook graduated from the M Street High School and earned a bachelor of literature degree in 1890 from Cornell University. In 1892 he was appointed to replace William V. Tunnell, who had taught both history and English, and in this capacity Cook introduced the first courses devoted exclusively to history. His courses in European and English history were based on his own research at Oxford and Heidelberg, and he proved a popular teacher. He agitated for the establishment of a separate department of history and the hiring of faculty members specifically to teach history. In 1906 the administration again appointed Tunnell to the faculty, this time to teach history alone.

Under Thirkield's administration, the university gradually dropped the old curriculum based on Latin and Greek, as other universities were doing across the country, paving the way for more courses in history and the social sciences. Unfortunately, Cook did not live to see the changes he had promoted: he accidentally drowned in 1910. In 1911, Tunnell introduced a course titled "History of the Reconstruction Period," which sparked interest in black history at Howard. Tunnell's course was especially important in counteracting the contemporary view of Reconstruction as, at best, a mistaken effort. The course also captured the mood of the black community, which was beginning to speak out openly against racial injustice, and through the NAACP was beginning to take a scientific approach to counteracting discrimination.

Tunnell's course inspired other faculty members to introduce courses designed specifically for African Americans. These courses played a large role in socializing the black elite to their connections with the race. In 1913 Kelly Miller began to teach "Problems of the Negro." Alain Locke petitioned for a systematic course on race relations in 1915, but the trustees rejected his proposal. In response, student groups such as the Howard branch of the NAACP and the Social Science Club sponsored a series of lectures in 1915 and 1916 to discuss race relations. In 1916 the Board of Trustees again refused to approve a course on race relations after the whole faculty had petitioned for it, claiming that it would be "inexpedient." The board's recalcitrance only further radicalized the faculty and student body. The board's action reflected the growing realization that the black community was indeed achieving cohesiveness, and that if its leaders were educated in the past wrongs of white society and taught how best to attack problems of current discrimination, they could become a threat to white hegemony.

In 1913 the official creation of the History Department with three full-time faculty members continued the process of improving the university while showcasing the talent of the race. Walter H. Dyson, appointed in 1905, had received A.B. degrees from both Fisk and Yale and was the first of the professionally trained historians to join the faculty. Dyson later became one of the first editors of the *Journal of Negro History,* and did graduate work at the University of Chicago, Columbia University, and the University of Pennsylvania. Dyson and Tunnell were joined in 1912 by Charles H. Wesley, who had an A.B. degree from Fisk and an M.A. from Yale. Both Wesley and Dyson were influenced by Carter G. Woodson, who would join them on the faculty in 1918 and who received a Ph.D. in history from Harvard in 1925. In 1915 Woodson founded the Association for the Study of Negro Life and History, which produced the scholarly *Journal of Negro History.* Under this nucleus of trained professors, the History Department expanded and raised its scholarship to a level equal to that of history departments at other universities.

By 1919 the department offered twenty-two courses in everything from Russia and the Far East to the United States as a world power. In addition, Tunnell offered two courses in constitutional history that essentially covered the African American experience. Not only did the department raise its reputation, it also offered one of the broadest bases for studying history at any university.[22]

What happened in the History Department mirrored the evolution of the other departments at Howard, and in society in general. Gradually the university moved away from the Latin and Greek curriculum and appointed professionally trained faculty in each area. The enlargement of the faculty allowed for increased specialization and a general improvement in scholarship. In addition, as more black students gained access to secondary education, it became less necessary to teach basic materials. When Howard abolished the secondary department in 1919, it was showing that it had truly become a regular university and wished to be accorded equal status with white colleges. Unfortunately for the faculty, this recognition did not come overnight.

The faculty at Howard came to encompass some of the brightest black scholars in the country by 1920, and an important portion of the black elite as well, but struggles with the administration limited the personal recognition that these scholars were accorded. The professors who succeeded at Howard were those who were willing to work for the institution rather than for themselves; but the scholars who could do the most to enhance the reputation of the university were those who achieved individual eminence and most deserved individual recognition.

Thomas W. Turner was one such professor. Turner had worked at Tuskegee Institute after getting his degree from Howard. He had taught at the Baltimore black high school and was recruited to join the faculty at Howard by his former professor and dean of education Lewis B. Moore. In 1913 Turner was appointed professor of applied biology and nature study, and charged with developing biology courses at Howard. He completed work for his master's degree at Cornell University while at Howard, with a thesis based on his research on potatoes. Turner continued his graduate studies, and in 1921 earned his Ph.D. from Cornell. As a professor at Howard he helped initiate the honor system and the Student Council, and he founded Honors Day to recognize students of superior academic achievement. In 1916 he helped to establish an organized athletics program, and he introduced courses in agronomy. During World War I, Turner served as acting dean in the absence of Lewis B. Moore.[23]

When ill health forced Moore to retire in 1919, Turner fully expected to be appointed to the deanship on a permanent basis, as he had never received criticism for his work as acting dean. President James Stanley Durkee, however, had other plans. Rayford W. Logan noted that Durkee had come to Howard with good credentials but with little experience with African Americans. Yet during Durkee's administration, from 1918 to 1926, Howard went through a complete and far-reaching reorganization that abolished the secondary course and centralized authority under the president. Durkee created new deanships to diffuse the power of the deans, combined the positions of secretary and treasurer of the university, and brought the professional schools under closer control. Durkee received as much criticism for his efforts as had Thirkield. Charles B. Purvis commented that "there is an eager desire in some quarters to have all the authority of the University concentrated in one person. I also feel that there is no desire to select colored teachers who will be potential in the affairs of the institution."[24] Durkee perhaps saw Thomas W. Turner as a threat to his authority, and appointed someone else to be the permanent dean. He offered Turner the position of registrar, inflating the job description to make it sound as though Turner would be studying education for the race, but Turner was not convinced and extremely angry.

Turner saw his conflict with Durkee in the context of the old industrial versus academic debate. The irony of the situation was that for the first time a Tuskegee supporter was in a minority position. In his memoirs he wrote that even in 1920 there was "little incentive to violate an old tradition around the college that the sciences were being taught there chiefly to satisfy the minimal requirements for entrance to the Medical College."[25] Undoubtedly Turner faced greater discrimination from the faculty because of the nature of his course and the fact that he had taught briefly at Tuskegee. Nevertheless, Turner was a first-rate scholar who deserved recognition for his efforts at the university. Turner was a victim of administration politics and of Durkee's attempt to strip power from all officials except himself. Durkee ultimately made life so unpleasant for Turner that in 1924 he resigned to accept a position at Hampton.[26]

Another brilliant scholar with a controversial tenure at Howard was Carter G. Woodson. When Woodson was recruited by Howard, he negotiated an agreement that the Association for the Study of Negro Life and History and the *Journal of Negro History* would remain entirely independent of the university. He resisted Howard's offers until 1919, when he accepted appointment to the Department of History. Woodson was a talented historian with an incredible ability to analyze information and a general ability to write in a scholarly manner. Woodson's public persona was at odds with his private one, however. Woodson demanded personal recognition and special treatment, so he came into conflict with Durkee almost immediately. Woodson had begun the reorganization of the College of Liberal Arts under the new president, but balked when Durkee asked him to report on the activities of certain professors. In a series of angry letters to the trustee Jesse Moorland, Woodson blamed the white leadership for his situation, threatened to resign, and accused Durkee of false representation. He was particularly outspoken against the dynasty of white clergymen who had served as presidents and faculty at Howard: "In as much as Northern teachers of the missionary spirit no longer come South to work among Negroes and those now coming for this purpose are less qualified in their fields than the average Negro teacher, will you permit such inefficient white leadership to bludgeon well educated Negro instructors among them into submission to their mediaeval methods thrown aside centuries ago by white educators?"[27] Woodson ultimately resigned from the Howard faculty to pursue a career as an independent historian, depriving Howard of yet another first-rate scholar. As Charles B. Purvis noted to Francis J. Grimké when commenting on Woodson's departure, "there can be but one general to command an army."[28]

Although not all of Howard's talented faculty came into direct conflict with the administration, the truth was that many of these professors were indeed nationally and internationally recognized scholars in their fields, but because of their race, they could not gain an appointment at a first-rate university in America. Many resorted to study abroad in the summers to gain research opportunities, but all felt somehow stunted at Howard. Ernest Everett Just was a prime example. Just graduated from Dartmouth in 1907 and taught at Howard from 1907 to 1941, first in English and then in his own field of biology. From 1912 to 1941, Just served as head of the Department of Zoology. He spent his summers studying at the Marine Biological Laboratory in Woods Hole, Massachusetts, and received his Ph.D. from the University of Chicago in 1916. In 1915 Just was awarded the first Spingarn Medal, and in his years at Howard he also received grants from the General Education Board, the Rosenwald Foundation, and the Carnegie Foundation for his research on cell construction. He wrote several texts on cell biology and numerous scholarly papers in his field, and received international renown for his work.[29]

Just enjoyed his teaching at Howard in the beginning. "If I can give the boys and girls [at Howard] a scientific start," he remarked, "it will help them in whatever they do later. It will clarify life. . . . I believe in mass action, and am here to raise the general level of race attainment."[30] Just gradually came to resent the disparity between his social and professional statuses, and began to request more leaves of absence to pursue work overseas.[31]

Just's feelings of deprivation must have been shared by many faculty members at Howard University. They were what motivated the effort to raise standards at Howard, and they were also the inspiration for greater involvement in racial uplift. Howard professors and black trustees knew that unless the reputation of the race improved, their personal reputations would continue to suffer. They also knew, like the teachers in the public schools, what it meant to have white control of educational institutions. Their experiences transformed them into leaders in the effort for racial uplift, and those they trained went on to become leaders in their turn.

Black colleges such as Howard struggled for independence from the white community as much as did other black institutions under segregation. The development of a solid curriculum and trained faculty at these universities ensured the availability of a first-class education to the children of the black elite. The gathering of so many educated and forward-thinking African Americans in one institution led to the development of radical approaches to racial uplift and the creation in Washington of a powerful leadership group within the black elite. The faculty reinforced the students' commitment to their race as they trained them for professional life. The experiences that black students underwent at college shaped their values, and hence the values of the next generation of leaders. With the development of black fraternities and sororities, those values increasingly came to include commitment to racial solidarity and uplift.

The environment at the university forced faculty members to work for the institution rather than for themselves, and that effort translated easily into working for the whole race. Although the white administrators of Howard attempted to control the course of the university, the faculty and black administrators were able to maintain their own control through racial solidarity. Again the black elite learned the importance of independent institutions and dedication to the race. The public school controversy had shown the black elite how not to protest discrimination; Howard presented the model of how best to resist it.

SEVEN

Occupation and Enterprise

For black elite men, probably the greatest incentive to become involved in racial uplift came from the need to earn an income. Black businessmen early realized that they could not compete with white businesses financially and so invoked racial solidarity to ensure the patronage of the black community. Black professionals were slower to realize the importance of good relations with the black community, since they offered services few could duplicate. Nonetheless, after being denied entrance to white professional organizations and facing lowered estimates of their abilities because of their race, black professionals soon found themselves in the vanguard of racial uplift. Black government workers and appointees depended on good race relations and the patronage of Booker T. Washington to keep their positions, but as segregation increased within the federal government and the influence of Tuskegee declined, they were only too happy to protest race discrimination, for their livelihoods depended on fair treatment in the workplace.

All three groups ultimately expected to participate in racial uplift activities as part of their responsibilities as members of the black elite. What began as a necessity to maintain an income appropriate to elite status became a qualification for that status. The new generation of race-conscious businessmen and professionals became the new leaders of the black elite.

While we most often associate elite status with wealth, economic security was more important to the aristocracy of color, and economic security meant employment. In a black community plagued by insecurity, a steady job could qualify one for elite status. Although many among the older elite blacks had earned their status through business enterprises, the Washington black elite counseled their children to enter the professions as well as to patronize black businesses. They also sought government positions that brought long-term security.

The occupational structure of the black elite changed over time to reflect larger trends in society. Before the rise of segregation in the late nineteenth century, black businessmen found it difficult to compete with more established white businesses. After the rise of Jim Crow, when many white shopkeepers refused to serve black patrons, African American entrepreneurs could find a steady market for their goods and services by appealing to racial solidarity. Early black professionals were heavily concentrated in the fields of teaching and the ministry, two professions that were open to educated blacks. By the turn of the century, however, greater educational freedom provided blacks with opportunities to study in a wider variety of fields. The black physicians and lawyers gradually became the community leaders that the ministers and teachers once were. In addition, as the professions opened to the black elite, more members of the younger generation trained as professionals rather than as entrepreneurs, realizing that fewer risks were involved in professional employment.

The rise of the younger black professional and business classes gave the black elite greater economic and social stability in the twentieth century. Rather than just relying on subjective qualifications to distinguish them from the masses, the black elite now rested on a solid foundation of income and education, and by the 1920s expected a commitment to using this foundation for the good of the race.

In the late nineteenth and early twentieth centuries salaries for blacks remained far lower than those for whites doing comparable work, and many blacks found it necessary to hold more than one job at a time. This was the plight of the teachers forced to teach night school to maintain a decent standard of living. It was not uncommon, therefore, for many members of the elite to don two caps simultaneously. Many lawyers, for example, also worked as clerks in government departments. W. Calvin Chase, editor of the *Bee,* also ran a law practice. John Anderson Lankford, the noted architect, studied law and was admitted to the District bar. Doctors often ran private hospitals, and

Whitefield McKinlay, who ran a real estate business, was constantly in search of a government appointment. William E. Matthews, a large property owner in the District, was a lawyer, money broker, real estate agent, post office employee, mortgager, and financier.[1] These men generally identified themselves as having one occupation, usually the one with the most prestige. Robert H. Terrell served in the Treasury Department, organized and maintained the Capital Savings Bank, and ran a law practice with John R. Lynch. He was always identified, however, as a lawyer, or sometimes as the former principal of the M Street High School, though he held the position only one year. After receiving an appointment as municipal judge, he was always referred to as Judge Terrell. George F. T. Cook was forever "former superintendent of schools" and Christian A. Fleetwood was Major Fleetwood long after the Spanish-American War. Whatever their occupations, most of these men supplemented their incomes with investments.

The evolution of black businesses in the District reflected changing objective conditions. By the 1890s, most towns had a black business district similar to the Shaw neighborhood in Washington. Centered on Seventh Street and Georgia Avenue, NW, Shaw stretched roughly between Florida Avenue and Howard University. The proximity of the university was not coincidental. Howard attracted a large community of educated blacks who came to teach or study there and resided close by. They provided a ready market for black-owned businesses, and created a demand for new services.

One such demand led to the rise of prosperous black undertakers in the late 1880s. Previously burial had been the responsibility of the family church burial society or fraternal association.[2] Now the new middle-class ethos of conspicuous consumption was absorbed by the black elite, and they wanted lavish funerals with all the trappings. Accounts of funerals took up much space in the black newspapers, naming active and honorary pallbearers and describing floral arrangements in great detail. The most prominent of the Washington undertakers was James H. Dabney, who by 1898 had three places of business—in Alexandria, in Georgetown, and on Third Street between L Street and New York Avenue. He arranged the funerals of many of the District's black elite, including that of Blanche K. Bruce. Dabney competed with, among others, James H. Winslow, the first undertaker to open for business in the Shaw District; Mason's Funeral Home in Anacostia, licensed in 1902; and William M. Davis, at 2053 Georgia Avenue, NW.[3]

In Washington as elsewhere, blacks often gained business experience by running beneficial societies and church relief organizations. The beneficial organizations laid the foundation for the black life insurance business—probably the most successful of all black business enterprises. The fact that most white insurance companies perceived blacks as poor insurance risks and refused to insure them enabled the black insurance companies to flourish. Milton M. Holland, after studying law, made most of his money as an insurance agent. Holland founded the Alpha Life Insurance Company in 1892, selling stock for $5 a share. His insurance policies were popular because they provided more benefits than the fraternal organizations could offer. Alpha Life Insurance soon had two subsidiaries: the Alpha Real Estate Banking Company, which dealt in mortgages, and the Alpha Law, Real Estate, and Collection Company. Holland had competition, however. The home office of the National Benefit Association, another black life insurance company, at 609 F Street, NW, coordinated branches in seven states, advertising itself as the "Premier Negro Insurance Company and Pride of the Race."[4]

Segregation did create opportunities for some blacks, for it provided them with a captive clientele. Nevertheless, segregation also endangered the very existence of these enterprises. Black entrepreneurs were often unable to get goods of the quality available to whites, and so could not offer comparable services to those white businesses that still served blacks. Other problems that black entrepreneurs faced were the low purchasing power of their clients, the difficulty of obtaining investment capital, and the lack of opportunities to gain modern business experience outside fraternal organizations.[5]

As a result of the many obstacles black entrepreneurs faced, the failure rate of their enterprises was fairly high. Since little could be done to change the objective conditions and handicaps under which black businesses operated, the black community quickly targeted feeble support of those businesses as a preventable cause of their failure. The *Leader* admonished in 1889, "If we do not encourage our own professional men, who will? Every colored man who rises lifts his people."[6] By 1898, failure to patronize black businesses was a cause for public censure. Andrew Hilyer concluded from his study of wealthy District blacks that elite blacks neither invested in black enterprises nor patronized them.[7]

While this statement may have been true of some of the wealthiest blacks, clearly not all the black elite felt the same way. Despite divisions between those who supported Booker T. Washington's ideas of economic progress before political rights and those who supported more radical efforts for civil rights, most agreed that economic security was an important priority for the black community. Tuskegee supporters believed that building up race businesses would lead ultimately to civil rights. Once African Americans gained an economic power base, the white community would have to accept them.[8] Yet even those with a more radical approach to civil rights supported the growth of black business, if for other reasons. W. Calvin Chase emphasized the development of black businesses as a means to train children, rather than forcing them into white businesses. In effect, Chase was advocating a separatist philosophy.[9] Building up black business was important to both factions, and therefore became an important priority for the race's leaders, and an important motivation behind the elite transformation.

Beginning in the 1890s, the movement to patronize black business intensified in Washington, and many black entrepreneurs made attempts to create new business ventures based solely on black patronage. The Hotel McKinley, which opened in 1897, provided a fashionable place to stay for visiting prominent African Americans. Founded by Henry Woodson, a popular and widely known black Virginian, the hotel offered meals at all times, a beautiful view of Southwest, a barbershop, "neat" furnishings, and smoking and reading rooms. The *Colored American* regularly listed guests registered at the hotel, suggesting its social prominence while providing free advertising. In 1910 the Whitelaw Hotel opened its doors at 13th and T Street, NW. The hotel was developed by John Whitelaw Lewis, one of a new breed of racially aware black entrepreneurs who wanted to provide accommodations exclusively for African Americans. The hotel became a fixture in black society in the following decades.[10]

Attempts to create black business institutions increased steadily after the late 1890s. Though many of these attempts failed, a significant number succeeded, transforming the Shaw District into the center of black commerce in Washington. Racial solidarity was ultimately the key to success in the perception of many business leaders. Ware's Department Store, in the Shaw District, advertised with a large photograph showing black clerks and customers. Most newspaper advertising stressed black ownership by showing photographs of the owners or emphasizing that a business was a race enterprise.[11]

By this time, African Americans were engaged in a variety of successful enterprises in Washington. Murray Brothers, Inc., Printers and Engravers, produced many works by black authors at their office in Shaw. They competed with Nathan Sprague, who published the *Washington Pilot*, and Manley Brothers, who printed the *Daily Record*. Washington boasted at least three black photographers—Moses P. Rice, Daniel Freeman, and Addison Scurlock at Scurlock Studio, in Shaw.[12]

Having a portrait taken at Scurlock's became a mark of distinction among members of the black elite. Founded in 1911 by Addison N. Scurlock, the studio was responsible for photographing most of the District's prominent black citizens. Born in North Carolina in 1883, Scurlock moved to Washington at age nineteen. His father was a politician and lawyer who also practiced in Shaw. Scurlock studied under Moses P. Rice and began photographing from his own home in 1904. He began with photographs of students at M Street, Armstrong, and Howard University. He soon made a reputation for himself, and was often called in to record visits of prominent African Americans to the District. Carter G. Woodson distributed Scurlock's portraits of black leaders to black high schools throughout the country. Scurlock's legacy was enduring. In 1976 a journalist noted, "For years one of the marks of arriving socially in black Washington was to have your portrait hanging in Scurlock's window."[13]

In 1901 there were 177 businesses in Shaw, and by 1910 over 200. Most of the growth came in "prestige" businesses—as jewelers, printers, undertakers, druggists.[14] In addition, four institutions were created to support black business in the District. The True Reformers Hall, built in 1903, held a business complex and meeting rooms. The Laborer's Building and Loan Association provided support to would-be entrepreneurs, as did the Lincoln Memorial Building Company. Finally, the Anthony Bowen YMCA, a building constructed largely through the efforts of prominent businessmen, particularly John W. Lewis, provided a place for black entrepreneurs to meet, exchange ideas on business techniques, and seek moral and professional support.

The key to the stability of black businesses, however, was the establishment of black-owned banks. Blacks found it difficult to get loans from white banks, and after the collapse of the Freedmen's Bank in 1874, there were no banks operated in the District specifically for African Americans until 1888. There were, however, building and loan societies. One of them, the Industrial Building and Savings Company, established in May 1885, proved to be the forerunner of the first black-owned bank in America, the Capital Savings Bank.

The group of men who organized the Industrial Building and Savings Company were of elite social status and were part of a concerted effort to reorganize black enterprise along modern business lines in order to make it more competitive. They wanted a voice in the management of their money as well as a chance to gain business experience in the companies this money supported. In addition, with their characteristic belief in noblesse oblige, they desired to create an institution that would teach thrift to the lower classes of the race and give them an opportunity to buy homes. By making a success of the enterprise they hoped to prove to whites that blacks were capable businessmen.

Officers of the Industrial went further in 1888 and created an unincorporated joint stock company with a twenty-year charter, designed to be a "general banking and discount business." Among those who served as officers for both the Industrial and the new Capital Savings Bank were Robert H. Terrell, William A. Warfield, and Lewis H. Douglass. In its first year the Capital Savings Bank took in $117,000 in deposits, and by 1892 it had over $300,000.

The bank's financial situation was far from sound, however. The investors were more idealistic than practical, and few had had any formal business training. Many of the promissory notes held by the bank had been signed by irresponsible persons and became uncollectable. The bank itself, located at 609 F Street, NW, was worth $18,500, but was mortgaged for $17,000 plus interest. The bank's securities consisted of insurance policies taken as security for loans, but many of these policies had expired or the insurance company had failed. At the time of the bank's closing in 1902 it had 1,400 depositors, but had given out more in loans than it held in deposits. In early 1903, a court order officially closed the bank, and an ensuing lawsuit by some of the depositors drove almost all of the officers into bankruptcy.[15]

The failure of the bank caused hostility in the community, particularly when the black community accused the officers of mismanagement. For many, the Capital Savings Bank was just a repeat of the Freedmen's Bank fiasco, only this time the officers had taken advantage of members of their own race. Robert H. Terrell, one of the few officers not bankrupted by the venture, still suffered from his involvement in the Capital Savings Bank every time he came up for renomination to the bench. Terrell kept his head above water until 1913, when he, too, filed for bankruptcy, listing $13,491.58 in debts and only $62.50 in assets above legal exemptions. Two years later, Terrell had to plead for exemption from paying a loan he had guaranteed because of his continuing debts.[16] Financial disaster on this scale could paralyze members of the elite and effectively stop them from investing in any further enterprises. Now the income they received from their main occupation became more important, particularly if it was steady.

The next attempt to establish an African American bank, in 1913, was more successful. John W. Lewis established the Industrial Savings Bank and served as its president until his death. The bank gained a strong reputation and avoided many of the mistakes of the Capital Savings Bank. A sizable portion of its assets consisted of stocks and bonds, and it issued a smaller percentage of loans. In addition, the bank owned real estate besides its own premises. All the same, the bank joined the many others that failed in 1932, after an unsound merger and embezzlement during the bank panic.[17]

The black venture into banking in Washington was not extraordinarily successful overall, but it showed efforts on the part of the black elite to support and create black enterprise and independent black institutions. These efforts were made at considerable personal risk but, unfortunately, without much financial experience. Nonetheless, the lessons of the Capital Savings Bank prepared men such as John Lewis for later attempts at black finance and at least made the elite more aware of the need for better training in business methods.

By the twentieth century, black entrepreneurs were imbued with the ideals of racial economic solidarity, and a new class of black businessmen came to prominence, not through their length of residence in the District or through longtime elite status but by building institutions to serve the black community and by helping the working classes and stressing racial advancement.[18]

With the establishment of Howard University and the opening of some white schools to blacks, the elite began to emphasize education as the key to elite status. They encouraged their children to enter professional occupations, to pursue careers that were open only to people with advanced degrees. As society became more complex, the black community expected its leaders to navigate the new system of restrictions that they faced and deal with problems they did not understand. Elite black parents realized that professionals such as doctors and lawyers would become the new race leaders, and wanted their children to maintain the family's social status in the community.

Historians of black communities in other cities have noted a change in elite occupations between 1910 and 1915 from entrepreneurship to professional endeavors.[19] That Washington experienced this shift nearly a decade earlier is not surprising. The leadership changed in other cities in part as a result of the migration of southern blacks to northern cities. As the black community grew, it was better able to support a new black professional class in an era when it was increasingly difficult for blacks to gain white clients. The lack of factories in Washington and the region's primarily southern outlook provided fewer inducements to blacks to migrate there in the twentieth century. The large influx of educated blacks to the District came during Reconstruction. Thus, essentially, the changes that occurred in the northern cities in the twentieth century had already occurred in Washington by 1915, because of the earlier existence and viability of a black professional community. Washington's black professionals played integral roles in the transformation of the black community, but they were only participants in the larger process.

Born in 1880 in Washington, Albertus Brown lived the typical life of a black professional. Educated in the District schools, Brown sold newspapers for seven years to support himself. In high school he was a messenger for the Republican National Committee and served as a stenographer for Mark Hanna and Colonel Charles Dick. In 1901 Brown entered law school at Howard University and upon graduation in 1904 moved to Toledo, Ohio, to practice law. In Toledo he helped found the Frederick Douglass Community Center for boys and girls, and was a member of the Bar Association, the Toledo Race Relations Commission, the Toledo Art Museum, the Masons, the Elks, the Shriners, and Alpha Phi Alpha. When he died, nearly a thousand mourners attended his funeral.[20]

Brown's experiences reflected most aspects of life for the new black professionals. With little family income, he had to support himself through school. While in Washington he was able to form important political connections with the Republican Party. His law degree from Howard University enabled him to pursue a profession and take a leading role in his chosen community. In a manner suiting his position, he joined both black fraternal organizations and presumably biracial groups to reinforce his connections with the white community. While it may have been family connections that introduced him to prominent Republicans, he chose to pursue a law degree to acquire the prestige he needed to become a community leader. By moving to Toledo, he ensured ties between the two cities that would reinforce the national black elite network. Brown's career was mirrored in the lives of most of Washington's black professionals, whether they lived in the District all their lives or moved there from somewhere else.

While any profession could bring high social status, physicians gained the highest respect in the black community. The doctor typically married the "best girl in town," lived in the finest home, entertained most lavishly, and sent his children to the best schools.[21] Washington had more black physicians than many other cities because its Freedmen's Hospital was one of the few hospitals for blacks that accepted black doctors as interns. Many doctors who went on to practice in other states interned at Freedmen's, thus extending the black professional network.

Freedmen's was also one of the first hospitals in the country to appoint a black surgeon-in-chief, a position that naturally brought the incumbent tremendous prestige. Since the hospital was administered largely by the Department of the Interior, white control remained a significant factor, and as at the public schools and Howard University, conflicts often arose. While Freedmen's was essentially an African American institution, it still had to conform to white ideas of what was appropriate for a black hospital. It was those ideas that governed the selection of the surgeon-in-chief, rather than the specific skills of the physician in question.

Dr. Daniel Hale Williams, a graduate of Northwestern University Medical School, was appointed surgeon-in-chief in 1892. Williams revolutionized the administration of the hospital. He organized the first training school for black nurses, installed the first black interns, and raised the standard of surgical work to make Freedmen's a centerpiece for the black medical community. He was one of the few black members of the American Medical Association, and from 1886 to 1889 was a member of the Illinois State Board of Health. He gained a reputation as one of the leading surgeons trained in the new methods, and performed the first successful open-heart surgery in the United States in 1893. He married Alice D. Johnson of Washington, thus consolidating his social status within Washington's black elite. In 1898, possibly because Williams was becoming too powerful, President William McKinley appointed him chief surgeon to a black Army corps on service in Cuba. After his return, Williams remained a well-respected member of the community until 1907, when he moved back to Chicago.[22]

The next appointment as surgeon-in-chief of Freedmen's was the most controversial. Austin M. Curtis, also a graduate of Northwestern Medical School, was appointed in 1898 amid much competition for the position. Before his arrival the *Bee* editorialized that his appointment was purely political and that the local doctors Furman J. Shadd and John R. Francis had equal qualifications, and still other candidates had received higher scores. W. Calvin Chase complained, "Washington is the dumping ground for state politicians."[23] The *Colored American* praised Curtis as a competent administrator and a great reformer but also expressed discreet criticisms. By the time of his arrival, however, both papers seemed willing to praise him.

After Dr. Williams's departure, an investigative committee from the Department of the Interior charged him with mismanagement of Freedmen's, including among its charges overpayment of several employees, provision of sumptuous food for the physicians, carelessness in the drug department, and nepotism.[24] Curtis saw his role as that of reforming the management techniques at Freedmen's and laying to rest the complaints of the Interior Department's investigators. Since Williams had himself been a reformer and had become immensely popular in the District, it was unlikely that Curtis, the outsider, would gain any friends by disparaging him.

Curtis, taking advantage of a three-week quarantine for smallpox in effect on his arrival, began a drastic reorganization of bureaucratic techniques, medical policy, and personnel. Curtis dismissed several people from Freedmen's who were intimately associated with Williams, including his sister. The *Bee* claimed that the Department of the Interior was using Curtis to remove any blacks who had gained power in the institution, and that the charges of mismanagement against Williams were simply part of this plan. The paper pointed out that the investigating committee had made no complaints about white employees. Chase noted that the committee itself was composed of white Democrats, who "found that negroes were learning too much dentistry and medicine." The committee recommended that Howard University remove these departments immediately, pending the approval of the Secretary of the Interior.[25]

Two factors lay behind the controversy. First, a white investigative committee appointed by a secretary of the interior who was less than sympathetic toward blacks was sure to incite response on the part of the black community. Whatever Williams had or had not done in his administration of the hospital, he had significantly expanded Freedmen's influence and independence in the black community and consequently his own. By so doing he had assuredly weakened the white community's control over the black hospital and touched some nerves along the way. When the investigators charged mismanagement, they could have been attempting to wrest some control of Freedmen's back from the hands of the black physicians, thus placating southern racists.

Second, the controversy was an issue of patronage. At a time when opportunities for black physicians and other medical professionals were severely restricted, affiliation with a steady institution such as Freedmen's ensured them a livelihood. Private practice was not always lucrative and certainly did not provide a steady income. In addition, Freedmen's was one of the few hospitals where black doctors could consult professionally and practice the latest scientific methods. The surgeon-in-chief of Freedmen's held a great deal of influence in hospital appointments.

While the *Bee* was quick to point out the racist elements of the report, most of its protest focused on the dismissal of the black matron, Mary J. Brown. According to the *Bee,* the white trainee supervisor had begun to assume some of Brown's responsibilities under Curtis's new rules. When Brown complained, she was accused of insubordination. Curtis complained that Brown could not get along well with others, but the *Bee* saw the problem as a matter of personal friction. Brown had served for many years as matron under Williams, and was associated with the old ways of doing things and the old circle of people loyal to Williams. Chase went around town seeking influence on Brown's behalf, but the publicity had upset Secretary of the Interior Cornelius Bliss, and he dismissed her himself.[26]

Naturally, many Washingtonians viewed Brown's dismissal as an omen of things to come, and more worried that Curtis might bring in outside competition for jobs. In a city that already had many members of the medical profession and where more were graduating each year from Howard University Medical School, this was indeed a serious matter.

After the initial uproar, Curtis settled into a relatively quiet tenure. He retired to private practice in 1902, after winning over most of the city's black elite and becoming an integral part of black society. In 1910 and 1911 he served as president of the National Medical Association. He was chair of the committee to raise $100,000 for the YMCA building fund, served as a member of the Anti-Tuberculosis Association, and gave talks in churches on sanitation and hygiene. In 1912 he was attending surgeon at Freedmen's and consulting surgeon at Provident Hospital in Baltimore and Richmond Hospital in Virginia. In addition, he was associate professor of surgery and lecturer in surgical pathology at Howard University Medical School and a clinical professor of surgery for the Medical School's postgraduate program.

Curtis's replacement, Dr. William A. Warfield, a noted specialist in abdominal surgery, was less of a shock to the District. A graduate of Howard Medical School, he had interned under Williams while he was surgeon-in-chief and had become his assistant. He had served as assistant to Curtis, too, and thus represented continuity.[27] Warfield found his tenure much freer of controversy than his predecessor had done, but even he aroused antagonism among the medical staff. Warfield fabricated stories about a rival, Dr. Charles I. West, the assistant surgeon-in-chief, and caused his dismissal in 1905. In 1907 Daniel H. Williams, who considered West a brilliant surgeon, urged Booker T. Washington to exert his influence to gain West's appointment to a different position, but Washington supported George C. Hall instead.[28] Despite the controversy surrounding appointments, Freedmen's attracted some of the country's leading black doctors, if only for temporary stays. All these physicians benefited from their association with the hospital and created ties with Washington's black elite that extended beyond the city.

Some graduates of Howard Medical School chose positions in the government, such as medical examiner of pensions, or sought appointments at Freedmen's, but most, even those in private practice, found an affiliation with an institution to be beneficial. William W. Purnell, born in Pennsylvania to an abolitionist family, came to the District at age eleven and enrolled in the District schools. He graduated from Howard with a degree in pharmacy in 1890 and got his medical degree in 1893 from the same institution. He became an assistant professor at Howard Medical School, instructing in diseases of the eye and ear. He served as medical director of the Alpha Insurance Company for three years and was also a hospital steward in the District National Guard. In July 1898 he became the assistant surgeon in the Eighth Regiment, U.S. Volunteer Army, with the rank of first lieutenant. A nephew of Furman J. Shadd, he moved in elite circles. He was a thirty-second-degree Mason, attended St. Luke's Episcopal Church, and married the heiress and social butterfly Theodora Lee of Chicago in 1895. The couple had one son and lived in an imposing house on New Jersey Avenue.[29]

Dr. Furman J. Shadd succeeded Charles B. Purvis as secretary and treasurer of Howard University Medical School in 1898. He was a professor of "materia medica and therapeutics" and assistant professor of clinical gynecology at Freedmen's. Shadd also lived in an "elegant mansion," called Arlington Terrace, at the corner of 9th and R Streets, NW. He had a nicely furnished and well-equipped office and was a prominent figure in the Fifteenth Street Presbyterian Church.[30]

Without an institutional affiliation, it was difficult for a black doctor to maintain a steady clientele. Independent physicians had to depend on the whims of the working classes for patronage and the unreliability of their paychecks. Some doctors countered this drawback by creating institutions of their own, thus furthering the move toward black economic independence.

Dr. John R. Francis operated a private hospital primarily for obstetrics. Since few hospitals admitted blacks, it was difficult for the black elite to obtain good care. As doctors gradually replaced midwives at the turn of the century, black women sought more professional care during pregnancy and childbirth. John Francis established his hospital "to guarantee [patients] the careful, scientific treatment of the hospital, combined with the comforts of home." Francis maintained that the home environment often prevented proper treatment or rapid convalescence and so offered his "sanatorium" as an alternative. Any doctor in good standing was welcome to bring patients to Francis's sanatorium for a fee. Thus he could offer his facilities to other doctors who might not have had equally modern equipment. Francis kept trained nurses on duty around the clock and barred any contagious or "objectionable" cases.

The cost of a stay in this private hospital was not small. Fees for room and board, nursing care, and medicaments could range from $15 to $50 a week. A private nurse cost $15 a week extra. Private hospitals such as this were purely a service for the elite, to enable them to avoid the embarrassment of a segregated public hospital. Such hospitals were not uncommon, as few black doctors could practice in white hospitals. They were of necessity operated for profit, and thus could prove financially detrimental to members of the community if no other hospital was available to them. However, some survived to serve as examples of successful business enterprises, and through employment of other doctors and nurses they contributed to the spirit of black capitalism.[31]

As prominent members of the community, black doctors were often sought as sponsors for business enterprises, as their names brought an undertaking prestige. They also lent legitimacy to an enterprise, for presumably men of such superior education would not back it if it were not sound. While these business involvements seldom brought profit in themselves, they did increase the doctors' connections with the community and their social standing. Black doctors in general were stable leaders of the community, the overwhelming majority of them married, with fine houses and rich libraries, and involved in community uplift efforts such as YMCA and Urban League programs.[32] Despite the irregularity of their incomes, black physicians increasingly gained the confidence of the black community that provided their patients, and thus earned more than any other black professional group. Their professional standing enhanced their social standing, and their social connections increased their professional practice. Black doctors on the whole made a commitment to the cohesion of the black community, even if it was only to serve their own purposes.

Dentists occupied similar positions in the community. John R. Francis, although primarily a doctor of medicine, held a dental degree also and operated Howard Dental Parlors at 7th and T Street, NW. Ten years after its establishment in 1906, this enterprise could advertise "Expert Colored Dentists of proven ability—No Students Employed."[33] Charles Sumner Wormley, dentist and member of the Howard University professional staff and Board of Trustees, was a highly visible figure in Washington black society. One newspaper reporter wrote that "he was, and looked the part of a natural aristocrat, with none of the artificial snobbery of the pseudo article which goes by that name." Wormley was a member of the Mu-So-Lit Club and was remembered for his Beau Brummel style, his funny stories, and his baritone voice. He was a professional singer briefly before settling back down in the District and studying dentistry. William S. Lofton, one of the District's most successful black dentists, was a member of the Board of Directors of the Capital Savings Bank and an active financier of black business. Lofton was regarded as one of Washington's leaders in racial advancement.[34]

Perhaps even more than doctors, dentists had to acquire standing in their community to support a profitable practice. The initial investment in equipment required to set up a practice was so large that lack of connections and financial resources deterred many men from entering the profession.[35] It was even more imperative for a dentist to cultivate good relations with the black working classes that would supply the bulk of his patients, so black dentists tried to stay prominent in any reform efforts that would help the community.

The medical profession closest to business was pharmacy. Most black pharmacies were small family operations that survived mainly through the patronage of black physicians. White doctors might send blacks to black doctors, but white pharmacists were businessmen and were quite happy to fill prescriptions for blacks; thus segregation did not stimulate a black pharmacist's business. In addition, in areas where race relations were good or where black doctors had ties to white druggists, the black pharmacist had little hope of gaining customers through referrals. In Washington, where personal animosities surfaced easily in the high-pressure competition for jobs, if a black pharmacist came in conflict with a black doctor, he could lose much of his patronage.

The twentieth century brought another competitor to the arena—the chain drugstore. An individual pharmacist, especially a black pharmacist, found it difficult to compete with a corporation. In order to survive, the black pharmacists emulated the white ones and turned their stores into variety stores, offering newspapers and a soda fountain, and they supported local racial uplift efforts by posting notices of meetings in prominent places. The pharmacist's commitment to the community made the black pharmacy a gathering place, particularly after church services on Sunday and after the movies. As Carter G. Woodson noted, however, many of the people who gathered there still took their prescriptions to white pharmacists, and the black pharmacy became a social center at the expense of the business side of the enterprise. Woodson attributed this development to an "idolatrous attitude toward the white businessmen who [working class blacks] believe can always give them a better bargain and more efficacious medicine than the Negro." Nevertheless, racial pride enabled some pharmacists to retain their clientele, because if blacks were refused service at a white pharmacy's soda fountain, it did not matter to them that they could buy their prescriptions there.[36] Black pharmacists became part of the black community by necessity, and were deeply interested in promoting racial cohesion, since they, more than any other professional, depended on the goodwill and confidence of black patrons.

In 1886 the only black pharmacist in Washington was Dr. S. A. Sumby, who was both pharmacist and physician. James Wormley had once been a pharmacist but had given up the business for lack of profit.[37] In the next forty years the situation changed radically as a black business community developed and as the number of black physicians in the District increased. Arthur S. Gray and his wife, Amanda, ran the successful Fountain Pharmacy until Arthur's death in 1917. Arthur Tancil, graduate of Howard Medical School in 1886, served as attending physician at the dispensary clinic at Freedmen's after 1899, and ran a successful pharmacy in Anacostia. R. F. Plummer and E. F. Harris also opened pharmacies in the first decades of the twentieth century.

Pharmacists became experts in marketing as well as dispensing. In 1919 the Colored Druggist's Association, Inc., of the District of Columbia advertised in the *Bee,* offering accuracy, honesty, and courtesy. The group of twenty-four pharmacists appealed to racial solidarity by implying they were better suited to meet the needs of the black community and would provide better service. They showed the diversity of their stores by offering over-the-counter remedies, cigars, and toilet articles, items generally sold in chain drugstores.[38] Pharmacists were forced to modernize and market aggressively, and their efforts contributed greatly to the general economic development of the black community. A by-product of their aggressive marketing was the promotion of racial unity.

Among the least common professionals in the black community was the architect. Few schools existed to train architects, and fewer still would accept blacks. Nevertheless, Washington boasted two of the race's leading architects, William Sidney Pittman and John Anderson Lankford. Not surprisingly, both men had strong ties to Tuskegee, since both had received their early training there. Lankford took courses at several black colleges before coming to Washington to study law. He was admitted to the District bar but practiced primarily as an architect. He was often a consultant on government buildings and became the official architect of the African Methodist Episcopal Church.[39]

William Sidney Pittman studied architecture at Drexel Institute of Art, Science, and Industry in Philadelphia, graduating in 1900. He was enabled to attend this school by a loan from Booker T. Washington, and returned the favor by teaching at Tuskegee for four years. Pittman gained even closer ties to Tuskegee when he married Booker T. Washington's daughter Portia. After a quarrel with the school's chief architect in 1904, Pittman and his family moved to Washington to set up an independent business. Pittman enjoyed little financial success, since few contractors were willing to hire a black architect, but he did design occasional churches, schools, and lodge halls and was involved with the Fairmount Heights development. He also designed the 12th Street YMCA building. In 1907 Pittman won the right to design the Negro Building at the Jamestown Exposition, an award that brought him national attention. Business did not increase substantially, however, and in 1913 he moved his family to Dallas.[40]

As few as black architects were (in 1930 there were only forty-five in the entire country), they could make little impact as a group on racial uplift. Individually they had to struggle to earn a living, although both Pittman and Lankford found time to serve on various committees for the race. However, these men set examples for the younger generation and showed them what opportunities there were for professionals in a variety of fields.

Of all the black professionals, those most concerned with racial uplift were the lawyers. This observation is partly a tautology, as many race leaders in the nineteenth century saw law as the best profession from which to help the race by entering politics. Washington boasted some of the nation's most distinguished lawyers. Archibald Grimké studied law at Harvard, as did D. Augustus Straker, before establishing a practice in Washington. Robert H. Terrell graduated from Harvard summa cum laude in 1884, and was valedictorian of his class at Howard University Law School in 1889. Terrell was admitted to the District bar in 1893 and entered into practice with John R. Lynch.[41]

Lafayette M. Hershaw graduated from Atlanta University in 1880 and ten years later moved to the District to take a government clerkship. After admission to the District bar he became a law examiner. Hershaw served as president of the Bethel Literary and Historical Society and was one of the charter members of the Niagara Movement, the precursor to the NAACP. James Adlai Cobb worked his way through Fisk University and Howard Law School as a Pullman porter. A strong supporter of Booker T. Washington, Cobb gained appointment as special assistant U.S. attorney from 1907 to 1915, and became a municipal judge in the 1920s. He also served as the local director of the NAACP and was a professor and dean of the law school at Howard University.[42] Other prominent lawyers in the District included Emmanuel M. Hewlett, Thomas J. Calloway, and Jesse Lawson.

Until the twentieth century, however, many black lawyers were objects of some suspicion. In 1898 W. Calvin Chase, himself a lawyer, editorialized on the need for reform in the legal profession. He noted that while some black lawyers were honorable, others were simply shysters who hung around the courts waiting for cases and charged low fees just to be able to say they were practicing. These shysters, Chase claimed, were the reason blacks were excluded from the Bar Association. He also warned the black community that the lawyer who guaranteed success in advance was not necessarily honest. The *Colored American* preferred to point with pride to the successful lawyers. "Washington has eight or nine excellent colored lawyers who are just as capable as the white men employed by our people to attend to their legal business, and we are glad to see our people beginning to put faith in them."[43]

Like other black professionals, lawyers suffered from a lack of confidence among the black community, which damaged their ability to earn a living as well as their status in the legal profession. In order to gain patronage the black lawyers had to prove their ability and their commitment to the community by taking on pro bono cases they could not afford, or tackling civil rights cases for which they did not have adequate experience.

The typical cases a black lawyer handled dealt with family matters—errant spouses, divorce, abandoned children, small estates, life insurance policies, petty crimes. Lacking experience in more sophisticated cases, black lawyers often did not perform well when they were confronted with one, a fact that reinforced the stereotype of the incompetent black lawyer in the minds of both blacks and whites. Although black partnerships were not unheard of—John R. Lynch and Robert H. Terrell created a partnership, as did E. M. Hewlett and John A. Moss, and James H. Smith and John F. Cook—most black lawyers worked in solo practices, and the paucity of opportunities for professional communication among them made it hard for them to acquire expertise.[44]

The negative view of the abilities of black lawyers led many blacks to seek white counsel rather than a lawyer of their own race. This bias could even damage a black lawyer's case, as white lawyers sometimes capitalized on the negative stereotype of their black opponents, and even more frequently the white judges ruled against black lawyers because of racial prejudice. One early way in which African American attorneys tried to bypass this discrimination was to affiliate themselves with a white lawyer, who would try the case if it got to court. This practice was particularly common in Washington, where judges consistently discriminated against black lawyers. An informal poll of Washington's black lawyers showed that they were unwilling to admit that prejudice prevailed, but acknowledged a lack of collegiality with white lawyers and blamed prejudiced juries for adverse decisions.

Black lawyers faced many clashes of perception and reality. Association with the lower elements tinged their own reputations. The intimate nature of Washington's black society caused many elite blacks to go to white lawyers to avoid letting their problems become widely known in their own community. Financial problems were particularly embarrassing when they became widely known. The lack of black brokers made it difficult for black lawyers to finance important cases. As a result, they could gain little experience with business law and thus had little interaction with the black business community.[45] The creation of a black bar association in 1906 did address some of the problems that black attorneys faced, but the organization did not flourish. Many black lawyers turned to fraternal organizations as a way of making connections with the larger community. Since the fraternal orders were often subjects of litigation themselves, some lawyers gained professional experience through their membership.

Gradually black lawyers began to realize that the best solution to their problems was to become active in racial uplift efforts. This strategy would accomplish two objectives: first, it would distinguish them as race leaders, and second, it would raise the status of their clientele and thus their own professional status. The District black bar association launched campaigns to allow blacks to use the white law library and to appoint a black probation officer. Younger lawyers took the forefront in racial leadership. Whereas older black lawyers tended to keep to themselves, the younger lawyers began investing in the community and helping out those less fortunate than themselves. Often their interest exceeded their investment because of their smaller incomes, but they were still involved in the black community. They were quicker to take up antidiscrimination cases and pro bono cases against extradition of blacks who would not receive a fair trial in another state. Many cooperated on cases with the NAACP, although few actually initiated a campaign for racial uplift themselves. The younger lawyers also began studying business administration in school in order to take business cases in the black community. By the beginning of World War I, black lawyers had increasingly moved into the black business districts, an indication of their greater affiliation with the black community.

Lawyers provided good examples and leadership in racial efforts. Traditionally involved with politics, they were sought out by white politicians during national political campaigns to rally the support of the black community. They used the organizational skills they received in the fraternal orders to organize civil rights campaigns. They also demonstrated the importance of knowledge of the law to the black community, for in order to fight discrimination, blacks had to know their rights and be able to protect them.[46] As younger lawyers moved into racial uplift efforts, the law profession gained increasing prestige in the black community.

Black professionals played key roles within the elite and in the formation of the black community. Most professionals gained social status on the basis of their occupation. Above all, elite and working-class blacks looked to professionals as the hope for the future, the group that would lead the race to greatness. Given the tendency of elite blacks to isolate themselves from the black masses, professionals such as lawyers, physicians, and pharmacists provided a bridge between those groups and created a sense of community. Professionals, excluded increasingly from white patronage, relied on black solidarity to make a living. Black professionals in the late nineteenth century may have formed ties with working-class blacks grudgingly or with little idea other than to increase their clientele. But simply by creating connections, they were forging a sense of racial solidarity, and many black professionals were already aware of their responsibility to their race.

The most stable source of employment for District blacks and the most peculiar to Washington's black elite was the federal government. Office seekers from far and wide came to Washington seeking appointments even to minor positions for the economic security they provided. The experience was not always pleasant or rewarding. Although employment in the government did not necessarily imply previous elite status, members of the elite were directly involved in gaining positions for many blacks and were deeply interested in who obtained which appointment. Government appointments often involved patronage power, which in turn could provide new openings for blacks in the government. The letters between elite family members and friends frequently touched upon the subject of influence in government appointments and how various election results would affect those appointments.

Of course, at the turn of the century appointments depended on the right connections—generally to the master of patronage himself, Booker T. Washington. But the competition for appointments was so fierce that even Washington's most loyal supporters were not certain of a recommendation. The chain of influence was often a tortured one. By 1908 Archibald Grimké had split with Booker T. Washington over issues of racial advancement strategies, yet he could still put powerful pressure on Washington when it came to appointments.

When Whitefield McKinlay sought appointment as recorder of deeds for the District of Columbia, he was unsure of Washington's support even though he had long been a supporter of Tuskegee. His wife, a friend of Angelina Grimké, asked her to ask Archibald to use his influence with Washington. Angelina wrote to her father that Mrs. McKinlay "has very little faith in Mr. Washington. She believes that unless you and some others of the [men] pin him down to a downright promise, Mr. MacKinlay will not get anything. . . . [He] makes scarcely enough to live on. Something ought to be done for him." Archibald Grimké replied that he had already written to Washington "with a strong statement for Mac's claim to recognition & I do hope that it will do some good."[47]

McKinlay was certainly not the only candidate for office who had to worry about Booker T. Washington's commitment. After 1895, Washington was publicly identified as an accommodationist, a black leader who could be counted on not to rock the boat. This image made him the perfect consultant to white politicians who wanted to gain black support by distributing patronage to African Americans but who wanted to appoint men who would not pose any threat to the established hierarchy.

During the presidency of Theodore Roosevelt, Washington was the de facto controller of black patronage, and those who wished appointments had to pay obeisance to the Wizard of Tuskegee. Roosevelt consulted him both formally and informally, and seldom failed to appoint a candidate Washington had recommended. For the black elite in the District this situation was particularly galling. Many considered Washington an upstart who was infringing on the influence of a more traditional leadership class. Many more felt that Washington was endangering the cause of civil rights for African Americans when he publicly excused some of the more blatant aspects of Jim Crow.

The status of the Four Hundred rested on an older power base with traditions born during Reconstruction, when integration seemed possible. Having fought for equal rights in earlier generations, they were too proud to sit back and see those rights taken away. Many members of the black elite in Washington had ties with counterparts in Boston, who followed a decidedly radical path in comparison with Tuskegee's. Booker T. Washington's approach took in the realities of segregation and worked within its limits to achieve influence for African Americans. The District's black elite took longer to accept those realities, and once they did, they were not willing to appear to compromise their beliefs or to kowtow to Tuskegee.

By the turn of the century the Four Hundred had come to realize that they no longer wielded influence in politics and social affairs. By that time Tuskegee controlled the only positions of importance in government that were still reserved for African Americans. Since government appointments were one of the mainstays of black social status, the older District black elite had little choice but to beg favors of Booker T. Washington. In addition, through the influence of the Tuskegee machine, many supporters of Washington had come to the District and joined the elite circles themselves. Blanche K. Bruce had been won over to Tuskegee before his death, and had received appointments for himself and his family and friends with Booker T. Washington's influence.[48] In 1901 Washington recommended Robert H. Terrell for a municipal judgeship that had become vacant, and succeeded in having appointed the first black judge in the District of Columbia. Terrell was one of the few black appointees to hold his position through the Democratic administration of Woodrow Wilson, and Terrell's loyalty to Tuskegee was strong, although his wife, Mary Church Terrell, often strayed from the fold.

Washington often used lieutenants to achieve his goals, so that he could maintain the fiction that he did not personally decide who would get appointments. Whitefield McKinlay, Thomas J. Calloway, James A. Cobb, Robert H. Terrell, Ralph W. Tyler, Richard W. Thompson, Edward E. Cooper, Roscoe Conkling Bruce, and Jesse Lawson served Tuskegee by visiting government officials to discuss appointments, writing articles for the local press, propounding the Tuskegee philosophy at public meetings, and reporting back to the Wizard on the opposition. With such formidable assistance and the ear of the president, Tuskegee ran patronage in the District with ease, much to the chagrin of those on the out list.

One of those not in the good graces of Tuskegee was Lafayette M. Hershaw, one of the leaders of the Niagara Movement. In 1907 Hershaw held a position in the Interior Department and was rallying opposition to Tuskegee and Theodore Roosevelt in the black press. Booker T. Washington decided that it was time to punish his opposition, which was growing more vocal every day. He sent Charles W. Anderson to Washington to discuss the matter with Roosevelt and other government officials. Anderson told Roosevelt that Hershaw was responsible for the problems in the press and suggested that Hershaw be given a reduction in rank, "or if that was impossible, a transfer to some very hard and disagreeable service." Roosevelt gave Anderson a note to take to Secretary of the Interior James Rudolph Garfield, who agreed to follow the recommendation provided Washington could guarantee that Hershaw was the ringleader. Anderson advised Washington to write immediately.

On the same day, Anderson met with William Howard Taft, then secretary of war, to warn him about a group of troublemakers who were opposing Taft's candidacy for president in 1908. Anderson related what had been suggested in the case of Hershaw, and noted that there was a similar troublemaker in the War Department, Freeman H. M. Murray, another active member of the Niagara Movement. Anderson suggested that Murray suffer a fate similar to Hershaw's. Taft found the proposition appealing. Continuing his rounds, Anderson then visited the State Department to try to have William Henry Hunt removed from his post as consul at St-Etienne in France. As Anderson reported to Booker T. Washington, it had been a productive day.[49]

After Woodrow Wilson was elected, Washington's situation changed drastically. Wilson did not consult the Wizard about most appointments, and, denied the ear of the president, Washington found his Tuskegee machine falling apart. Those members of the District's black elite who had supported Tuskegee in order to gain appointments now split openly with Booker T. Washington. The District branch of the NAACP grew into one of the largest branches in the country. Even the *Bee*, under obligation to Tuskegee for funds since 1906, began to reassert its independence. Ralph W. Tyler reported to Emmett J. Scott in 1914 that the leaders of the NAACP were "either avowed opponents of the Doctor or indifferent friends." Many members of the black elite were switching from strong support of Tuskegee to a middle-of-the-road stance in order to keep their government appointments. "We have friends," reported Tyler, "who were with us strong when we were serving their meals and washing their clothes. Now that they believe we can no longer feed or clothe [them] they are preparing to hurdle the fence. We held them by favor then. We must hold them now by fear."[50]

The threat was empty, however. Later in the same year, James A. Cobb asked for Washington's influence in his efforts to keep his appointment as special assistant United States attorney in the District. Scott wrote Cobb a rather facetious letter, explaining that Washington was not in a position to have any influence with the new attorney general. Deeply offended, Cobb reported to Scott that he was no longer certain of Washington's motives, and that he had heard from W. Calvin Chase that Washington did not really support him. Scott thought Cobb was simply spoiling for a fight at Chase's provocation, but Washington wrote a letter of recommendation for Cobb anyway, because he feared that if Cobb lost his position, the attorney general would appoint a white man in his place.[51] Cobb gradually distanced himself from Tuskegee and later became a leading figure in the local NAACP.

Clearly Tuskegee was losing power. Washington later reported to Andrew F. Hilyer that he could not help with an appointment because he had opposed Wilson in the election and would be embarrassed to ask for favors. He suggested that Hilyer go see the officials himself. Scott noted on the letter that Hilyer should consult Bishop Alexander Walters, a prominent black Democrat.[52] After Washington's death in 1915, the split from Tuskegee was complete. The District black official elite gradually began to resume the radical mantle that it had worn in the nineteenth century.

Competition for government jobs was so fierce that the office-seeking process acquired a circus atmosphere at times. Washington's black elite received as much gratitude from successful job seekers as they did criticism from losers. Archibald Grimké intervened on behalf of many grateful African Americans. One such applicant wrote, "When things look so very dark for the thousands of little people of our race it is good to know that we have some leaders of integrity in high places who are constantly using their influence to secure justice for the many."[53] Such fawning praise, however, merely shows the importance of influential connections in the black community.

An office seeker described the process by which one obtained an appointment in 1903, noting there was nothing wrong with "pull" as long as the applicant was qualified for the position. To get a job one had to urge "the appointing officer to make the appointment when the name is certified to him . . . appointments are to be made from a sort of combination [of factors, the results of civil service examinations being only one] and a little reflection will indicate to you that it is done to leave an opening so that fellows can get in who have a little influence behind them."[54]

But influence was not always enough to gain federal employment in the face of increasing racial prejudice. In her autobiography, Norma Boyd described the process by which employers decided whom to hire. "Although there was no impediment to Blacks taking the Civil Service Examinations, photographs were a part of the application. . . . There would always be a reason for overlooking the top Black candidates. Accordingly, at that time, a job as a Printer's Assistant was a job of status in the Negro Community."[55]

Ironically, while the federal government grew larger during the Progressive Era, job opportunities for blacks in the government decreased. During Taft's administration, the number of black employees declined substantially. In 1910 the federal government employed 22,540 blacks, who accounted for 5.86 percent of all federal employees. In 1912 the number of black employees was down to 19,729, or 4.98 percent. Of course it was under Wilson's administration that segregation became fully institutionalized in the federal government. Memos began to circulate, such as one from R. W. Woolley, auditor of the Treasury Department, by order of the secretary of the treasury, reserving a toilet facility for whites only and relegating blacks to the third-floor facilities.[56] Ralph W. Tyler, auditor of the Navy until 1913, when he was replaced by a white appointee, reported that screens were erected to keep him from the view of his fellow workers and he was limited to the use of the basement facilities.

Reorganization of a government bureau was often an excuse to eliminate black positions. When the Department of Commerce and Labor became two separate departments in 1913, for example, blacks did not receive any important positions. In 1914 blacks were "honored" by the creation of a "Negro Bureau" in the Department of the Interior. In the District post office there were no black foremen by 1914, and it was common for groups of ten to fifteen blacks to be transferred to branches that were slated to be closed shortly.

The practice of requiring a photograph to be attached to a civil service application came into wide use under Wilson. The practice originated with applications for service in the Philippines or the Panama Canal. Because of the expense of sending someone to such distant places, the government wanted to be sure it was not paying the passage of impersonators. However, the photographs facilitated abuse of the rule that the appointing officers were to select one of the top three qualified candidates. In 1913 the *Boston Record* noted the increase in segregation in the Post Office Department when blacks were shifted to the dead letter department and then transferred all over the country. Since few blacks could afford to move, the transfer forced them out of their jobs. The Navy Department became segregated, and even the Pension Office began asking blacks if they would prefer to have their own room. When all said no, they were moved to dark corners away from windows.[57]

It was protests against government segregation that focused the attention of elite blacks on the larger issues of discrimination. Blacks organized petitions and committees of protest. A delegation headed by William Monroe Trotter visited President Wilson in 1913 and again in 1914. Some of these campaigns were successful in eliminating segregated facilities or at least in removing the signs, but in general the government was unsympathetic to the black cause. Segregation in the federal government was of interest to blacks all over the country as it was symbolic of American racist attitudes. Rolf Cobleigh, associate editor of the *Congregationalist and Christian World,* observed from Boston that without continued protest "the segregation movement may then be extended slowly and quietly before the public realizes what is going on."[58] During World War I, protest against segregation became extremely heated, since black soldiers were called upon to defend an ideal of democracy that for them did not exist.

When Francis J. Grimké received a Labor Department circular on segregation in government departments, he returned it with an impassioned plea: "It is surprising that you did not see the impropriety of sending out such a paper. The assumption running through it is that colored people are to be limited to certain grades of work only. By what authority is this done? Are they not citizens, entitled to the same considerations as other citizens?"[59]

A letter from Grimké to a black newspaper shows how government discrimination was forcing blacks into protest. "These outrageous damnable discriminations that are being made against us in the Departments here . . . call for loud, persistent, unceasing protest. . . . The time to voice our dissatisfaction is now, while the war is going on; while we are going across the sea to lay our lives down in order to safeguard democracy in the world. . . . I cannot believe that the subordinates in the various departments of the Government here and elsewhere would dare discriminate as they are doing unless they felt pretty sure that they had the sanction of those higher up."[60] Such statements, eloquent though they were, had little effect on the government. Between 1912 and 1918 the size of the federal workforce more than doubled, yet blacks made up only 4.9 percent of it.[61]

More distressing than the decline in black civil service employees was the decline in black presidential appointments. Three blacks, Blanche K. Bruce, Judson Lyons, and William T. Vernon, served as register of the Treasury between 1881 and 1913, but from 1913 on no African American held this position. When Henry Lincoln Johnson was appointed recorder of deeds by McKinley, he followed a long line of black appointees, but the next black to serve in this position was appointed in 1921. Blacks felt particularly cheated by the Wilson administration. Carter G. Woodson noted that the only member of Wilson's cabinet who spoke well of blacks was the secretary of the interior, Franklin K. Lane, who had been born in Canada.[62] In all, the black community was as ambivalent about the federal government as an employer as the government was about blacks as employees.

Protest against conditions of employment in the federal government led to the growth of the District NAACP, a group that was founded in Washington largely under the impetus of black professionals and government workers. The organization's initial campaigns were to protest segregation in the government departments, but its members soon extended their vision to encompass larger issues of discrimination. After the death of Booker T. Washington in 1915, the black elite felt free to protest segregation openly. The former Tuskegee antagonist Lafayette M. Hershaw was particularly active in the NAACP, gathering statistical data on black government employees. Since the steady income that the civil service offered was important to many of the city's elite blacks, protest against working conditions in the federal government was a good rallying point to begin a concerted effort for racial uplift. Once organized, the NAACP was able to expand its efforts into a variety of areas, carrying the leaders of the black community with it. Once again, in their need to make a living the Talented Tenth found themselves making common cause with the entire black community.

The black elite still faced many problems in their efforts to earn an income commensurate with their social status. Business ventures were risky when blacks with little financial backing had to compete with whites for customers. Professionals had difficulty keeping a steady clientele and maintaining a regular income without affiliation with an institution or a professional organization. Federal employment may have offered a steady income and served as a necessary supplement for most elite families, but conditions within the federal government were at times humiliating and generally gave little hope for promotion. In addition, to receive an appointment one often had to make political concessions or incur political debts. Most elite blacks found investment in real estate the only sure way to increase their financial resources. Yet employment not only defined the elite, it helped forge bonds in the black community that had not previously existed. It tied the race together inextricably and provided the foundation for black institutions and racial uplift organizations. Elite blacks soon realized that they relied on the rest of the black community for their incomes, particularly after the advent of segregation. From there it was no great leap to the realization that if the community united and created a firm economic base, everyone would benefit. Once the elite began to create these community ties, they could create a more stable environment in which business could flourish and the elite could take the lead in the movement for racial uplift.

By the twentieth century, although incomes for the black elite were still precarious, the younger professionals, particularly lawyers and doctors, took a more idealistic approach to their roles as community leaders. By 1920, these professionals and a new breed of racially conscious businessmen were seriously challenging the concepts behind racial discrimination in the form of protests and black institution building. They organized petitions against discriminatory legislation and sent delegations to the president to protest segregation in the federal government. They created black institutions, such as the Industrial Savings Bank, that would strengthen the independence of the black community. Though black businesses still frequently failed, they had begun to be founded on the principle of racial solidarity as well as on a drive for personal gain. And though a steady income still eluded many black professionals, they were now able to specialize in their fields and still maintain a livelihood and high social status. Gradually, as a result of changes in objective conditions in the larger society, the black elite began to view their means of employment as a way to help their race. Through their occupations and enterprises black elite men had begun to render obsolete the old standards for membership in their status group.

Archibald and Angelina Grimké. Abandoned by her white mother, Angelina grew very close to her father. (*Courtesy Moorland-Spingarn Research Center.*)

Annette Church, Mary Church Terrell, and Anna Church.
In this case the stepfamily was as close as the nuclear one.
(*Courtesy Moorland-Spingarn Research Center.*)

Phyllis and Mary Terrell, the natural and adopted daughters of Robert and Mary Church Terrell. (*Courtesy Moorland-Spingarn Research Center.*)

Fifteenth Street Presbyterian Church, under Francis J. Grimké, was nationally renown among the black elite for its progressive minister and racial advocacy. (*Martin Luther King Jr. Public Library, Washingtoniana Division.*)

Anna Julia Cooper in her M Street Latin class. Cooper came under attack for trying to ensure a classical curriculum in the black high school. (*Courtesy Moorland-Spingarn Research Center.*)

Roscoe Conkling Bruce, assistant superintendent of colored schools, was attacked for his allegiance to Booker T. Washington but promoted racial pride in the black schools. (*Courtesy Moorland-Spingarn Research Center.*)

Dunbar High School, completed in 1917, replaced the overcrowded M Street School, but maintained its reputation as the premier black high school in the country. (*Reproduced from the Collections of the Library of Congress.*)

Ernest E. Just, while at Howard University, earned international recognition for his work on cell structure but struggled to gain respect in the United States because of his race. (*Courtesy Moorland-Spingarn Research Center.*)

Daniel Hale Williams, surgeon-in-chief of Freedmen's Hospital, was the first doctor of any race to perform open-heart surgery in the United States. (*Courtesy Moorland-Spingarn Research Center.*)

Wormley's Hotel, owned by one of the richest black men in the District, catered primarily to whites. (*Reproduced from the Collections of the Library of Congress.*)

Residents of the National Training School for Women and Girls, run by Nannie Helen Burroughs, which emphasized the civilizing effects of "Bible, bath, and broom." (*Reproduced from the Collections of the Library of Congress.*)

Nannie Helen Burroughs was known nationally for her charitable work and race advocacy but was never accepted socially by the District black elite. (*Reproduced from the Collections of the Library of Congress.*)

Odd Fellows Hall provided not only a meeting place for the fraternal order but space for black entrepreneurs to coordinate institution building. (*Martin Luther King Jr. Public Library, Washingtoniana Division.*)

EIGHT

Charitable, Professional, and Fraternal Organizations

Joining and forming organizations were part of the experience of most Americans in the Progressive Era. Elite blacks were no different in this respect. Because the Progressive Era was also the era of Jim Crow, however, black organizations took on an added dimension. In their charitable, professional, and fraternal organizations the black elite established an independent basis from which to approach racial uplift while ensuring social status. Black charitable and reform organizations allowed black elite women to continue to discharge their obligations to those less fortunate than themselves while making connections with the black working class. Black professional organizations enabled elite blacks to reinforce their social status while becoming more aware of their racial identities. In black fraternal organizations elite blacks created connections with the rest of the community while gaining valuable experience from a business and professional standpoint.

For black elite women, charitable and reform activities took the place of occupation as the key to transformation of values. Although many women held jobs, they did so more for freedom as women than for racial uplift. Some women, such as Mary Church Terrell and Anna J. Cooper, did combine work with racial uplift through their lectures on race issues, but these women were not moved to feel sympathy for the race by their employment. That transformation came through their activities as clubwomen and churchwomen.

Charitable activities brought elite black women closest to the rest of the black community and provided the strongest link to racial uplift activities. As these women became aware of the importance of defending their honor against charges of immorality, they realized that they had more in common with all black women than with the white "sisters" with whom they usually conducted charitable efforts. Increasing discrimination in biracial organizations contributed to this conviction. Black elite women had first seen themselves as intermediaries between the races through their joint activities with northern white churchwomen. Gradually they began to believe that they must take on the task of racial uplift without white help. Such beliefs furthered their sense of racial solidarity and convinced them that their efforts were not simply a matter of noblesse oblige but were of vital importance to the race and to their own social status.

Their philosophy was best expressed in the slogan of the National Association of Colored Women (NACW): "Lifting as We Climb." Their participation in charitable activities enabled elite blacks to further their own status in the community by performing traditional elite services. When they assisted the black working classes, they also assisted their race by eliminating the causes of the degradation that had fostered negative stereotypes of African Americans. The impact that black charities had on the black community was profound. White charities were improving living standards for the disadvantaged; black charities were practicing racial uplift.

In the 1890s the black women's club movement flourished. Inspired by the churches' efforts to uplift the race, as well as by other community efforts, women formed groups of more or less exclusivity to discuss the issues of the day and in some cases to try to improve conditions. In Washington some of the race's most prominent women were responsible for founding black women's clubs and organizations. While they lived in Washington, women such as Mary Church Terrell, Mary Ann Shadd Cary, Hallie Q. Brown, and Fannie Barrier Williams had the additional stimulus of the Bethel Literary and Historical Association, which inspired their efforts to uplift the race on a regular basis while providing the women with a chance to become involved in the discussions and to present papers. Both informal and formal meetings led these women to a common understanding of what was necessary to improve the race. Since most black elite women had taught at some point in their lives, they also realized the importance of education to racial uplift, and their own responsibilities as educated women to lead the reform.

As business leaders appealed to racial unity to support black business, so black elite charity workers used race to shame their community into action. This tactic showed clearly that black elite women were aware of their responsibilities to the race, even if at times they needed prodding in the right direction. Those who invariably accomplished this conscience-pricking were women such as Amanda R. Bowen, who dedicated their efforts to charity and racial uplift. In 1898, Bowen made an appeal in the *Colored American* for black leaders to get involved in charity work among the black working classes. "Why don't we who say we are interested in our people step to the front, put ourselves to a little inconvenience and do something at once.... One has only to pass through our city with open ears and eyes, and if he does not carry with him at the same time an aching heart, he has no real love for his race. He is minus race pride, without which no human being can claim full development in true manhood or womanhood."[1] Such calls for service typified the views of Washington's elite black clubwomen, who felt it their mission to reform society's ills. The subelite of charitable workers in the District was an impressive group of talented women.

Amanda R. Bowen, known as Mattie to her friends, was a teacher in the public schools, with a second profession as a public lecturer before black women's church groups. She was president of the Sojourner Truth Home Association and active in the NACW. With Emma F. G. Merritt she founded the Teacher's Benefit and Annuity Association in the 1890s. She was one of a handful of elite black women in Washington who gained social prominence through her affiliation with charitable organizations.

Included in these ranks were women such as Helen Appo Cook, the first president of the Colored Woman's League, who championed the cause of disadvantaged women and children. Cook served on the Board of Managers for the National Association for the Relief of Destitute Colored Women and Children (NARDCWC) in the 1890s and later became president of the Women's Protective Union, a coalition of forty-two women's societies in the District. Anna Evans Murray also championed the cause of black children and was almost wholly responsible for the creation of the kindergarten movement in Washington. She established a program to train kindergarten teachers, was head of the kindergarten committee of the Colored Woman's League, and in 1898 was the league's delegate to the interracial Congress of Mothers, which convened to discuss issues surrounding the proper care of children. After the early 1900s she ran her own school for neighborhood children.

Bettie Cox Francis was also active in the NARDCWC and served as a trustee of the Colored Social Settlement. Francis served several terms on the school board and was active in the founding of the Phyllis Wheatley YWCA. Francis crossed paths frequently with Mary Church Terrell and Josephine Bruce. Terrell was president of the Colored YWCA in Washington and a trustee of the Colored Social Settlement. She helped found the Colored Woman's League and was the first president of the NACW. Josephine Willson Bruce was an original member of the Colored Woman's League, later joined the NACW, and worked with the Colored YWCA.

Most of the black women who became involved in charity work in the District at the turn of the century already had high social status in the community by virtue of their families or spouses, but some, while associating with these elite women in organizational work, did not otherwise move in elite circles. One of the most prominent of these women was Nannie Helen Burroughs. Founder of the National Training School for Women and Girls, affiliated with the Baptist church, Burroughs was a member of the NACW and corresponded with black leaders all over the country on racial matters, but never really was interested in elite social affairs in Washington. Burroughs preferred action to socializing, and she had intense race pride. She served on the International Council of Women of the Darker Races and worked with the Association for the Study of Negro Life and History and the NAACP. As the first elected secretary of the Women's Auxiliary of the National Baptist Convention, she worked tirelessly to give women a greater voice in the affairs of the black Baptist church.[2]

Bowen, Terrell, Bruce, Murray, Cook, Francis, and Burroughs worked unceasingly for various causes throughout their lives. They served on the boards of numerous charities, raised incredible sums of money, and showed unwavering dedication to any benevolent activity that might improve conditions for African Americans. They mastered the techniques of effective organization and shared their experiences with all the organizations they joined. Together these women and other like-minded souls transformed the charitable activities of the black elite in the District from expressions of concern and well-meaning gestures into methodical approaches to racial uplift.[3]

The founding of the NACW was an important step in the transformation of elite black women's attitudes toward reform. The NACW was formed in response to attacks made against black women in the media, and was designed to promote a positive image of African American women. The association also created a national network for black women that facilitated the sharing of ideas and further extension of the black elite.

It was hardly surprising that the NACW originated with the Colored Woman's League in Washington. Organized in 1892, the Colored Woman's League aimed to promote education and uplift black women. Its members included many former teachers, such as Terrell, Cooper, Cook, Bruce, and Murray. The organization was designed to coordinate women's reform efforts in the District. The women soon declared a desire to make the Colored Woman's League the coordinating body for women's clubs nationwide. The newly renamed National League of Colored Women was able to gain affiliates in several cities, but rival claims to leadership, particularly from Boston's Woman's Era Club, prevented a national coalition, although the League claimed national membership as a representative to the National Council of Women in 1894.

In 1895, after the publication of a particularly slanderous letter against the character of black women, the Woman's Era Club invited black women all over America to the First National Conference of Colored Women of America. Helen Appo Cook served as vice president of the conference, and the Colored Woman's League was well represented. The delegates voted to create the National Federation of Afro-American Women, dedicated to redeeming the reputation of all black women.

In 1896 the two organizations, the National Federation of Afro-American Women and the National League of Colored Women, decided to merge after much bickering over leadership of the new organization. The resulting NACW became the vehicle for a national network of black clubwomen, influenced in large part by Washington's black elite women. Mary Church Terrell served as first president of the NACW, and District reformers remained active in the organization's leadership.

By the time of the 1896 meeting, many of the older generation of black women reformers had died. Sojourner Truth, Mary Ann Shadd Cary, and Mary J. Patterson were gone. These pioneers had often risen from lower social status to prominence in the abolition movement. The new leadership, as exemplified by Terrell, Cook, and Sara Iredell Fleetwood, was predominantly elite, well-educated, and dedicated to scientific methods of reform.[4] Most important, this generation had begun to see racial uplift efforts as not only important to the rest of the race but essential to the maintenance of their own social status.

The earliest efforts of black women to coordinate charitable activities in Washington resulted in the settlement house movement. In 1895, inspired by the efforts of their sisters in Boston, New York, and Philadelphia, District clubwomen established the Sojourner Truth Home for Working Girls. Mattie Bowen managed the center, which was loosely affiliated with the Metropolitan AME Church and was designed to help young women from other areas adjust to city life. The home suffered from lack of financial support, however, and needed greater coordination with other reform organizations in the city.[5]

Better resources and coordination led to the creation of the Colored Social Settlement in 1902. Founded with the help of interested whites in the Associated Charities, who served on the advisory board, the settlement combined the efforts of elite black men and women to provide for those African Americans less fortunate than themselves. Located first on M Street, the organization offered programs for men, women, and children designed to provide positive examples. Sarah Collins Fernandis, one of the first professional black social workers in America, served as the settlement's first head resident and helped the women organize programs of benefit to the needy.[6]

Incorporated in 1906, the Colored Social Settlement stated as its objectives the creation of a social settlement and center with clubs, educational activities, industrial work, and social gatherings; investigation of the conditions that caused poverty and work for their improvement; promotion of volunteer personal service; and promotion of "cooperation and mutual helpfulness among the colored people of its vicinity by enlisting all who may be interested in united efforts for the common good."[7]

The settlement offered programs for everyone. It sought to develop character and sound morals in boys, to mold them into "strong and wholesome men and sober citizens." It taught girls to dance, sew, and play basketball. The men of the center created a civic association, "A Better South Washington," to offer alternatives to saloons and brothels, such as meals of baked beans, coffee, and bread at reasonable prices. For women the center provided lessons on how to be a model cook, mother, and homemaker. Such efforts certainly reinforced the middle-class morality accepted by both elite blacks and whites, but the Colored Social Settlement went beyond these efforts to truly improve the situation of the black working classes. It was largely as a result of the investigations of social workers affiliated with the settlement that the Sanitary Housing Company was created to build affordable brick apartment houses. The women worked with the government to create new playgrounds and to increase school opportunities for neighborhood children. They operated a neighborhood laundry, and inaugurated a Back Yard Garden and Beautification project that encouraged residents to grow fresh vegetables and in the process to clean up the neighborhood. They opened a public library for two nights a week and gave extension lessons in homes around the settlement house.

The Colored Social Settlement proved beneficial to both the residents of the neighborhood and the women and men who donated their time and money. The women provided a day nursery for working mothers for 5 cents a day, where local normal school students gained practical training. Local high school students became "big brothers" to neighborhood fatherless boys, creating friendships between different social groups. In general the settlement took advantage of the generous impulses of the whole black community and earned praise from Mary White Ovington, among others. In 1918, despite the organization's success, George W. Cook, one of the trustees, reported that war work was detracting from local support to the settlement and asked for help to pay its debts.[8] Ultimately the settlement house of the Progressive Era was replaced by the community center of the 1920s.

The success of the settlement house movement encouraged other reform efforts among members of the black elite. The clubwoman Mary E. Cromwell compared conditions in Washington in 1895 and 1909 and showed just how much the organizational techniques and dedication of the District's charity workers had accomplished for the black community in less than fifteen years. In 1895 there had been no school attendance law, no truant officer, and no regulation of child labor. By 1909 legislation had been passed to make it illegal for any child under fourteen to work during school hours, and children were required to obtain permits to sell papers or conduct a street trade after school. Since many black children worked to augment the family income, this legislation at least ensured that work would not interfere with education, one of the key elements of racial uplift.

Since the crime rate among black youths was high in Washington, the establishment of a juvenile court system with probation officers was of vital importance. Attacking some of the causes of criminal behavior among black youth, black charitable organizations sought to organize healthful activities into which children could channel their energies. Among the results of these efforts was the creation of supervised municipal and school playgrounds with organized recreation. The first of these playgrounds was established in 1902.

The following year three more opened, and after positive response from the public, eleven more opened in 1904. By 1927 each municipal playground was supervised by a director and two or more paid workers. The playground at Howard University also boasted a pool. In addition, most schoolyards were opened as playgrounds during the summer.[9]

Another concern shared by the black community was poor health among the working classes. Poor blacks lived in alley dwellings in crowded and unsanitary conditions, with little access to fresh air. In 1895 there was no organized attempt to address these health issues, and the death rate among blacks from tuberculosis alone was 283.3 per 100,000 residents. In the next fifteen years charitable and reform organizations pushed for a law condemning unsanitary dwellings, created the Washington Sanitary Improvement Company to create low-rent housing for poor blacks, and formed the Alley Improvement Association as a result of the report of the President's Homes Commission. In addition, they demanded compulsory registration of all tuberculosis victims, provided free disinfection of homes, started an education campaign with nurses, lectures, and leaflets, and established a public tuberculosis hospital. As a result of these efforts, deaths from tuberculosis dropped to 209.5 per 100,000 District residents.[10]

Attacking the causes of health problems as well as treating the symptoms, various groups organized "fresh-air day excursions" to the suburbs on the trolley. In the summer of 1902 the biracial Committee on Summer Outings was established "to provide fresh-air excursions for children and mothers who could not otherwise obtain the rest, refreshment, instruction and inspiration which comes from even a short summer outing." The three-person committee coordinated picnics for hundreds of people the first year of its existence. By 1903 the committee had expanded to thirty-eight members. In 1904, the Board of Commissioners of the District gave free use of a farm at the city limit to create a permanent day camp, Camp Goodwill, which catered to whites. Two years later Camp Pleasant was established for African Americans at Tuxedo, Maryland, through the efforts of teachers, ministers, and volunteer social workers. The camp was funded with contributions by blacks and whites, particularly through the efforts of Mary E. Cromwell, the attorney Charles Tignor, Samuel Middleton, and George W. Cook.[11]

Camp Pleasant provided a relaxed, healthy, and educational setting for working-class black mothers and children. From 1906 to 1909 it was managed by Julia N. Wilson; it was then moved to Notley Hall, in Oxon Hill, Maryland,

and taken over by the Associated Charities. Dr. J. H. Waring, a Howard University trustee, reorganized the camp along scientific lines in 1910 and moved it back to the District. Waring began the practice of talks on hygiene and other educational programs to teach mothers how to keep their homes efficient and disease-free. Under the reorganization, Camp Pleasant provided longer stays for some campers as well as the traditional day visits. Campers rose at 6 A.M., breakfasted at 8, then followed a structured regimen of exercise, crafts, patriotic activities, and education; only an hour each day after dinner was set aside for free time. Meals were nutritious—lunch typically consisted of soup, meat, two vegetables, dessert, bread, butter, and milk—and activities were designed to develop both mind and body.[12]

Of all the biracial charitable efforts, those for improved housing for blacks had the greatest impact. Small alleyways within blocks of respectable houses, often invisible from the street, were crowded with ramshackle houses and were breeding grounds for disease and crime. Since the majority of alley residents were African Americans, the issue of alley improvement was of particular concern to the black community. In the 1870s the Board of Health had begun the process of condemning some of the alley dwellings, but the Organic Act of 1879 stripped the health officers of the power to condemn residences.

Beginning in the mid-1890s, reform groups agitated for the elimination of the alleys, and the movement slowly picked up steam. Reformers went on tours of the alley dwellings and brought in Jacob Riis in 1904 to photograph and report on living conditions. As a result of Riis's report, Congress created the Board for Condemnation of Insanitary Buildings in 1906. In 1907, President Roosevelt established a fifteen-member commission to investigate conditions in the alleys and to make recommendations for their improvement. This President's Homes Commission, combined with the new board, was successful in bringing the plight of the alley dwellers to the notice of the general public.

In 1913 a new campaign succeeded in converting one alley into a playground. Woodrow Wilson's wife, Ellen, spearheaded the new campaign, which attracted the elite of both the black and white communities. Mrs. Wilson asked for legislation to abolish alley dwellings, and a law was enacted to go into effect in 1918. The deadline for enforcement was extended into the 1920s, however, and the courts struck down the legislation in 1927.[13]

Black leaders formed the Alley Improvement Association as part of the housing reform effort. Among the directors of this organization were some of the city's leading black citizens, including the Reverends J. Milton Waldron and Walter H. Brooks, Professor Lewis B. Moore of Howard University, and Rosetta E. Lawson, the noted temperance advocate. With a combination of reforms such as low-rent housing and the razing of some alleys, the alley-dwelling population declined from 19,000 in 1906 to 11,000 in 1915.[14] Many of the alley residents found housing in the new buildings erected by the Sanitary Improvement Company. With the joint participation of black and white elites, this particular charitable effort attracted many of the District's leading black citizens and certainly provided a measure of social status.

The Associated Charities established a separate conference for black charity workers in 1900, hoping to persuade more black leaders to volunteer. This attempt proved singularly successful, both in gaining volunteers and in the results of their activities. Black charity workers concentrated their efforts in the alleys and encouraged personal savings accounts through the Provident Stamp Saving System. A visiting charity worker would collect money in exchange for stamps that could be redeemed at the central office. Mary Cromwell noted that the collectors as well as the inhabitants benefited from these visits, for they received "an education about the people and the construction of society. Perhaps for the first time [they realized] what is meant by the brotherhood of man."[15]

Home visits brought the realities of poverty home to the black elite. The story quickly spread that after making a "friendly visit" to an alley dwelling, a black student contracted tuberculosis and died. Reports of the young man's death rocked the respectable community and led to the creation of the Committee on Consumption, which established educational programs in churches and provided free dispensaries.[16]

The interest that the members of the black elite showed in charity for poorer blacks had marked effect. Applications for charity by African Americans dropped substantially. In 1899, 66 percent of applications to the Associated Charities were from blacks; in 1900 the rate had declined to 60 percent, and in 1905, only 53 percent of all applications were from the black community—despite the fact that most alley dwellers were African American. The 1906 annual report of the Associated Charities admitted that the idea that all black women lived on charity was a myth that had arisen because of the large number of black women seen at the central offices. In truth, most of these women were actually coming to deposit savings.[17] Such myths, however, undermined interracial cooperation in charity work, which at best was based on a sense of noblesse oblige on the part of white workers.

Overall, despite much parallel effort, the record of biracial cooperation in the District was poor. Black charity workers in biracial organizations rarely achieved positions of importance. Whites often perceived little difference between these workers and the objects of their charity. The white organizers of the Associated Charities truly believed that blacks could accomplish more in segregated groups when they offered a separate conference to blacks in 1900. Undoubtedly, there were also a few white charity workers who did not want to spend time and money on what they saw as a degenerate race and who were more than happy to leave charitable efforts among the black working classes to African Americans. There was little true communication between the races at the turn of the century, and both races harbored distorted views of each other.

A statement in the 1913 yearbook of the Associated Charities recognized the hypocrisy of racial prejudice but still revealed a lack of true empathy for the black community. The writer acknowledged that whites did little about conditions for blacks in Washington except complain, but still saw nothing good coming from the black community. Instead, whites "permitted" blacks to create miserable conditions, as if they had a choice in the matter. As a result, most institutions created in the District to help African Americans were segregated. By 1913, only one white church-related charitable institution, the Lucy Webb Hayes Training School, still opened its doors to black girls; otherwise African Americans had to rely on their own charitable institutions.[18] Fortunately, black women had been creating these independent institutions since the turn of the century.

Although black elite women cooperated with white umbrella organizations, they did not find the racial atmosphere reassuring. Unfortunately, the white organizations had ready access to funds that the black women's organizations, resourceful as they were, could not match. The women also realized that organized charity was the best approach to poor relief. Mary Cromwell noted that in 1894 and 1895, $84,000 had been distributed "more or less indiscriminately" to the poor in the form of direct relief, but by 1909 the united charities, pursuing more scientific methods, were able to accomplish far more with much less money. Instead of police relief and independently operated free soup kitchens, for example, the Citizen's Relief Association now distributed relief funds through the agents of the Associated Charities with much more efficiency.[19] The black community could not yet provide relief on the scale of the predominantly white Associated Charities, and so black leaders bore the condescension of their fellow white charity workers in silence.

Several attempts surfaced to unite black charities under an umbrella organization, but none proved successful. In 1898 the attorney Jerome A. Johnson, "a gentleman of high social standing and well known business Capacity," proposed to unite the Banneker Relief Association, the United Aid, the Frederick Douglass Relief Association, the Protective League, the Immediate Relief Association, and two chapters of the Knights of St. Augustine, for a total of 838 members. An organization of close to a thousand, Johnson believed, could do much more than simply pay sick dues and conduct burials. He proposed the purchase of a home for the elderly in the suburbs. Although the *Bee* supported Johnson's proposal, little happened in the way of unification. Other attempts did follow to establish a home for the elderly.[20] With efforts to unite black charities foundering, except in the case of compartmentalized coalitions such as the Women's Protective Union, the black elite either worked under white supervision in charity matters or, as in all other aspects of their lives, had to create parallel black institutions.

One of the most publicized of these efforts was the establishment of the black YMCA in Washington. Washington had a strong tradition of black YMCA work. In the 1850s Anthony Bowen and a group of free blacks had organized the first black YMCA in the country. It survived only a few years, however, and was not actively revived until the late nineteenth century. Jesse E. Moorland, one of the first black secretaries of the international YMCA, expanded his interest in YMCA work in Washington while he was a student at Howard University. In 1892, the local chapter appointed Moorland secretary of the organization, a position he held until he graduated from Howard a year later. During his short affiliation with the District chapter, Moorland made important contacts with the national YMCA, particularly with William A. Hunton, who later recruited Moorland to become an international secretary.

YMCA work held special appeal for elite blacks. The emerging profession of association secretary provided a new career path for African Americans that carried high social status. Moorland also considered appearance, education, and personal conduct as important factors in recruiting international secretaries. He promoted nonconfrontation in dealing with racism, an ideology that appealed to an elite still dependent on white patronage. Conceiving of YMCA secretaries as diplomats between the races, he believed that "a man with the spirit of John Brown could not very well be an International Secretary."[21] The YMCA also provided a sheltered atmosphere in which men could gather without fear of discrimination and discuss business or professional strategies. The Y placed great emphasis on building character and leadership qualities in boys, so many members of the elite joined it to reaffirm their own status.

The campaign to build a YMCA building in Washington led to the cooperation of white philanthropists and black YMCA workers. Previously it was difficult for the local organizations to raise money for a building, and thus few had been built. In 1904 the Washington YMCA started a plan to raise a building fund of $20,000, but even after appealing to the white YMCA for assistance, the group was not able to raise enough money. Then John D. Rockefeller Jr. offered to match any donation of $25,000, and that promise sparked a massive fund-raising campaign among the entire black community.

By 1909, however, it was clear that many of those who had pledged money were unable to pay. Costs for the building itself increased, and the black YMCA asked Rockefeller for more money. Rockefeller was enraged by the request, and although he did not withdraw his money from the project, he never again contributed to any black YMCA. His offer of matching funds nonetheless inspired other white philanthropists to donate money for the creation of separate African American YMCAs. The black and white YMCAs in Washington continued to raise money for the building, designed by William S. Pittman, which was not completed until 1912. Theodore Roosevelt attended the opening ceremonies and heaped praise on the efforts of the black community in creating a permanent home for its institution.[22] The building became a meeting place for local black businessmen and created a visible symbol of black independence, despite the necessity of white funds for its creation.

The most successful independent black effort was the creation of the Phyllis Wheatley YWCA. Whereas the black YMCA was largely the product of black businessmen who sought to protect black masculinity in an era of racial humiliation and to build character to create racial uplift on an individual level, the YWCA came from the traditional charitable efforts of the black women's club movement. Led by Emma F. G. Merritt, Marion P. Shadd, and Mary E. Cromwell, a group of women founded the Phyllis Wheatley YWCA in 1905. It preceded the creation of a white YWCA by several years, and as the oldest YWCA in the city, the Wheatley should have become the central branch in Washington. However, racial hostility made it impossible for a black group to take precedence over a white organization. As a result, the Phyllis Wheatley YWCA never affiliated with the central Y organization. Bettie Cox Francis was the first president and served in that capacity for ten years.[23]

The Wheatley YWCA aimed to provide positive role models for young black women much as did the black YMCA for young men. It organized clubs to channel the girls' energies, such as the Girl Reserves, which emphasized health, knowledge, service, and spirit. The Girl Reserves produced plays and made gift boxes for the elderly and indigent. The Y offered Sunday services and incorporated the life of Jesus into daily activities. The Hostess Group, whose members included some of the more popular girls on the social scene, were charged with contacting the young men of the city and providing respectable, chaperoned entertainments. Although one observer noted that the girls could become rather petty in their competition for the attentions of these men, in general the group was favorably regarded and its social affairs were patronized by the elite.[24]

The women who operated the Wheatley YWCA were superb organizers and fund-raisers. The group occupied a series of temporary headquarters at first, one of them a floor in the Miner Institution building. By the end of its first year the Y claimed 193 members, and by its third year it occupied the entire building. In 1910 Emma Merritt negotiated the purchase of a house in Le Droit Park, near Howard University. In the next two years the women raised the $4,300 required to pay off the mortgage and expanded the Y's programs.[25]

The social services provided by the Wheatley YWCA were similar to those offered by the settlement houses. Since a frequent problem for the alley dwellers was a lack of good-quality clothing, the Y offered a sewing class. In addition, the women organized weekly entertainments and "at homes," to which they invited speakers on devotional work and literary matters. They also offered travelogues and musicales, at which the hot cocoa they served probably increased attendance. The women had their share of elitist views, but Mary Cromwell, among others, encouraged friendships with poor women in an effort to raise them up and act as a good influence on them.

The women who ran the Wheatley Y also served an important traditional function by greeting strangers to the city, particularly helping those who did not have much money or any social connections. They operated a Traveler's Aid service, meeting trains at Union Station to help southern migrants and other newcomers to the city. They also provided furnished and heated rooms for 50 cents a week, which gave the occupants access to the library and Christian hospitality, and offered the Hope and Help Dormitory for those who could not afford the weekly rate. The 1911 annual report noted: "Our women need help and it is our duty to help them. A race cannot rise above its women."[26]

Although men, too, became active in charity and reform work, it was clearly black elite women who were the driving force behind charitable organizations in the District. For the women of the Talented Tenth, charitable activities were considered an important part of elite status. As charity turned into reform of society's problems, black women began to connect reform and racial uplift. As they began to feel their own social status threatened, they realized that their fates were intimately linked with those of other black women and that "Lifting as We Climb" was more than simply a nice motto. Through the local and national networks they created the women were able to organize effectively. Since the women had always embraced charity work as their special contribution to the race, they now saw racial uplift as a natural extension of that contribution and an intimate part of their own social identity.

While black elite women believed they had a special mission to uplift the race, black elite men were far from certain of their role in the black community. As professionals, they were denied the basic respect given to white men of their occupations. As men they were often denied a chance to support their families in a style commensurate with their social status, or even to ensure that their wives did not have to work for pay. Although they had attained a measure of social status in the black community, that status was precarious at best. What they needed was a sense of their proper place in society and a means of gaining the respect they deserved for their accomplishments. They found these things in professional and fraternal organizations.

The primary motivation for forming black professional societies was a desire for recognition as legitimate professionals. Most national white professional organizations, such as the American Medical Association and the American Bar Association, excluded all but the most prestigious black doctors or lawyers. State professional organizations, particularly in the South, were even more exclusive. Yet at the turn of the century the professions were in flux. Snake-oil salesmen flourished, as did quack doctors and lawyers with bogus credentials. The legitimate professionals fought back with licensing requirements and accreditation of schools, and in keeping with the organizational tendencies of the era, they also formed groups that accepted only approved members of their professions. Membership was a stamp of approval that gave clients confidence in the abilities of the professional.

Black professionals, denied access to these organizations because of their race, were handicapped in their efforts to attract clients. In addition, the already negative opinion that many whites held of their abilities was simply confirmed by these restrictions. Their defense was to create organizations of their own that would grant similar recognition to worthy professionals of their race.

Although some black Washington lawyers were accepted as members of the ABA or other state or local organizations in the 1880s, as discrimination increased in society at large, it also increased within the professions. After the 1890s professional legal organizations found various reasons not to accept black candidates for admission, although they would admit them to the District bar. White professionals in general believed at best that black professionals did not have adequate training to be admitted to professional fraternities; at worst they believed that blacks were intellectually inferior and incapable of learning a profession. Even those whites who supported black professionals did not necessarily want to belong to a biracial organization. In an era when professionals were trying to weed out persons unqualified for professional titles and protect themselves against charlatans, it was easy for prejudiced white professionals to justify excluding blacks from their organizations.

Black lawyers responded to the situation by creating a black bar association in 1899. The chief organizers were Emmanuel M. Hewlett, Thomas L. Jones, Perri W. Frisby, Jerome A. Johnson, and W. Calvin Chase. That they formed a separate black organization shows that these attorneys no longer expected acceptance in the white professional organizations. They were therefore doing the next best thing, creating a professional fraternity that could monitor its members, ensure a certain level of competence, help regulate fees, and promote the exchange of professional experience and research. Unfortunately, the group's limited financial resources and small membership made success unlikely. Many black lawyers were not ready to believe that they could not gain acceptance from the white community and felt that membership in a black organization represented capitulation to segregation. In addition, such affiliation might antagonize the white societies, since they did not recognize the legitimacy of the black organizations.[27]

Probably the best-organized professionals were those in the field of medicine. The great need for standardization of the profession led to the formation of the American Medical Association and a series of state and local professional organizations. The AMA accepted as members any doctors who were members of their state or local medical society, but did not allow independent members. Since few local organizations admitted blacks, few blacks were members of the AMA. Even by 1934 there were fewer than 150 African American physicians in the AMA, and fifty of those resided in New York.[28]

The Medical Society of the District of Columbia, one of the oldest in the country, was founded in 1819 and incorporated under an act of Congress in 1838. A shadow organization, the Medical Association of the District of Columbia, encompassed the same membership but claimed to be a strictly social organization. During the entire history of the Medical Society only five blacks applied for membership. Although arguably those five were the most qualified men of their race, none gained admission. In 1869 and again in 1870 Charles B. Purvis, Alexander T. Augusta, and A. W. Tucker were proposed for membership, declared eligible, but not elected. Furman J. Shadd was similarly rejected in 1891, as was John R. Francis in 1894. Lack of membership in the Medical Society was a handicap to the careers of black physicians in the District. Nonmembers could not consult with member doctors, whatever their area of expertise. Charles B. Purvis recalled a severely ill patient whose family had called for Purvis, but in their concern they had also called in two white doctors. Purvis was not included in the consultation, despite the fact that the patient was his, and ultimately the white doctors took his patient away from him.[29] Similar incidents caused great resentment between the white and black physicians of the city.

The black doctors' struggle to gain acceptance in the Medical Society led to a debate before the American Medical Association's annual meeting in 1870 and the creation of the National Medical Association, which represented itself as a biracial organization. The predominantly white AMA capitulated to pressure from the District Medical Society and refused recognition of the National Medical Association. This was a setback in the formation of independent black medical organizations.

When Shadd and Francis were rejected by the Medical Society, they appealed to Congress to void its charter on the grounds that such discrimination was unconstitutional. The white physicians maintained that it was the unincorporated Medical Association that had adopted discriminatory rules, and therefore the Medical Society was not to blame. Congress censured the practices but could do little else.[30]

Since neither society nor the government seemed willing or able to address the issue of racial discrimination in professional organizations, black physicians in the District decided to take matters into their own hands. The biracial Medico-Chirurgical Society had ceased meeting in the 1880s because of a persistent belief that separate organizations for blacks were unnecessary and detrimental to the goal of assimilation. After the congressional investigation of Francis's rejection brought no results, however, interest in a new organization revived. In 1895, under the leadership of the white physicians Samuel Rogers Watts and Robert Reyburn and the black physicians Arthur W. Tancil, Daniel H. Williams, Thomas B. Hood, and James R. Wilder, the Medico-Chirurgical Society gained a new lease on life. By 1920 the membership had become all black, as the original white members died and no new white members replaced them. The society aimed "to provide opportunities for mutual conferences, the interchange of thought, the presentation of the results of experience, and the consideration and promotion of all subjects relating to medicine and the collateral branches of that science," as well as to promote health and the general welfare of the profession. Nevertheless, William Montague Cobb, professor of anatomy at Howard University and a member of the society, still wrote that its founding "was a loser's best alternative after prolonged and angry strife."[31]

Although the group suffered a few lean years, by 1920 it was a strong organization, and most of the District's prominent black physicians (and some dentists and pharmacists) belonged to it. The society sponsored reading groups to encourage the dissemination of new research, and provided the doctors with a sense of acceptance and fraternity within their profession. Nonetheless, it was difficult for the Medico-Chirurgical Society, in straitened circumstances, to accomplish much more than provide a professional atmosphere twice a month. Ultimately the group depended more on individual drive than on any institutional structure.

Other professionals in the medical field gained inspiration from the Medico-Chirurgical Society. In July 1913 a group of twenty-seven black dentists from Washington, Maryland, and Virginia formed the Tri-State Dental Association. They attempted to make it a national organization by incorporating representatives from other states each year. In 1915, North Carolina dentists joined the coalition, and an article in *Crisis* extolled the efforts of the organization to turn national: "None but ethical practitioners are admitted and must be members of a state or local society." Such a requirement promoted the formation of local black dental societies, further encouraging racial solidarity. In 1919 the Colored Druggist's Association organized an aggressive marketing campaign, guaranteeing good service and products at member pharmacies. In 1922 the local dental association, the Colored Druggists' Association, and the Medico-Chirurgical Society hosted the twenty-seventh annual meeting of the National Medical Association, an organization that itself flourished as a separate black organization.[32]

Although black professional organizations generally could accomplish little in the way of reform of their professions, they did provide a measure of respectability that helped their members maintain their practices. More important, they gave the professionals a chance to share information with other doctors, dentists, or lawyers and to learn from their experiences. Perhaps the most unexpected outcome of the formation of these societies, however, was that they committed the black elite professionals to racial solidarity and strengthened their involvement in issues of racial uplift. Forced to cry discrimination to protect their reputations, black professionals found themselves de facto spokespersons for the cause of civil rights. Of course they supported the cause to begin with, but their special circumstances made a stand against discrimination necessary if they wished to keep their practice and their social standing in the community. Since the white community would not accept even well-educated blacks as equals, the black elite was forced to reject assimilation as an option and look for social status within the black community.

Joining fraternal organizations was one way in which members of the black elite sought to enhance their status. Although most fraternal orders were segregated, they provided a sense of belonging that shielded the elite from some of the harsher aspects of society. In addition, since many fraternal orders attracted men who were considered "respectable" but not elite, members of the black elite generally found respect within the orders. Respect translated into positions of leadership, which gave these men valuable practical experience. Leadership also brought them closer to the rest of the black community and thus increased their sense of responsibility while it fostered the nonprofessionals' willingness to patronize black professionals and businesses.

The most important reasons for joining a fraternal organization were practical. Disfranchised and handicapped by Jim Crow practices, black leaders had few opportunities to gain administrative and business experience. Most members of the District black elite who joined secret organizations assumed leadership positions and learned the ins and outs of group politics while reinforcing their social status. Any black businessman or professional who joined a fraternal organization made important social contacts that enhanced his social status while building confidence in his abilities. This confidence was as important in maintaining a clientele as any seal of approval from a professional organization. For the black elite, membership in a fraternal organization was simply good business.

The black fraternal orders had been home to a number of leading black politicians during Reconstruction, and membership in them, particularly the Prince Hall Lodge of the Masons, seems to have been another indicator of elite status in the nineteenth century. Certainly the Masons were highly exclusive. As the numbers of black leaders of the Reconstruction era dwindled, however, a change appears to have taken place within the black Masonic order. This change coincided with the widening of the order's membership base to include blacks of slightly lower social status. By the end of the nineteenth century, when membership was becoming less exclusive, the Prince Hall Masons gave in to popular pressure and began adopting insurance features common to working-class fraternal orders.

Most prominent families had one or two representatives in the order—George W. Simms, James A. Wormley, and George W. Cook were members—but few seem to have accorded the Masons high priority by the 1890s. In 1899 James A. Wormley was actually dropped from the roll of the Prince Hall Lodge for nonpayment of dues. Of the ten or more lodges in the District of Columbia, only two, the Pythagoras Lodge, No. 9, and the Prince Hall Lodge, No. 14, had many elite and professional blacks on their rolls. During most of the 1890s, few elite blacks seem to have held membership in the order in the District.[33] This period also coincided with the deaths of many of the old leaders of the race, such as Alexander Crummell, Blanche K. Bruce, John Mercer Langston, and Frederick Douglass. Perhaps the Masons lost much of their direction with the loss of their leaders and did not appeal to the new generation of professional elite blacks. Many of this generation saw the Masons as a hypocritical group that forced segregation on its black members while preaching universal equality.

Some of the most blatant cases of discrimination against black Masons occurred at the end of the nineteenth century. The 1899 proceedings of the Grand Lodge of Illinois reported that blacks were too degraded to be Masons. "They are ignorant, uneducated, immoral, untruthful, and intellectually they are more impotent than minority or dotage—both of which we exclude. It would be rare if any locality could furnish the requisite number of sufficient capacity to open a lodge." The Grand Lodge concluded that all-black lodges were a de facto threat to the Masonic character and integrated lodges would be an impossibility.[34]

White Masons faced a moral paradox. The central tenet of Freemasonry was the equality of man, yet few were willing to accept African Americans as equals. At the turn of the century, many white Masons were also members of the Ku Klux Klan. The Masonic fraternity had to officially disparage racial discrimination or appear hypocritical, but most white Masons were so opposed to the idea of black Masons that they went to court to deny the Prince Hall Masons the right to the name. In order to avoid public racist arguments, the Masons argued that the Prince Hall Lodge had been granted a charter by a heretical lodge in England that pursued an ancient rite no longer accepted by the rest of the Masonic fraternity. The white Masons pursued any legal challenge they could find, but their time-consuming tactics did little but widen the gap between black and white lodges.[35]

In the late 1890s a splinter group of black Masons appeared. They followed the Cerneau Rite, which allowed individual lodges to confer the higher degrees of masonry, thus superseding the powers of the grand lodges. The practitioners of this "spurious and fungus Masonry" were expelled or suspended from the main order but established their own lodges and grand lodge.[36] The dispute led to a series of lawsuits over jurisdiction and legitimacy.

Around 1900, black professionals and other members of the black elite in Washington again began joining the Masons. One reason was the benefits that Freemasonry had provided, despite segregation: a sense of belonging, ties to the national elite, and social status. Charles Sumner Wormley, George W. Cabaniss, Edward E. Cooper, and William A. Joiner entered the Pythagoras Lodge in 1899. By 1915, Henry C. Scurlock, William A. Warfield, John E. Syphax, James T. Wormley, Walter Dyson, William T. S. Jackson, Jesse E. Moorland, and Roscoe Conkling Bruce had all joined the fraternity. Professionals such as Robert H. Terrell, Emmanuel M. Hewlett, William Montague Cobb, Arthur W. Tancil, and W. Calvin Chase also joined the Masons at the turn of the century, many assuming leadership positions.

Robert H. Terrell had a distinguished Masonic career. He joined the

Prince Hall Lodge in September 1895, became the senior warden in 1896, was elected master of his lodge the same year, was named right worshipful deputy grand master the next year, and became grand master of the District in 1898. He served as grand master for many years and remained active in the order for the rest of his life. In 1917 he served as chairman of the Jurisprudence Committee of the District Grand Lodge. At his death he had acquired a long list of honors, titles, and degrees, all testifying to his active involvement in the Masons.[37]

It appears that in the early twentieth century the Masonic lodges had become social clubs where black elite men could go to discuss the issues of the day with like-minded men. Most of the professionals tended to join Prince Hall Lodge, No. 14, while those who had ties to Tuskegee and the older generation of leaders became members of the Pythagoras Lodge, No. 9. For this measure of social comfort they were willing to accept segregated organizations, and may in fact, have welcomed them.[38] In addition, the rising professional class had realized the practical benefits of membership in a fraternal order. With diminishing opportunities to gain administrative or legal experience in the larger society, holding an office in a fraternal organization provided one of the few chances to gain leadership experience. In addition, the frequent legal actions by both black and white rival lodges gave attorneys such as Robert H. Terrell a chance to work with complex business law and increase their professional abilities and standing in the community.

The Masons were not the only fraternal order to experience discrimination or offer such practical benefits as a result. When the first black Elks lodge was established in Cincinnati in 1898, the group expected protest from the white Elks. Anticipating a lawsuit, the leader of the black Elks had the name of the order copyrighted after learning that the white Elks had failed to do so.[39] Legal difficulties were often a way of life for the black secret societies, and having a lawyer as a member enabled an order to function effectively while giving that member valuable training.

The Odd Fellows provided many opportunities for members to gain business or legal experience. A description of the duties of officers reveals the complexities of the organization. The noble grand presided over the lodge, enforced the laws, decided points of order, appointed tellers to inspect ballots, named ad hoc committees, and in general learned the ins and outs of running an organization. He was assisted by the vice grand, who was particularly charged with maintaining order and decorum. The permanent secretary and his assistants kept the seal of the lodge, collected dues, kept the membership rolls up to date, and served as overall accountants. For anyone desiring business experience, the permanent secretaryship was undoubtedly a prime position, attested to by the longevity in office of many incumbents.

The treasurer had to be a man of means, as he was required to present a $500 bond upon assuming office. He acted as bursar and collected and distributed group funds. He was aided by the Banking Committee, which deposited all monies over $30 in the bank. Other standing committees included the Committee of Correspondence, the quarterly Audit Committee, and the Finance Committee, all of which provided training in various areas of business expertise.[40]

Charles H. Brooks, a clerk in the Pension Bureau of the Department of the Interior, revealed the demand for educated blacks in fraternal orders in the nineteenth century with the story of his early experiences with the Odd Fellows in Paducah, Kentucky. He joined the order in 1882, at the age of twenty-two, and was immediately called upon to serve as the lodge's permanent secretary. "This lodge was composed almost entirely of unlettered men—but men of age and experience, who were devoted to the principles of the Order. The Lodge at that time was very much in need of young men capable of filling the important positions."[41]

Because of his social status, Brooks was also elected a delegate to the Kentucky Grand Lodge convention as well as to the Biennial Moveable Committee, the national convention of Odd Fellows. Brooks held his position as permanent secretary until 1889, when he moved to the District. In Washington he remained active in the organization and served as grand director of the Fifth Biennial Moveable Committee and grand secretary of the Subcommittee of Management.[42]

Prominent Odd Fellows such as Brooks had the potential to gain widespread recognition in their community. A group of young men organized the first Washington Odd Fellows chapter in 1855 and named it in honor of John F. Cook Sr., a prominent Odd Fellow. The first chair of the group was John A. Simms Sr. Simms went on to open several other lodges in the District, and served as delegate to the national conventions. He was also the first district noble grand.[43]

Thomas H. Wright, a free black from Washington, worked in the Justice Department for forty-five years and was appointed to the Board of Trustees of the District schools to take the place of his father, James H. Wright, who was going blind. Thomas Wright gained a reputation as a loyal Odd Fellow. In 1889 he suggested that the Odd Fellows build a new home for their society and led a great fund-raising campaign. In 1892 the Odd Fellows Association Hall was completed, to much acclaim.[44]

The benefits of membership in fraternal organizations were both tangible and intangible. Although the nature of these orders changed over time, the elite generally found it in their interest to join. Most of the lodges served as sheltered places in which race leaders could meet to discuss common concerns. This was the factor that most appealed to the black elite in the nineteenth century. As racial discrimination increased in the 1890s, the organizations seemed to lose their attractiveness. When the white organizations denied the legitimacy of their black counterparts, black elites became disillusioned with the secret societies. In the twentieth century, however, the practical aspects of the orders reasserted themselves, and a growing class of professionals sought to increase their ties with the community to enlarge their practices. In addition, the paucity of opportunities for practical business, professional, and leadership experience made the litigious secret orders with their fund-raising capabilities very attractive. By the late 1910s, the lodges had once again become places where both local and national African American leaders met to discuss the issues of the day in a congenial and informal atmosphere. For the black elite, membership in a secret society did far more than reaffirm social status.

The organizational impetus among the black elite at the turn of the century evolved in parallel with that in the white community, but it was driven by different motives. Membership in some charitable, professional, and fraternal organizations bestowed social status in itself, but there were other important reasons for the elite to join these organizations. Charitable and reform activities, which elite black women originally viewed as a matter of noblesse oblige, ultimately became linked to racial uplift. Since white charities often excluded black charity workers and biracial organizations relegated them to inferior positions, elite black women had to turn to independent efforts to maintain their social welfare activities. Working for racial uplift transformed these women. Always convinced that they were uniquely qualified to help right social wrongs, they saw themselves as in the vanguard of race leadership when righting social wrongs became fighting to elevate the race. Noblesse oblige was transformed into self-identity.

The exclusion of black professionals from white-dominated professional organizations pushed them, too, to create independent organizations. In order to establish their qualifications to practice in their fields, black professionals needed to establish associations that would grant a seal of approval to their work. They also benefited from the opportunities for interaction with other professionals that such organizations provided. Although at first black professionals preferred to associate with the white professional groups when they could, when the whites systematically excluded them, they became more aware of the realities of racial discrimination. Many opposed the idea of segregated societies, seeing them as implicit admission that the races were somehow unequal. By the twentieth century, however, most black professionals recognized the value of independent organizations. In the process of protesting their personal exclusion from white organizations, professionals often found themselves leading the fight against racist practices. As a result, many of the younger professionals began consciously to equip themselves to lead the fight for civil rights.

Fraternal organizations offered elite blacks exclusivity, leadership responsibility, and the chance to increase their business or professional clientele and experience. The black elite lost interest in fraternal activity in the late nineteenth century, as increased racism underscored the hypocrisy of segregated orders such as the Masons. By the turn of the century, however, black professionals had once again discovered the practical benefits of membership in fraternal organizations, and they welcomed the chance to discuss race issues with like-minded men in a secluded environment.

Organizations of all three types brought the black elite closer to the rest of the black community. Businessmen and professionals were forced to cultivate connections with other African Americans in order to maintain a viable livelihood. In fraternal organizations they could make these connections while gaining professional and leadership experience. Black professionals in particular found themselves closely involved with civil rights issues for the community when they contested their exclusion from white organizations. Black charitable and reform organizations, while embracing middle-class morality, also involved an element of racial uplift that brought charity workers into greater sympathy with the poorer members of their race. The precariousness of the black elite's economic status made the Four Hundred acutely aware of the plight of the masses. Their exclusion from white charitable organizations only made them realize that their fate was linked to that of their race, and that racial uplift would also benefit their own status.

Organizational affiliation both affirmed the status of the black elite and encouraged the development of independent institutions. In building these parallel organizations, the black elite found themselves drawn toward racial solidarity. The development of black organizations furthered the transformation of the black elite from a nineteenth-century aristocracy into a twentieth-century leadership class.

NINE

Race and Racial Uplift

Between 1880 and 1920 the black elite underwent a transformation. Continually disillusioned by increasing segregation, they attempted to find new methods of reinforcing their social status. With a proud heritage of race leadership both before the Civil War and during Reconstruction, the members of the black elite fully realized their responsibilities to their race. Increased educational opportunities after Emancipation created a leadership class stronger than that of any previous era, one better equipped to create a social and economic base from which the race could advance. Ironically, or perhaps as a result of this strengthening process, the late nineteenth century was a period of heightened racism in which economic and social opportunities available to educated blacks were increasingly restricted.

In *The Secret City*, a history of race relations in Washington, Constance McLaughlin Green characterized the turn of the century as a period in which black leadership degenerated into backbiting and petty squabbles as each member of the black elite sought his own advantage. Although conflicts were certainly plentiful, it is undeniable that the black elite contributed greatly to the cause of racial uplift despite them. The disputes resulted from heavy pressures placed on the elite. Limited in resources and offered only sops from the white community while trying to hold on to their social status, members of the elite often found themselves fighting for positions and influence.

Nonetheless, the Four Hundred had intense race pride and fostered the growth of this pride, even if only to counter their rejection by white society as individuals. They criticized those who tried to become more white, either cosmetically or by "passing" into white society. For the most part they were critical of intermarriage and sometimes even of integrated schools, although they fought official proscriptions of social intermingling and were sensitive to any violation of their civil rights. For many the "drop of African blood" that determined their racial designation in American society was the defining aspect of their identity.

It is true that in the 1880s, while most elite blacks believed that they were race leaders, few black aristocratic families associated regularly with the rest of the race. Most preferred to separate themselves from the working classes in an effort to pursue assimilation into the majority culture. For these people, elite status depended on emphasizing differences between the working classes and themselves. Without that differentiation, elite blacks would simply be lumped into the same group as those they considered the undesirable members of their race. In their efforts to perpetuate their social status, members of the black elite sought to better their own condition and gain acceptance in the white world. These attitudes developed from a decade of Reconstruction, when blacks and whites cooperated toward common goals and American society seemed destined to evolve to a state of racial equality once the South recognized the error of its ways.

In the nineteenth century, when "white" features were highly prized, blacks turned to cosmetic products to straighten their hair and lighten their skin. By the turn of the century most African Americans had realized that skin bleaches and hair straighteners were only temporary expedients, since, as the *Colored American* noted in 1898, "Negroes as white as the Executive Mansion, or as black as the subcellar of the Capitol, are lumped together and discriminated against alike."[1] Elite blacks showed evidence of pride in their skin color. John E. Bruce wrote to a Nigerian Baptist minister that "I am Black all over, and am as proud of my black skin, and that of my forebears, as the blackest man in Africa."[2] Paul Laurence Dunbar's 1906 obituary in the *New York Age* noted that Dunbar's success was proof that dark skin was not a sign of ignorance, and that Phillis Wheatley, Alexander Crummell, and many others had proved that intellect did not correlate with skin color.[3]

Washington's black elite expressed their pride in personal and public correspondence. In 1895, while completing a legal transaction with William A. Joiner, Robert H. Terrell warned: "We don't need any court guardian to probate [the] will. Won't have that white man. Must have someone in family. . . . Don't let Mr. Anglo Saxon get his finger in anywhere."[4] Terrell's wife, twenty years later, wrote to Lansburgh & Brothers to protest the use of "Nigger Brown" as a description of a color in an advertisement. The owner apologized, since he catered to blacks, but claimed that it was too late to make a change. Thomas J. Calloway complained to Booker T. Washington that Richard T. Greener's wife, who was fair-skinned, associated only with whites in New York.[5]

Having light features could in fact be a disadvantage in the black community. When Ida Gibbs Hunt described her sister-in-law to her own sister, she seemed to disparage the characteristics that made her sister-in-law seem less African: "She is just about my complexion with dark hair, worn a la pompadour, and, alas! grey eyes. She has grown up with white people and shows it in her talk and manner."[6] Josephine Bruce was a candidate for president of the NACW in 1906, but her fair skin disqualified her in the eyes of the delegates, because the organization wanted to show that Africans were capable of leadership.[7]

Nevertheless, the black elite, most of whom were light-skinned themselves, generally treated the darker-skinned masses with condescension. Angelina Weld Grimké wrote in her diary that "as fair as I am I find I am very sensitive [to any mention of color]. How much harder it must be to be black. God pity them! They [not] only have the white people's prejudice to contend with [but] the light people's too. Light people are very [small?]. What difference does color make anyway it is only skin-deep."[8]

Even the black press sometimes ran material of questionable taste for a black audience, such as a grotesque cartoon showing a black man with simian features asking a white man at an upstairs window for some watermelon. The "Sam" got the watermelon when the white man dropped it on him. This cartoon, which appeared in several issues of the *Colored American* as part of its boilerplate material, was followed by a story in dialect about dumb "niggers" fooling each other and generally behaving like buffoons.[9] Such public humor at the expense of working-class blacks reveals the elite blacks' low opinion of their poorer brothers and hardly paints a flattering image of the black elite.

Elite blacks distinctly disapproved of those who tried to enter white society through marriage or pretense. Nonetheless, while many elite blacks publicly opposed intermarriage as distasteful and somehow insulting to black pride, others saw it as a solution to racial discrimination. The *Colored American* editorialized: "Let the races intermarry without restraint and the race problem will soon be settled. Amalgamation is our only salvation."[10] Most blacks, however, realized that public pronouncements of this sort put fear in the hearts of white men and women and only reinforced the stereotype of blacks as somehow more lascivious than whites. Thus, while most elite blacks opposed laws against "miscegenation," publicly they were careful to assert that they themselves did not think intermarriage was a good idea for either race.

Many members of the black elite were themselves products of interracial couplings, generally under conditions of slavery, when the coupling was not a matter of choice. As a result, the children of these unions had additional reasons for hostility toward whites. In 1932, when Anna J. Cooper was in her sixties, she still resented her father. When she responded to a survey of black college graduates, she wrote: "I owe nothing to my white father beyond the initial act of procreation. My mother's self sacrificing toil to give me advantages she had never enjoyed is worthy the highest praise and undying gratitude."[11]

Racial issues were increasingly complex at the turn of the century, but none more so than the issue of "passing." In 1895, Francis J. Grimké sermonized on the subject, characterizing the practice as a sin one must resist. He noted that it was insincere to "sail under false colors, to masquerade," even though there were many good reasons for doing so. Grimké advised his congregation not to give in to temptation but to try to be accepted for what they truly were.[12] Ray Stannard Baker also spoke of "the temptations that beset fair colored people to pass for white and the number who have yielded to it" in "Tragedy of the Mulatto," which Mary Church Terrell read with interest in *American Magazine*.[13]

For those who knew someone who had passed for white the issue was often more complex. Norma Boyd, a founder of Alpha Kappa Alpha, had an uncle who had passed. Her family told her that he had been "lost in the crowd," but Norma understood that "while this was a hurtful practice to those families involved, they understood and accepted it because it was brought about by economic necessity resulting from the racial prejudice of the times."[14] When Mary Church Terrell was in London in 1919, she ran into an old acquaintance who had passed, and he refused to acknowledge her until she forced him to do so. Terrell absolved him of all blame for this embarrassment: "Jack Durham is very much better off today as a white man than he could ever have been as negro! It would be a crime for him to bring his son up as a negro with all the damnable prejudice he would have to face!"[15]

Elite blacks were not averse to passing temporarily when it was convenient to do so. William Hunt, upon his return to New York City from his consulate in Madagascar, needed a temporary place to stay while he looked for permanent lodgings. He chose a hotel that did not accept blacks, more because of its convenience and comfort than anything else. He explained to his wife how he was managing: "As *I speak only French* I came here to the Brevoort [Hotel Lafayette-Brevoort] to pass a day or two."[16] Since white America was often more courteous to foreign visitors than to African Americans, Hunt avoided discrimination by pretending he was foreign. At a train station a black maid mistook Mary Church Terrell for white and helped her onto the train with her bags. Terrell noted that the maid certainly would not have carried her luggage had she known Terrell's race, but it amused her to play along with the charade, which enabled her to sit in the white waiting room and gain a seat in a whites-only car. On several occasions the ticket seller had been unable to determine her race and had punched her ticket for both black and white seating on the train.[17] Robert H. Terrell was also conscious of the advantages of having light skin. When their daughter Phyllis married a light-skinned man, he told his wife: "Phyllis should now appreciate what it means to have a husband who looks like Billie. She can go and travel anywhere."[18]

Ultimately, it was essential to the elite's sense of self-worth that race not be a matter of shame. When discrimination was at its harshest, racial pride was a citadel in which the race's leaders could defend themselves. Although the black elite did not always wish to associate with the black masses, they were quick to defend the race as a whole when it was under attack. Racial pride was an important motivating factor for the black elite throughout the Progressive Era.

As black leaders repeatedly met defeat in their attempts to assimilate peacefully, their frustrations were transformed into anger with the system that excluded them. Through their fight over the public schools, elite blacks learned the importance of an independent power base in efforts to resist discrimination. During the 1890s, however, black leadership was still dependent on white patronage. Realizing that the strident rhetoric adopted during Reconstruction would now only bring retribution, the black elite adopted the tactic of nonconfrontation. Nonconfrontation did not mean giving up the struggle for equality, it just meant keeping that struggle at a level that would not bring repercussions against the black community.

Between 1890 and 1910, the elite focused on strengthening black pride and building up the YMCA, the black school system, and other institutions that would provide an independent basis for survival and bring the black community together on the path to common goals. As they worked to attain those goals, however, elite African Americans were careful not to challenge any established hierarchies, except in extreme cases of discrimination, and they used methods that would not bring undue negative publicity to their efforts. They followed social guidelines until they had the power to make overt moves effective and until the leadership could no longer withstand the frustration and humiliation that accompanied a segregated society.

As early as 1879 blacks had sensed a change in white tolerance of black outrage. P. B. S. Pinchback worried that a speech he had recently given was too bold for a black man. "Such utterances on our part," he wrote Blanche K. Bruce, "are generally considered impudent and impertinent."[19] The *Leader* editorialized that going to the courts to gain admittance to segregated facilities was perhaps not the best solution: "It seems to us that when our people attempt to force these accommodations, they take an undignified action. They attempt to enter where they are not desired. . . . While colored people desire such conveniences and feel it unpleasant to be excluded from them, the only hope of complete emancipation in this as in other directions is a favorable public opinion."[20]

Keeping one's hostility private was particularly difficult for elite blacks who had succeeded economically but were still denied equality. James A. Wormley was overheard angrily protesting the condition of race relations at a private dinner for Edward Blyden, the former president of Liberia College and Liberian minister to the Court of St. James's. But by the turn of the century, most elite blacks had come to accept the new climate under Jim Crow and realized that, in the words of a *Colored American* editorial, "if absorption into the white race is to be the destiny of the American Negro, agitation will not help the idea along, nor will it increase the comfort of the Negroes of the present generation."[21]

In 1902 Charles S. Hunt, of the *Boston Transcript,* made it very clear to Angelina Weld Grimké that confrontation was not acceptable to the American public. When he refused to publish a poem she had submitted because it implied the threat of a black uprising, he was simply echoing the opinion of a majority of people in the white community: "God knows the negro has suffered enough in the past to warrant a good deal. But the worst of his evil days are over and he is now beginning his peaceful fight for political and social equality which as sure as the world stands, will sometime be successful."[22] Most whites preferred to believe, as Hunt did, that African Americans had overcome the worst of their problems and now had only to be patient.

It was this atmosphere that had caused Andrew F. Hilyer to declare, "There are some phases of this race question which it is not well to discuss in public, in our Lyceums, and in the press. They are strictly family matters and should be discussed and settled among ourselves when no unfriendly ears are listening."[23] In 1906 the *New York Age* praised the late Paul Laurence Dunbar by saying that although Dunbar was keenly aware of racial discrimination, one of his better qualities was that he was not an agitator. "Thus unheralded and unperceived his works have found their way into most of the circulating libraries in the country.... And therefore, in his own way our author was all along furthering a better understanding between the races."[24] Members of the black elite had faith that if they worked quietly behind the scenes to contradict negative images of African Americans, they could bring whites to accept them as equals without open conflict.

This nonconfrontational strategy prevailed even into the 1920s, although by the second decade of the twentieth century more blacks were advocating open protest. Despite an increase in open protest, the black elite still praised those who accomplished racial uplift without making waves. A 1922 description of the magazine *Opportunity* was designed to appeal to this sensitivity: "It is not a magazine of protest, of satire, the organ of a clique of 'sore heads.' There is nothing hysterical about it.... It believes that the problems of the Negro have grown out of misunderstanding on the part of those who would seek to hamper and oppress him. By its rigidly consistent presentation of the facts of the Negro and of Negro life it endeavors to correct this attitude."[25] By emphasizing the pacifist tone of the journal, the authors of the pamphlet hoped to appeal to those members of the black elite who favored nonconfrontation, and probably to reassure the white community that they did not challenge its authority.

One of the best ways to strengthen the black community without challenging the social order was to counteract negative stereotypes. Studying black history was an important part of this effort. Dr. C. V. Roman, a Nashville accommodationist, thought that studying the history of African Americans would "furnish an atmosphere of mutual cooperation and helpfulness that will change the winter of our discontent into the glorious summer of racial solidarity."[26] Even radicals such as W. E. B. Du Bois devoted their lives to creating and collecting works of black history and presenting them in a scientific manner to disprove white stereotypes of African Americans.

By studying their past, African Americans were able to reach beyond the heritage of slavery to cite examples of greater civilizations in the African past, and perhaps prove that civilization arose in Africa while Europeans were still living in the Stone Age. In addition, they could discover examples of black men and women who had succeeded despite the odds against them and who could provide inspiration for others. Armed with these examples, African Americans hoped to combat the rising tide of racism at the turn of the century while encouraging racial pride.[27]

Many non–Anglo Saxon groups responded to intolerance by forming historical and literary societies. It seemed to ethnic and minority groups that historians not only generally ignored their past but distorted it when they did mention it.

African Americans had early seen that knowledge was a powerful weapon and since 1828 had established a series of literary societies to collect and preserve books by and about blacks. The movement to study black history did not become widespread until after the Civil War, however. Participants in the National Equal Rights Convention in December 1873 passed a resolution to start a historical society for persons "who desire to know the true history of what our lifelong opponents have conceded to be the most remarkable race."[28]

In Washington, the Bethel Literary and Historical Association took the lead in promoting the study of black history. Its members took the information they had learned at the meetings and brought it to a larger audience. In December 1902, Professor Edward A. Johnson gave a paper on the importance of teaching black history in the public schools. He noted that "many of the histories now taught in our public schools . . . [are] simply referring to us as slaves; not even remarking that we made *good* slaves."[29] John W. Cromwell Sr., an officer of the Bethel Literary and its historian in the 1890s, completed a manuscript titled "The Negro in American History," designed as a textbook to supplement school history texts. Cromwell corresponded frequently with a fellow bibliophile, Arthur Schomburg of New York, in search of pictures of prominent African Americans to place in black schools.[30]

Charles H. Shorter, for forty-eight years an employee of the Pension Office, collected many clippings and books on African American history. He was a staunch member of the elite community, serving at various times as superintendent of the Union Bethel AME Sunday school and teaching at the Sunday school of St. Luke's Protestant Episcopal Church. A member of the Odd Fellows and the Grand Army of the Republic, Shorter had attended the John F. Cook School for free blacks as a child. His study of the past made him uncompromising on issues of race and led him to a radical stand on race relations, although he was not widely known in the white community.[31]

When members of the American Negro Academy formed the Negro Book Collectors Exchange, it was not surprising that three of its top officers were Washington residents. Carter G. Woodson, a frequent participant in Bethel Literary debates, founded the Association for the Study of Negro Life and History in 1915, and in his role as director of the organization found time to give talks on black history at colleges and high schools and helped collect materials to form the basis for courses in African American studies.[32]

Increased awareness of black history did indeed bring racial pride. Arthur Schomburg reported to Cromwell that at the Spingarn Medal award ceremony in 1915, a white woman had asked if African Americans were proud to have been brought from barbaric Africa under the mantle of Christianity. "We were pleased to hear groans and no's from people of refinement."[33] In a speech at Hampton Institute in 1921, Woodson commented, "It is not going to be long before we can so sing the story to the outside world as to convince it of the value of our history . . . and we are going to be recognized as men."[34] Woodson's pronouncement showed the value that the black leadership placed on knowing its true heritage, but it also showed the belief that with increased pride the race would be able to lift itself in the eyes of the white community.

The American Negro Academy was an unsuccessful attempt to extend the concept of racial uplift through nonconfrontational methods. In 1894 William H. Crogman and Alexander Crummell proposed the creation of an African Institute, comprising about fifty of the race's best scholars and "devoted to literary, statistical, ethnographical, folk-lore investigation, pertaining wholly and entirely to Africa and to the world wide Negro race. . . . Its work should be so real and thorough . . . that it would command the respect of the scholarly sentiment outside."[35] Essentially the organization would be a national extension of the Bethel Literary, with a more formal status, publishing capabilities, and the best black scholars in the country. The idea for the African Institute finally evolved in 1897 into the American Negro Academy, with Crummell as its first president. Since many of the academy's members lived in Washington, partly because Howard University was one of the few places where the nation's black scholars could find gainful employment, the organization's headquarters were established in the District, and it was members of Washington's Talented Tenth who ultimately ran the organization through its executive committee.

The academy never met its goal of fifty members. Many scholars declined to join or never participated actively after they were elected. Others participated enthusiastically at first, but lost interest and were dropped from the rolls. The academy never considered accepting women. The Washington contingent was probably the most active, including Kelly Miller, the Grimké brothers, John W. Cromwell, Lewis B. Moore, John A. Johnson, and many others affiliated with Howard University. But even the Washington contingent could not broaden the appeal of the organization.

After Crummell's death in 1898, Du Bois was elected president of the academy, but he was an inactive president and attended only two of the five annual meetings during his administration. When Du Bois resigned in 1903, the academy elected Archibald Grimké as its leader. Grimké revitalized the academy and made a conscious effort to promote publication of the annual addresses and other papers written by members. Although many complained that Grimké published more of his own papers under the academy's auspices than those of anyone else, in truth he was one of the few who wrote specifically for this purpose. Other members, such as Du Bois, James Robert Lincoln Diggs, and Richard Robert Wright Jr., found a wider audience and better remuneration in other publications.

As the twentieth century progressed, the greatest obstacle the American Negro Academy faced was its members' involvement in other organizations. They were so busy with the NAACP or the National Urban League that they had little time to devote to the academy. In addition, since the organization concentrated mainly on research rather than action, many of those who were eligible for membership shunned it as too conservative. This belief reflected the increased activism of the black elite in racial uplift efforts as well as the transformation of attitudes toward race issues. Grimké, who was affiliated with the NAACP, attempted to involve the academy in protest activities in 1917 in an effort to stimulate support for it. In December the academy sent a telegram to Woodrow Wilson asking for an end to Jim Crow railroad cars in the South.[36] Such efforts, however, were not enough to attract significant attention.

The academy struggled for support in its later years, without attracting any of the new generation of scholars for any length of time. Alain Locke alone maintained his affiliation with the academy. Woodson left the organization after a short membership, and in a sense duplicated its efforts with greater success when he founded the Association for the Study of Negro Life and History in 1915. By relying only on nonconfrontational efforts, the American Negro Academy limited its own life span. In the late nineteenth century such methods were the accepted way of improving the status of the race, but as the twentieth century progressed, those methods became outdated.

Another way to further the race without rocking the boat was through lectures designed to highlight the positive achievements of African Americans. Mary Church Terrell put to good use her skill at walking the path between outright confrontation and accommodation when she toured extensively as a lecturer between 1895 and 1910. Her entrance into a public career came after the lecturer Robert Nourse heard her speak at a meeting of the Congregational Association of Maryland. Upon his recommendation, the Slayton Lyceum Bureau offered her a contract sight unseen.

Terrell soon began a successful (if not well-paid) speaking career. Her papers show that she was constantly bombarded with requests for engagements and tried to fit as many as she could into her schedule. If she had to stop somewhere overnight when she was traveling, she often tried to find a group to address in the town. More often than not, however, people pressed her into service at a moment's notice. Once she was shanghaied at the Milwaukee train station to address a group of normal school students, with no opportunity to prepare her remarks.[37]

Terrell's stock speeches reveal her dedication to the spirit of uplift. In "The Bright Side of a Dark Subject," Terrell discussed the progress of the race and stressed the positive rather than dwelling on what still needed reform. In "The Progress of Colored Women," she recounted charitable works accomplished by black women, particularly through the NACW and church clubs. She also discussed the intellectual achievements of black women in the nation's colleges and the obstacles they were required to overcome. By nature a feminist, Terrell stressed the fact that black women had two burdens to bear, those of race and those of sex. In "Uncle Sam and the Sons of Ham," she described forthrightly the attitude of the government toward race relations and examined disfranchisement and the convict lease system. Above all, however, she took every opportunity to stress the progress the race had made during and after slavery.[38]

Even as she was attempting to publish an article on the need for antilynching legislation in the *Atlantic Monthly,* Terrell stressed the rosier aspects of racial progress in her lectures. She portrayed black women in roles similar to those of white women but used the rhetoric of proud achievement to make white audiences feel less threatened. She often commented on how she avoided any remarks that might arouse controversy or opprobrium.

During World War I, however, even Mrs. Terrell had a hard time finding speaking engagements. The lyceums with which she dealt had nothing to offer her, and most of her speeches she solicited herself through her formidable network of friends and acquaintances and with the help of the NAACP.[39] The distraction of the war could explain a lack of interest in other speakers, but it is likely that despite her efforts to appear conservative, many lyceums came to view her as too controversial to sponsor. Lecturing combines show business with politics, both notoriously fickle masters.

By the second decade of the twentieth century it was clear that many members of Washington's black elite wanted to take a more radical stand on civil rights. Many had allied with W. E. B. Du Bois in his criticism of Booker T. Washington's methods. Perceiving the realities of their situation, these leaders realized that gradual assimilation was not a possibility and that conservative rhetoric was actually damaging to the cause of equal rights.

The years from 1905 to 1915 were therefore marked by great turmoil between those who clung to the nineteenth-century ideal of assimilation and those who wanted to try new approaches to racial uplift. Unfortunately, circumstances again limited open protest, since the Tuskegee machine controlled white patronage in the black community and the elite was not yet strong enough to survive without it. Tuskegee still promoted gradual assimilation, and many of those who favored open protest still owed personal allegiance to Booker T. Washington.

The situation began to change in 1895, with Washington's famous "Atlanta Compromise" speech at the Cotton States Exhibition, in which he spoke in favor of economic growth without social or political integration. At first the reaction in the District was fairly mild. Francis Grimké congratulated Washington on the speech, and reported that the majority of discussants at the Bethel Literary and Historical Association had spoken favorably of it.[40]

W. Calvin Chase and the *Bee*, however, almost immediately attacked the speech, editorializing that it was as poisonous as Cleopatra's asp. The editor of the *Colored American*, Edward E. Cooper, rushed to assure Washington that although the "small fry of the colored press, as well as a few of the so called 'big guns,' are worrying a little about your speech [y]ou have a champion in the COLORED AMERICAN at all times."[41]

As the twentieth century opened, however, Chase was joined by other members of the District's black elite in questioning Washington's leadership both publicly and privately. Kelly Miller, who had always tried to maintain an independent stand, began to challenge the Tuskegee political agenda, although he still supported the idea of industrial education.[42] Washington responded to criticism by securing appointments for moderates such as Robert H. Terrell, in order to secure their loyalty. In 1903 Du Bois initiated his public attack on Washington, and other members of the elite found the strength to question Tuskegee.

Archibald H. Grimké considered Washington's silence on civil rights issues unconscionable. He asked Washington to clarify his position on black disfranchisement, since Washington had counseled acquiescence in the discriminatory laws going into effect in the South. Grimké was later joined in his efforts by District Attorney Louis G. Gregory, although Gregory's rhetoric was more conciliatory than Grimké's.[43] As Grimké maintained residences in both Boston and the District, he was influenced by the vocal opposition to Tuskegee among the Boston black radicals. He was determined that he, too, must speak out openly against injustice. Besides, since Grimké had obtained his former position as consul in Santo Domingo without any help from Tuskegee, he had acquired political influence of his own and was not so dependent on Washington for support.

Archibald and Angelina Grimké were present at the so-called Boston Riot in July 1903. Booker T. Washington had been invited to defend his views before a mass meeting in Boston, and supporters of both sides came prepared to do battle. The meeting degenerated into a disorderly melee, and two of Washington's opponents were arrested for disturbing the peace. Although Grimké was not directly involved in the fracas, Washington took the opportunity to brand him as dangerous to the race. In a press release issued under an alias, Washington blamed his opponents for causing the "riot," and he mentioned Grimké as one of the rabble-rousers. He saved most of his venom for those who had "in the most cowardly manner stood in the dark, urging them on, without showing their own hands."[44] Such criticism further alienated Grimké and made him more vocal in his opposition. In addition, the Boston Riot made many members of the elite aware of the number of people willing to oppose Tuskegee.

Opposition to Washington in the District grew in the next few years, and Washington had to spend more time trying to find appointments for his lieutenants than before. He recognized that the District, along with Boston and Chicago, was rapidly becoming a center of criticism that could cause him a great deal of harm.[45] What he needed was a way to stop the opposition before the president realized that he did not have the full support of the black community.

In late 1903 Washington began to organize what would become the Carnegie Hall Conference in an attempt to orchestrate an agreement between the factions. Of course he hoped to choose delegates who favored the Tuskegee philosophy. He courted Francis J. Grimké, who had not yet quarreled with Tuskegee, but told him that Archibald could not attend the conference because there were already too many delegates from Boston. This was Washington's first tactical error. Francis Grimké took offense at Washington's obvious manipulation of the invitations and implied that he might not attend the conference after all. Reluctantly Washington agreed to invite Archibald as an alternate to Francis. Since Du Bois had insisted that no officeholders be invited, Washington did not inform Robert H. Terrell, one of his chief supporters in the District, about the conference until after the fact. Though Terrell claimed to understand why he was not invited, it is likely that his exclusion bothered both him and his wife.[46]

The conference ultimately achieved little. Although a new organization, the Committee of Twelve for the Advancement of the Interests of the Negro Race, emerged from it, Du Bois and many others felt that Washington had dominated the proceedings, as usual, and had loaded the committee with Tuskegee supporters. When in 1904, soon after the conference, Washington publicly described blacks as a child race, the District's elite were quick to criticize.[47]

Archibald Grimké and Kelly Miller were among Washington's few critics to be appointed to the Committee of Twelve. Grimké held out for a few months, then resigned in July 1904 when the committee refused to issue a statement opposing southern disfranchisement of blacks; but at Washington's urging he rescinded his resignation.[48] Du Bois also resigned in August, but the committee continued to function actively for another year. For many years after its other activities ceased, the committee continued to publish pamphlets on the race issue. When Grimké and Miller tried (unsuccessfully) to steer the group in the right direction, Du Bois questioned their loyalty. "It was my unalterable decision from the first," he wrote them, "that unless the committee was so organized as to allow real work by indiv. membs. that I would not be a member of it," and he expressed disappointment in them for their failure to sever all connections with the group, as he had done.[49] In August 1905 Du Bois invited Miller and Grimké to become charter members of the Niagara Movement. Although neither accepted immediately, Grimké later became highly active in the NAACP.

By the end of 1904, when it had become clear that Grimké and other members of the District elite would not be appeased by any joint meetings, Booker T. Washington launched an all-out campaign against his opponents, speaking in the District whenever possible, using his influence for appointments in the public schools, and sending his lieutenants to put pressure on any recalcitrants. He also subsidized the District's black press to ensure maximum favorable coverage of Tuskegee events and create the illusion that most of the black community still supported him.

Edward E. Cooper, editor of the Washington *Colored American,* was the first journalist to receive Washington's largess. Having shown his loyalty to Tuskegee, he frequently appealed to Washington's friends for contributions to his paper. Washington told Charles W. Anderson, "While he has many weak points he has some strong points and one is that he always stands by his friends."[50] Cooper printed consistently pro-Washington editorials and articles, and for his loyalty the *Colored American* received regular subsidies from Tuskegee.

Tuskegee's support of the press did not go unnoticed. Du Bois charged on several occasions that Washington distributed hush money to manipulate the black newspapers. These charges, supported by some documentary evidence, contributed to the view of Booker T. Washington as a power-hungry tyrant who controlled public opinion by threats and bribes.[51] This image provoked some members of the District elite to defect. Francis Grimké regularly gave sermons criticizing Tuskegee and Washington. The District school board became a center of the debate, and hostilities became more open. John W. Cromwell gave Du Bois evidence of Tuskegee's subsidies to the press. Added to this public outrage was the growing frustration of the black elite with Washington's nonconfrontational policy. The rebellion against Tuskegee's domination spread.

Between 1904 and 1915 the turmoil in the District intensified. Washington stepped up his press subsidies, switching to support of the *Bee* in 1906 after the *Colored American* failed. Chase was a longtime opponent of Washington but he needed money to keep his paper afloat, and under the circumstances he sold to the highest bidder. He was an unsteady ally, however, and quickly shifted his allegiance when more benefits seemed likely to flow from the anti-Washington side.

Using various expedients, Washington tightened the noose around the necks of the District's black elite. He used his political influence with Roosevelt and Taft to try to remove Lafayette Hershaw and Freeman H. M. Murray from their government positions. He sent lieutenants to spy on meetings of the Niagara Movement and report to him. When allies seemed to be wavering, as Richard W. Thompson and Calvin Chase did, Washington defrayed their expenses. Washington infiltrated the opposition center at Howard University by securing an appointment to the Board of Trustees from the university's white president in 1907. In the same year he solidified his influence in the District public schools by getting his protégé Roscoe Conkling Bruce appointed as supervising principal and later as assistant superintendent. In short, Washington used every weapon in his arsenal to keep the District elite from publicly opposing him. As the anti-Washington faction strengthened, however, these efforts became increasingly futile.

The tide began to turn in 1909 with the formation of the NAACP, but change was slow. It was not until the arrival of a Democrat in the White House that tensions approached the breaking point. With Woodrow Wilson in the executive office, Booker T. Washington no longer held the president's ear. As it became clear in the early months of the new administration that most of the Tuskegee-supported officeholders would lose their positions, the black elite increasingly paid only lip service to the Tuskegee ideal. With Washington's death in 1915, the community leadership began to reunite and made the District branch of the NAACP one of the largest and most active branches in the country.

The Reverend J. Milton Waldron of the Shiloh Baptist Church, the charity worker and teacher Carrie Clifford, Archibald Grimké, and other members of Washington's black elite organized the District branch of the NAACP in March 1912. More than a thousand people attended its first rally. The organization was primarily an elite group at first; among its officers were three ministers, three teachers, two women civic leaders, and one government clerk. Waldron served as the branch's first president, and his prominence in the Democratic Party caused a split along party lines. As a result, the organization foundered until 1913, when Archibald Grimké was elected president to close the rift. One of the branch's first actions, at the suggestion of Oswald Garrison Villard, was to form a delegation to visit President Wilson to discuss his position on segregation and disfranchisement of blacks. Wilson refused to meet the delegation, and his refusal sparked a summer of protest against his administration's segregationist policies.

Working with Villard, Grimké organized a dual campaign to gain access to the president through Villard's private diplomacy and open letters and through protest by the NAACP. The main focus of the branch's protests was segregation of the government departments. When the protests failed to change government policies, various members of the NAACP, among them George W. Cook and Francis Grimké, launched a letter-writing campaign aimed at sympathetic members of Congress. At the same time the District NAACP was collecting data on segregation from members who worked in the government.

For the black elite government workers to collect data on their employers, they must have had a strong commitment to the work of the NAACP. Discriminatory practices, such as requiring photographs on job applications, were often applied surreptitiously, and the government departments were not eager to have them revealed to the public. Government workers who protested openly were likely to become targets of greater discrimination and could even lose their jobs. Nevertheless, Lafayette M. Hershaw and Thomas H. R. Clarke managed to collect the data to publicize the extent of segregation in the federal government. Hershaw, at least, was not unfamiliar with political pressure, as he had been a target of Booker T. Washington's manipulation in 1907.[52]

Even before Washington's death, the NAACP served as a unifying force for the District elite. The group had learned its lesson from the controversy surrounding Waldron's presidency and avoided personal publicity for its members. This policy tamed many egos and made it possible for such diverse personalities as Roscoe Conkling Bruce, George W. Cook, Edward C. Williams, and Lafayette M. Hershaw to work together.

Bruce became a leading fund-raiser for the NAACP in the District, even while Washington was still alive. Ralph W. Tyler reported to Washington that

Bruce "is a grand high priest now in the N.A.A.C.P. movement, hurdling from his past friends who saved him to hoped for new friends."[53] Bruce may have been trying to curry favor with the black community at a time when controversy surrounding him was high, but he clearly saw the NAACP as an elite organization worth his efforts.

Mary Church Terrell was another former Tuskegee supporter who worked actively with the NAACP. Mrs. Terrell had always retained her independence from her husband's political debts, and was generally more outspoken than he on educational and civil rights issues. Many people in the Tuskegee camp regarded her as a loose cannon, although she generally drew the line at open opposition for the sake of her husband's judicial appointment. In 1906 Charles Anderson reported that Mrs. Terrell had participated actively in a meeting of the Constitution League and had received much praise from the "Anti-Bookerites." "It seems to me, Doctor," he wrote Washington, "that it is high time that this woman should be called down a little." Anderson also reported that he believed that both Robert and Mary Terrell were leaking information to the enemy and had been working to alienate many of Washington's followers.[54]

As early as 1907, it was rumored that Robert Terrell was edging out of the Tuskegee camp. Anderson reported that Terrell was speaking against Washington in private. He theorized that Terrell felt safe now that he had been reappointed for the remainder of Theodore Roosevelt's term.[55] Too, Terrell may have been smarting from his exclusion from the Carnegie Conference. He knew that as an officeholder he could not be an active participant, but he had probably expected to be consulted.

Mary Church Terrell was proving more trouble to Tuskegee than her husband. When she spoke at an NAACP meeting in New York in 1910, Washington made veiled threats to scuttle Robert's reappointment. The abuse heaped on President Taft by the NAACP, he explained, made it hard for Terrell's friends to support him when he came up for renomination. Mrs. Terrell convinced Washington that by being on the inside of the NAACP, she could monitor its activities for him, or at least stir up trouble in the organization. Certainly she did pass on some information on the NAACP to Tuskegee.[56] This could not have been the whole story, however, for both Terrells continued on a course that led them away from Tuskegee. An anonymous letter informed Washington in 1911 that Terrell had removed Washington's picture from his office and "on inquiry as to why, he simply shrugged his shoulders and winked."[57] Although Robert and Mary Terrell followed their own consciences, ultimately they led them to the same place. One by one, Washington's admirers among the District's black elite withdrew their support from Tuskegee and gravitated toward the more appealing NAACP.

Washington's death removed barriers to unity among the black elite, and increasing outrage also served to unify the black leadership. Accelerating segregation in the federal government, bills introduced in Congress to segregate the District's blacks further, and above all the treatment of black soldiers during and after World War I pushed to the limit even the most conservative black leaders. Public outcry in the black press increased, and complaints became more vehement. It was one thing to practice nonconfrontation when the federal government supported equal rights in principle; it was another to remain peaceful when America seemed to be committed to democracy for everyone but African Americans. With their contacts in the white community, the elite knew better than anyone else the barriers of prejudice they faced.

J. G. Schmidlapp, a white hotel proprietor of Cincinnati who had known Mary Church Terrell in Memphis, where she grew up, took it upon himself to lecture her regularly on matters of race. He condescended to her without even realizing that he did so. In 1917 he wrote: "As far as I can learn a race must be built up within itself, and for that reason I have favored segregation. I avoid using the term, because the negro, being American, is opposed to force, which the word indicates. I prefer to call it community." Schmidlapp also helpfully explained to her the usage of such terms as "negress," which he found objectionable, and "colored," which he believed applied only to people of mixed blood. He proposed using language that would "instill pride of birth into your people."[58] Exposed to such unknowing condescension on a regular basis, the black elite could not help but despair of achieving racial equality gradually.

Discrimination extended into reform movements as well as charity organizations. In 1919 Carrie Chapman Catt asked a friend to write unofficially to the president of the Northeastern Federation of Women's Clubs, a black women's organization in which Mary Church Terrell was active, regarding the group's admittance to the National American Woman Suffrage Association (NAWSA). Ida Husted Harper asked the group to delay their application until after the Nineteenth Amendment had passed, because the admittance of an organization representing 6,000 black women might antagonize southern senators.[59] If even the supposed friends of African Americans could not publicly acknowledge that friendship, race leaders had little hope of influencing enemies through their white connections.

Increasing prejudice led to a proliferation of resolutions on Capitol Hill calling for segregated facilities and bans on interracial marriage. Discussion of bills to segregate streetcars in the District and nationally began in 1906 with debate over the Hepburn Bill to regulate railroad practices. The bills were usually introduced by southern members of Congress. J. Tom Heflin of Alabama, who served eight terms in Congress, alone introduced six bills to segregate streetcars in the District. Few of these bills came to a vote and all were defeated. In February 1915 the House Committee on the District of Columbia favorably reported the Clark Bill, yet another attempt to segregate streetcars in Washington. The full House, under pressure from northern members and the NAACP, disposed of the bill by eliminating the last District Day in the session, when it would have come up for a vote.[60]

Three bills banning intermarriage were introduced in the Sixty-second Congress, the first a general ban and the second to apply specifically to the District of Columbia. House Resolution 1486 stated: "There is no law against such intermarriages in the District of Columbia, and we feel that the District should be in line with the general sentiment of the States of the Union upon the subject of intermarriage between the races." House Resolution 1710, applying to intermarriage of whites with blacks only, was reported favorably in the House; violators would be subject to a fine of $250 to $1,000 or incarceration for six months to one year at hard labor. The bill died in the Senate, however.[61] Although many people in the black community opposed intermarriage themselves, few were willing to have Congress curb their freedom to marry the person of their choice.

The NAACP organized a committee against the bills to ban intermarriage in 1915. Mary Church Terrell, Mamie F. Hilyer, Archibald H. Grimké, and Naomi Curtis worked together to coordinate opposition to the bills and to organize public protests. A group of women, headed by Hilyer and Terrell, started a petition opposing the bills, stating that telling a man that a woman was "not for marriage" put the woman in a horrible light, making her a victim.[62]

In 1916 the House District Committee simultaneously considered seven measures on intermarriage and segregation of streetcars. Archibald Grimké, in his capacity as president of the District NAACP, requested a hearing before the full committee but was refused. He did manage to bring a delegation before a subcommittee. Kelly Miller, George W. Cook, Whitefield McKinlay, James A. Cobb, and Rosetta Lawson testified against the measures. Two of the three members of the subcommittee were absent from the hearings, however, so it was a symbolic gesture at best.[63] Nonetheless, constant public pressure by the NAACP and other groups seems to have had its effect, for as late as 1920 none of the bills to ban intermarriage or segregate streetcars had passed both houses of Congress.

Part of the success of the NAACP and other racial uplift movements was due to the younger people who were beginning to take active leadership roles. These people had come to maturity after the assimilationist years of Reconstruction, when the black community had already begun to look to itself for answers. These young lawyers and businessmen had trained to help their race become strong and independent and harbored no illusions of assimilation into the white community. They became active in civil rights protests and were the forerunners of the civil rights activists of the 1950s. Working with the older members of the elite, they openly challenged the status quo and worked to solidify the ties to the black working classes that their elders had created.

In 1898 the national black press began a discussion of these post-Reconstruction leaders. Frederick Douglass had died in 1895, John M. Langston, Alexander Crummell, and Blanche K. Bruce in 1898, and the black community was ready for a new kind of leadership. The leaders who had reached prominence during Reconstruction were generally optimistic that blacks would achieve political equality, and focused on political means of racial advancement. Bruce had never accepted the idea of separate but equal accommodations.[64] His aristocratic bearing, however, kept him aloof from the black masses he claimed to represent politically. The rise of Jim Crow in the late 1880s called for new approaches.

The *Bee* editorialized that in the light of new educational opportunities and technical advances, the new leader should be of a new sort. He had to be genuine in his attitudes toward the race and "his energies must be bent toward uplifting the entire race, without regard to section or social caste." In 1902 Booker T. Washington recommended Robert H. Terrell to Theodore Roosevelt as an example of the "New Negro" who would take the place of the old leadership.[65] These men shared the common bonds of education, professional training, and political connections, all elements that were to define the new leadership.

Descriptions of the new leadership invariably contained the element of commitment to racial uplift, a factor that the younger generation of the elite took into consideration when they chose their careers. Whereas their forebears had seen a career in politics as the ultimate goal of a law degree, thus ensuring individual advancement, many black elite men now chose law as the best profession in which to help the entire race. They studied complex business laws and gladly took on pro bono cases if they would help the cause of civil rights. Few people in the younger generation could remember a time when race relations were fluid and there was hope for assimilation. Most now saw only the ever-present Jim Crow and increasing disfranchisement. Since this new generation worked within the black community almost exclusively, they had less dependence on the white community for patronage and after 1913 little hope of political patronage. As a result, they were more willing to speak out against injustices, having a solid social and economic foundation within the black community.

The attorney Charles H. Houston, the historian Carter G. Woodson, and the businessman John W. Lewis were but a few members of this younger generation who protested discrimination but did not expect the white community to support their endeavors. Houston trained in the law in order to challenge discrimination from within the legal system. Woodson concentrated on disproving negative stereotypes and raising the quality of higher education for blacks. Lewis helped to develop the black business district in Washington to enable African Americans to maintain a livelihood without having to depend on white businessmen for their basic needs. It was these race leaders, along with others such as the Terrells, the Cromwells, the Grimkés, and the younger generation of Bruces, who gave the impetus to black community development in Washington. For them, attention to racial issues was part and parcel of race leadership, and therefore part of what it meant to be elite.

It was the frustrations of the black elite that led to the new strategies for racial uplift. In the years after Washington's death, the most upsetting situation for the black community was the treatment of black soldiers during the Great War. African Americans had loyally served their country in its military in every war in the nation's history. The black community felt a strong sense of duty to the government that had granted their freedom, and felt that military service was a way to repay their debt while showing their loyalty. Many blacks also believed that the example of black soldiers would convince the white community that they were equal citizens, willing to take on national responsibilities.

During past wars the black press had occasionally debated the wisdom of fighting in a segregated military, but generally ended by supporting the war effort.[66] By 1917, that confidence was practically broken. Blacks still volunteered in large numbers for the military, but few were accepted. At the same time, blacks who were drafted generally found it harder to get exemptions than white draftees. None of the officer training camps admitted blacks, and it was only after a campaign by the NAACP, largely under the impetus of the chapters at Howard and other black universities, that the Army established a black officer training camp at Fort Des Moines. The officers trained there were all assigned to the black 92d Division and served under white superiors. The camp was closed after graduating one class.

Even when blacks were accepted in the Army, few were given an opportunity to fight. Of those black soldiers sent to France, only one in five saw actual combat. The rest served as menial laborers. In 1918 General Pershing placed four black infantry regiments under French command, and these units did see action under less prejudiced French control.[67] A member of one of these regiments was Napoleon B. Marshall, graduate of Harvard and husband of Harriet Gibbs Marshall, of the Washington Conservatory of Music. Marshall fought with the French in the Vosges in September 1918 and in the Argonne in October. He and his unit led a night raid on enemy lines south of Metz in late October. Marshall emerged from the raid with a concussion of the spine and shell shock.[68] The French Army decorated three of the black regiments, including Marshall's, with the Croix de Guerre for bravery. This praise did not lessen discrimination against black soldiers, however, and when the praise came from French civilians as well as officers, it sparked a white backlash.

American officials pressured the French to acquiesce in the American stand on race relations, and in August 1918 French officers were advised not to overpraise the black soldiers or treat them as equals, or to allow French civilians and black troops to become too friendly.[69] A government employee and prominent member of the Fifteenth Street Presbyterian Church, Louis R. Mehlinger, enlisted in the 92d Division with high ideals but ended with only bitter memories. In an eloquent letter to Francis J. Grimké, Mehlinger told of discrimination against black officers:

> In a word the color question would not down. It followed us when we said goodbye to Meade. It embarked with us at Hoboken and remained rampant

> throughout the voyage, disembarked with us at Brest, followed us throughout our training areas all over France and, not satisfied with having been everywhere and ever with us he walked side by side up in the front line trenches with us and even went over the top in death gripping struggle. . . . It is only necessary to say one [of the commanding officers] was from Texas and the other from Virginia, and another from the Lord only knows where, but from where the Rebel Yell is not forgotten because a certain high officer suggested that it be adopted for our battle yell when we went over the top.[70]

Mehlinger reported that efficiency had little to do with keeping a position in the military; only toeing the line kept black officers in the good books of their white superiors. The French generally welcomed all American soldiers, but when the white officers preceded the black soldiers in a village, Mehlinger, who was in charge of finding civilian lodgings for his men, discovered that the French had been told terrible things about them. The French had been convinced that African Americans would steal and kill if given the opportunity, and one youngster asserted that the black soldiers all had tails like monkeys. Fortunately such stereotypes were not easy to maintain under personal exposure. Once the civilians got to know the soldiers and had discussed the race question with them, they tended to side with the blacks against Jim Crow. Wrote Mehlinger: "France knows us now and our cause which is one of the many things the war has made possible."[71]

Not only did the soldiers discuss the race issue with the civilians, they undoubtedly discussed it among themselves, a factor that led to further radicalization of the black community after they returned home. Mehlinger clearly faced a difficult choice between his strong feelings of patriotism and his outrage at the humiliation the black troops suffered. Rayford Logan's war experiences in France convinced him that he could no longer passively accept racial prejudice. He began to rebel against any overt form of discrimination, and ultimately became so disillusioned with the United States that he moved to France in the 1920s.[72] Both black soldiers and civilians were shocked that the government seemed to care so little for men who were fighting for it. For those who had already realized the trend in the federal government, this disregard was just another example of how little the United States truly believed in democracy for all Americans.

Disillusionment led to rebellion for many of Washington's black elite. Francis J. Grimké was particularly outspoken against wartime discrimination.

When asked why he had never declared loyalty to the government or spoken in praise of the Red Cross in any of his sermons, he replied that he would do so only when the government showed its appreciation of the services of the black community and when the Red Cross ceased to discriminate against black nurses and doctors. In 1918 he wrote to James H. Odell, a white minister: "The Germans have shown themselves to be savages of the worst kind, they have been guilty of the most atrocious deeds; but has anything occurred in the nature of German brutality that may not be matched by things that are going on in our own country?"[73]

Other elite blacks recognized the danger of discrimination in and out of the armed forces. William H. Crogman, a member of the American Negro Academy, "knew that the latent, deadly prejudice of the white Americans in the army would be aroused and inflamed by the generous recognition given our black troops by the gallant people of France, and determined effort would be made to keep them in a 'nigger's place' on their return."[74] Charles B. Purvis lamented that the war had revealed race hatred to exist throughout the world, but he believed the United States should concentrate on conditions at home. Patriotism, said Purvis, was "a reciprocal relationship existing between a government and its citizens. While the colored people have always displayed patriotism to this country, the country through its administrations has never displayed any patriotic desire to serve their best interests."[75]

Frustration reached a head in June 1919. The *Washington Post* had been running a series of articles sensationalizing black crime. On June 19 a white woman was briefly jostled by two black men. She screamed and the men ran away. The headline in the *Post* the next day: "Negroes Attack Girl." On the following evening, a group of white sailors and marines gathered near the White House vowing to avenge the alleged spate of black violence. They marched from Pennsylvania Avenue into Southwest Washington, attracting other white men as they went and attacking black men, women, and children at random. On Sunday the violence was repeated, and on Monday the *Post* reported erroneously that all servicemen had been "ordered" to report that night for a final "cleanup" of the area. On Monday night blacks began a counterattack focused on white military men.

The major scenes of conflict during the three days of violence were the streetcars. Mobs of both races pulled people from the cars and beat them, and individuals started fights on the streetcars themselves. The violence slowed on Tuesday night, but many Washingtonians observed that while it was the white mobs that generally provoked the conflicts, the majority of the persons arrested were black. Most alarming to the white community was the fact that African Americans had armed themselves with guns and other weapons in self-defense.[76]

Black counterattacks during the race riot of 1919 were a long-overdue release of frustrations. It is unclear if any members of the black elite actually participated in the rioting, but it is certain that most supported the actions of the militant blacks. Arthur A. Schomburg wrote to John W. Cromwell that he "enjoyed the recital of the Washington riots. I have been expecting the outbreak for a long time and am glad it happened when the august President had returned from Telling Europe how to conclude a lasting peace."[77] Charles B. Purvis told Francis J. Grimké that he had looked for such an outbreak since the Wilson administration had come to power, bringing with it many southern prejudices and expanding institutional racism.[78] Many other members of the Washington elite felt the inevitability of this violence, and some actually welcomed its arrival.

William H. Crogman Sr. noted that the Washington and Chicago riots had awakened the country to the seriousness of the race issue and showed that blacks would not take attacks lying down. Grimké advised fellow African Americans, as he had done in response to the Atlanta riot of 1906, to protect themselves when attacked and not to accept their situation passively. In a sermon before his congregation, Grimké quoted a southern black woman as exclaiming: "The Washington riot gave me a thrill that comes once in a lifetime. . . . I stood up, alone in my room, held both hands high over my head and exclaimed aloud, 'Oh, I thank God, thank God!' . . . The pent-up humiliation, grief and horror of a lifetime—half a century—was being stripped from me."[79] For Grimké to repeat words of such joy in private would hardly have been surprising; that he did so in front of his influential congregation shows that the black elite were thoroughly aroused about racial injustice. Archibald Grimké was so disillusioned by the events surrounding the war that although he had generally been Republican in politics, he began subscribing to socialist newspapers.[80]

In the aftermath of the riot, tensions between the races surprisingly lessened. African Americans had shown their willingness to stand up for themselves and their ability to do so. The white community, alarmed by the riot and further disturbed by the prospect of radicalism during the red scare of 1919, saw the wisdom of treating black protest with more respect. Both the black and white communities had released a great deal of tension through the riot and were willing to negotiate. Black leaders felt that they had finally made their voices heard and began to believe that an organized plan for protesting segregation might once again be a possibility. There were many obstacles to overcome before civil rights for blacks could be guaranteed, but under the guidance of the NAACP, African Americans began to address these obstacles one at a time.

The Progressive Era marked a transformation of race leadership and racial uplift strategies that reflected the objective conditions the black community faced. Immediately after Reconstruction, African Americans held on to the possibility of gradual assimilation, but that hope was dashed by the rise of Jim Crow. Many members of the black elite at first clung to the hope and attempted to dissociate themselves from the black masses in the vain belief that once whites saw that members of the black elite were superior to the rest of the race, they would accept them as equals. As racism increased, however, that belief, too, was crushed.

Struggling to maintain a sense of identity, members of the black elite realized that the basis for their social status lay in the same black community from which they had attempted to dissociate themselves. Some black professionals felt forced to lead protests after they had been excluded from white organizations that bestowed professional status. Others of the black Four Hundred found it necessary to establish ties with the black working classes in order to maintain a business. Gradually they perceived that the fate of the black elite was inextricably tied to that of the entire race.

The leaders of the black community began to look for ways to uplift the race, and therefore their own status, within an increasingly segregated society. Although the races had been separated, the black community had not yet developed independent means of survival, and was largely dependent on white financial and political support. The black elite therefore concentrated on building up black institutions and businesses to reduce this dependency, and pursued forms of racial uplift that would not antagonize the white community. The nonconfrontational methods of racial advancement they adopted included building a basis for racial pride through literary groups and educational reform. In charity work they employed scientific methods that proved highly effective in reducing poverty and providing alternatives to crime for poor black youths. They established parallel organizations and institutions to provide for the black community when the white community would not.

They created a foundation from which protest could once again become a possibility.

In the process of moving from assimilationist ideals to nonconfrontational strategies and then to open protest, the black elite transformed its vision of itself. In 1880 black aristocratic families had secluded themselves from the working classes with exclusive social groups and prided themselves on their free ancestry, both black and white, on their connections with the white community, on their familial affiliations, and on their occupations, limited though they were by the restricted opportunities available to free blacks. By the turn of the century many of these distinctions had faded in importance in the face of new educational opportunities and the new atmosphere in race relations. Education, professional occupation, and involvement in the community became equally important indices of social status. The elite had become less an aristocracy and more a class of people trained in their responsibilities as leaders of their race.

Washington was not the only city to undergo this transformation within the black elite; the national network of elite blacks ensured that ideas would be transmitted around the country. Since Washington was one of the leading centers of African American culture at the turn of the century, however, and produced more national race leaders than any other city, what happened in the District had the greatest influence on what happened to the race.

The younger generation of the black elite in Washington never experienced the disillusionment of their parents; they had known only a segregated society. They were impatient with the conservative ideology of Booker T. Washington. They shed the mantle of nonconfrontation as outdated and turned to organized protest under such groups as the NAACP. They came into the twentieth century with new priorities and goals for the race, and with the education and independent power base to attain those goals. Yet they did not completely break from their parents' generation. They simply operated under different objective conditions, made possible through the efforts of the black elite at the turn of the century. Ultimately, leading the race came to define not just individual assimilation but commitment to uplift of the race as a whole.

NOTES

ABBREVIATIONS

REPOSITORIES

MLC   Manuscript Division, Library of Congress
MSRC Moorland-Spingarn Research Center, Howard University

NAMES

AFH	Andrew F. Hilyer	CGW	Carter G. Woodson
AHG	Archibald H. Grimké	FJG	Francis J. Grimké
AJC	Anna Julia Cooper	JWB	Josephine Willson Bruce
AWG	Angelina W. Grimké	MCT	Mary Church Terrell
BKB	Blanche K. Bruce	RCB	Roscoe Conkling Bruce
BTW	Booker T. Washington	RHT	Robert H. Terrell

Introduction

1. Joe W. Trotter, "African Americans in the City: The Industrial Era, 1900–1950," in Goings and Mohl, *New African American Urban History,* 314–15.

2. See Meier, *Negro Thought in America,* 156–57; Spear, *Black Chicago,* 71–79; Kusmer, *A Ghetto Takes Shape,* 190–205; Gatewood, *Aristocrats of Color,* 67–68.

CHAPTER 1. *The Washington Black Elite: An 1880s Overview*

1. RCB to AHG, 7 Dec. 1922, folder 87, box 4, AHG Papers, MSRC; unidentified manuscript, folder 55, box 1, Mary Ann Shadd Cary Papers, MSRC.

2. John E. Bruce, "Washington's Colored Society," John E. Bruce Papers, Schomburg Center for Research in Black Culture, New York Public Library.

3. See *Bee,* 24 Feb. 1883, 2.

4. Alexander Crummell to FJG, 30 June 1886, in Grimké, *Works,* 4:4–6.

5. Richard T. Greener to FJG, 27 Dec. 1890, ibid., 25.

6. BTW to FJG, 23 Mar. 1901, ibid., 70.

7. Gatewood, *Aristocrats of Color,* 39–41; Johnson, "Mary Ann Shadd," 89–90.

8. Gatewood, *Aristocrats of Color,* 39–44.

9. Ione, *Pride of Family,* 16; Gatewood, *Aristocrats of Color,* 167–68.

10. Gatewood, *Aristocrats of Color,* 41–43.

11. Ibid., 51–52.

12. *Bee,* 25 June 1898, 4; 24 June 1882, 3.

13. Gatewood, *Aristocrats of Color,* 44; AHG to "Frank and Lottie," 6 Sept. 1895, folder 118, box 3, FJG Papers, MSRC.

14. MCT Diary, 29 Jan. 1908, reel 1, MCT Papers, MLC.

15. *Bee,* 30 Dec. 1882, 2.

16. Ibid., 19 Jan. 1884, 2; 2 Feb. 1884, 3; 16 Feb. 1884, 2; 15 Mar. 1884, 2.

17. Ibid., 6 Jan. 1883, 3; 10 Feb. 1883, 3; 23 June 1883, 3. See also Gatewood, *Aristocrats of Color,* 226–27.

18. *National Leader,* 8 Dec. 1888, 3; Gabel, *From Slavery to the Sorbonne,* 35.

19. *Bee,* 3 Mar. 1883, 3; 30 Dec. 1882, 3.

20. Ibid., 2 June 1883, 2.

21. Cromwell, *History of the Bethel Literary,* 26, in folder 48, box 3, Cromwell Family Papers, MSRC.

22. FJG, *A Look Backward,* 10–15.

23. See, for example, 15 Mar. 1881, in "Records of the Session and the Church Records, 1874–1890," II, folder 2, box 1, Records of the Fifteenth Street Presbyterian Church, MSRC; March 1890–March 1893, in "Minutes of the Official Board [of Trustees], July 28, 1884 to April 23, 1894," folder 47, box 3, Records of the Metropolitan AME Church, MSRC.

24. See 7 Jan. 1886, in "Records of the Session and the Church Records, 1874–1890," II, folder 2, box 1, Records of the Fifteenth Street Presbyterian Church, MSRC; 2 Apr. 1894, in "Minutes of the Official Board [of Trustees], July 28, 1884 to April 23, 1894," folder 47, box 3, Records of the Metropolitan AME Church, MSRC. In the same collection, see, for example, the settlement of a divorce case, 22 Mar. and 5 Apr. 1880, in "Minutes of the Official Board [of Trustees], January 20, 1879 to July 1884," folder 46, box 3.

25. Carter G. Woodson, "Things of the Spirit," in Sernett, *Afro-American Religious History,* 330–33; William Wells Brown, "Black Religion in the Post-Reconstruction South," ibid., 239.

26. Woodson, *History of the Negro Church,* 225, 229–31.

27. Clarke, *History of the Nineteenth-Century Black Churches,* 17–18.

28. Obituary [1896], Martha Ann Simms, folder 20, box 1, Simms Family Papers, MSRC; obituary, 23 Sept. 1900, John A. Simms Jr., folder 14, ibid.

29. John Wesley Cromwell Sr., "First Negro Churches in the District of Columbia," 7, folder 37, box 2, Cromwell Family Papers, MSRC.

30. Pamphlet, 13 June 1881, folder 37, box 2, Simms Family Papers, MSRC; Cromwell, "First Negro Churches," 8.

31. Cromwell, "First Negro Churches," 28; Charles H. Wesley, "A Century of Methodism at Metropolitan, 1838–1938," folder 44, box 2, Simms Family Papers, MSRC.

32. *Bee,* 23 Dec. 1882, 2; 3 Mar. 1883, 3.

33. Cromwell, *History of the Bethel Literary,* 4.

34. Cromwell, "First Negro Churches," 8; 15 May to 7 Aug. 1882, in "Minutes of the Official Board [of Trustees], January 20, 1897 to July 1884," folder 46, box 3, Records of the Metropolitan AME Church, MSRC.

35. Woodson, *History of the Negro Church,* 233–34; Cromwell, "First Negro Churches," 11.

36. Mary Ann Shadd Cary, undated typescript, folder 19, box 1, Mary Ann Shadd Cary Papers, MSRC.

37. Martha Cromwell Brent, "Education for Negroes in the District of Columbia: Our Leaders and Builders for Tomorrow," undated manuscript, ca. 1940, folder 165, box 15, Cromwell Family Papers, MSRC; Schweninger, *Black Property Owners,* 138; William A. Joiner, "Brief Review of the Origins and Development of the Colored Schools, District of Columbia," in *Supplemental Exhibit at Charleston, S.C., 1901–2,* folder 83, box 2, James C. Wright Papers, MSRC.

38. Dabney, *History of Schools for Negroes,* 197–200, 216–17.

39. Null, "Myrtilla Miner's 'School for Colored Girls,'" 254, 268.

40. Logan, *Howard University,* 91–92.

41. Schweninger, *Black Property Owners,* 204.

42. Unidentified clipping, scrapbook 3, box 1, Thomas H. R. Clarke Papers, MSRC.

43. Schweninger, *Black Property Owners,* 178, 217.

44. Woodson, *Negro Professional Man,* 23.

45. Ibid., 15, 54–56.

46. John A. Simms Sr., undated employment record, folder 3, box 1, Simms Family Papers, MSRC.

47. Biographical notes, folders 15, 17, box 1, ibid.

48. *Colored American,* 11 June 1898, 3; 25 June 1898, 5.

49. *Bee,* 14 Apr. 1883, 2.

50. Ibid., 10 June 1882, 3; 14 Apr. 1883, 3.

51. Ibid., 10 June 1882, 3; 30 Dec. 1882, 2.

52. For more on the masculine aspects of secret societies see Carnes, *Secret Ritual and Manhood*.

53. Gatewood, *Aristocrats of Color*, 212–13; Muraskin, *Middle-Class Blacks in a White Society*, 18–19, 4, 24–25, 27, 40, 191.

54. Severson, *History of Felix Lodge No. 3*, 8, 18, 25.

55. *Bee*, 24 June 1882, 2.

56. Ibid., 6 Jan. 1883, 2.

57. Ibid., 17 Mar. 1883, 2; 25 June 1898, 4.

58. Ibid., 1 Mar. 1884, 3.

59. Meier, *Negro Thought in America*, 54.

60. Hine, *Black Women in America*, 1:201–5.

61. *Bee*, 24 Mar. 1883, 3.

62. Cobb, *First Negro Medical Society*, 1. The organization reemerged in the 1890s when Washington's black doctors realized the futility of trying to gain acceptance in the American Medical Association, as we shall see in Chapter 8.

CHAPTER 2. *The Family*

1. Frederick Douglass speech, unidentified typescript, folder 351, box 19, AHG Papers, MSRC.

2. Billingsley, *Climbing Jacob's Ladder*, 72, 333.

3. Levey, "Scurlock Studio," 43.

4. For an excellent theoretical discussion of the problems surrounding research on the black family and a semihistoriographical essay see Allen, "Search for Applicable Theories of Black Family Life," 117–29.

5. Bernard, *Marriage and Family Among Negroes*, 28–30, 47–49.

6. Ione, *Pride of Family*, 167–68, 129, 177, 16–17, 18.

7. Biographical notes, Cromwell Family Papers, MSRC.

8. Levey, "Scurlock Studio," 43.

9. *Colored American*, 2 Apr. 1898, 4; 17 Sept. 1898, 5.

10. Bruce, *Archibald Grimké*, 37–41.

11. Ione, *Pride of Family*, 17.

12. *Bee*, 18 Mar. 1899, 5; 30 Dec. 1882, 3.

13. Ione, *Pride of Family*, 191.

14. Boyd, *A Love That Equals My Labors*, 22.

15. See JWB to RCB, 5 Feb., 18 Sept., and 21 Sept. 1896, folder 41, box 2, RCB Papers; BKB to RCB, 30 Apr. 1897, folder 8, box 1, BKB Papers; RCB to BKB, 30 Apr. 1897, folder 2, box 1, RCB Papers; all in MSRC. See, for example, BKB to RCB, 24 Jan. 1897, folder 1, box 1, RCB Papers.

16. MCT Diary, 6 Oct. 1909, reel 1, MCT Papers, MLC.

17. Terrell, *Colored Woman in a White World,* 173–74. See, for example, MCT Diary, 5 Sept. and 7 Oct. 1908, reel 1, MCT Papers, MLC.

18. MCT Diary, 24–25 and 28–30 Aug., 1 and 11 Sept. 1909, reel 1, MCT Papers, MLC.

19. Terrell, *Colored Woman in a White World,* 249–50.

20. M. C. Stanley to Sarah Stanley, 27 Feb. 1879, folder 5, box 1, AHG Papers, MSRC.

21. AWG, "Archibald H. Grimké," undated manuscript, folder 51, box 3, ibid.

22. Gatewood, *Aristocrats of Color,* 55; *Bee,* 21 May 1898, 4; FJG, "The Douglass Centenary," in Grimké, *Works,* 4:179.

23. *Bee,* 21 May 1898, 4; FJG, "Douglass Centenary," in Grimké, *Works,* 4:179.

24. Ione, *Pride of Family,* 189–98, 149–56, 36.

25. Ibid., 16–17, 29.

26. Mintz and Kellogg, *Domestic Revolutions,* 108–9.

27. *Colored American,* 25 June 1898, 8; *Bee,* 19 Mar. 1898, 5; 25 June 1898, 5; 4 June 1898, 7.

28. MCT Diary, 28–31 Aug. and 7 Sept. 1911, box 1, MCT Collection Additions, MSRC.

29. Mintz and Kellogg, *Domestic Revolutions,* 108–17.

30. MCT Diary, 24 Nov. and 4 Dec. 1909, reel 1, MCT Papers, MLC.

31. Compare, for example, comments on Mary's Latin, ibid., 23 Nov. 1909, with comments on Phyllis's reading and music, ibid., 15 Aug. 1909, 17 Feb. 1908.

32. Ibid., 1–2 Aug. 1908.

33. Ibid., 25 Nov. 1909.

34. RCB to BKB, 18 Apr. 1897, folder 2, box 1, RCB Papers, MSRC.

35. BKB to RCB, 9 Oct. 1897, folder 3, box 1, ibid.

36. RCB to BKB, 1 Jan. 1897, folder 1, box 1, ibid.

37. Sarah Stanley Grimké to AHG, 25 Apr. 1887, folder 62, box 3, AHG Papers, MSRC.

38. AHG to "Home Ones," 16 June 1895, folder 117, box 1, FJG Papers, MSRC; AHG to AWG, 19 June 1895, folder 66, box 4, AWG Papers, MSRC. See AHG to AWG, 29 Oct. 1895, folder 66, box 4, AWG Papers; Bruce, *Archibald Grimké,* 75–77.

39. AHG to AWG, 18 Nov. and 6 Oct., 1897, folder 67; 1 Dec. 1898, folder 68, all in box 4, AWG Papers, MSRC.

40. AHG to AWG, 25 Feb. 1899, folder 69, ibid.

41. AHG to AWG, 26 Nov. 1899, ibid.

42. MCT Diary, 17 Feb. 1908, 23 Nov. 1909, 28–30 July 1909, 15 Aug. 1909, reel 1, MCT Papers, MLC.

43. AHG to AWG, 7 Feb. 1895, folder 66, box 4, AWG Papers, MSRC; BKB to RCB, 24 Jan. 1897, folder 1, box 1, RCB Papers, MSRC.

44. Harriet Willson to JWB, 15 May 1895, folder 40, box 2, RCB Papers, MSRC.

45. RCB to JWB [1922], folder 53, box 3, ibid.

46. JWB to RCB, 19 Oct. 1897, folder 43, box 2, ibid.

47. See MCT to Florence M. Fitch, October 1913, box 4, MCT Papers, MLC.

48. See BKB to RCB, 30 Apr. 1897, folder 8, box 1, BKB Papers, MSRC; RCB to BKB, 30 Apr. 1897, folder 2, box 1, and RCB to JWB [1922], folder 53, box 3, RCB Papers, MSRC.

CHAPTER 3. *Culture and Leisure*

1. Jones, *Recreation and Amusement,* 98–99.

2. Terrell, "Society Among the Colored People," 155.

3. See, for example, the account of the visit of Mrs. Harry L. Kemp of Brooklyn, New York, in *Colored American,* 17 Sept. 1898, 6.

4. *Bee,* 10 June 1882, 3; *Colored American,* 11 June 1898, 8.

5. Jones, *Recreation and Amusement,* 100.

6. MCT Diary, 21 Feb. 1908, reel 1, MCT Papers, MLC; undated clipping, box 4, ibid.; MCT Diary, 20 Apr. 1911, box 1, MCT Collection Additions, MSRC.

7. MCT Diary, 2–3, 17, 20, and 29–30 Nov. 1905, reel 1, MCT Papers, MLC.

8. Ibid., 8 June, 12 and 13 Dec. 1908.

9. AHG to AWG, 31 Oct. 1898, folder 68, box 4, AWG Papers, MSRC.

10. MCT Diary, 6 and 10 May 1905, 30 and 20 Oct. 1909, 17 and 19 Nov. 1909, reel 1, MCT Papers, MLC. See *Washington Post,* 19 Nov. 1909, 8, for MCT's views on football.

11. MCT Diary, 31 Aug. 1908, reel 1, MCT Papers, MLC.

12. Ibid., 27–28 July 1908.

13. Ibid., 3 Sept. 1908.

14. *Colored American,* 7 May 1898, 4.

15. Gatewood, *Aristocrats of Color,* 200–201.

16. *Colored American,* 20 Aug. 1898, 5.

17. MCT Diary, 14 Aug. 1908, reel 1, MCT Papers, MLC.

18. Souvenirs, folder 62, box 3, AHG Papers, MSRC.

19. *Bee,* 24 June 1882, 3.

20. Gatewood, *Aristocrats of Color,* 201; Jones, *Recreation and Amusement,* 52.

21. MCT Diary, 6 Aug. 1908, reel 1, MCT Papers, MLC.

22. MCT to Thomas A. Church, 10 Aug. 1917, box 3, ibid.

23. MCT, "Society Among the Colored People," 155–56.

24. Jones, *Recreation and Amusement,* 52.

25. Gatewood, *Aristocrats of Color*, 182–209.
26. Ibid., 193–94.
27. Woodson, *Negro Professional Man*, 253.
28. Green, *Secret City*, 207.
29. Terrell, *Colored Woman in a White World*, 247.
30. Ibid., 248–49.
31. *Howard Theater District* (film).
32. Davis, 'Missing Link,' 10–11.
33. *Howard Theater District*, commentary; Davis, 'Missing Link,' 12.
34. *Howard Theater District*, commentary; "The Colored Man," clipping, in Walter J. Singleton to [MCT or RHT], 5 Dec. 1913, box 4, MCT Papers, MLC.
35. RHT to Phyllis Terrell, 26 Jan. 1914, box 3, MCT Papers, MLC.
36. Jones, *Recreation and Amusement*, 132, 138–39.
37. *Colored American*, 17 Sept. 1898, 6.
38. Ibid., 16 Apr. 1898, 4; Jones, *Recreation and Amusement*, 141–43.
39. Jones, *Recreation and Amusement*, 29–34.
40. *Colored American*, 16 Apr. 1898, 7; 7 May 1898, 2; 21 May 1898, 5; 17 Sept., 1898, 8.
41. Gatewood, *Aristocrats of Color*, 47–48, 231.
42. Mrs. Terrell describes one such meal in MCT Diary, 9 Feb. 1911, box 1, MCT Collection Additions, MSRC; see also the entry of 6 Apr. 1911.
43. Unidentified clipping [1913], box 1, Mu-So-Lit Club Records, 1915–20, MSRC.
44. *Chicago InterOcean*, 28 Sept. 18[95], in Washington, *BTW Papers*, 4:37–38.
45. Letterhead found in box 5, MCT Papers, MLC.
46. *Colored American*, 28 Jan. 1899, 6; 15 Apr. 1899, 4.
47. See, for example, the description of a recital ibid., 23 July 1898, 8.
48. Gatewood, *Aristocrats of Color*, 217.
49. Prospectus [Oct. or Nov. 1902], folder 31, box 3, AFH Papers, MSRC.
50. Program, "Hiawatha, 16 Nov. 1904," folder 67, box 2, ibid. See folder 47, ibid.
51. Nellie A. Plummer to AFH, 29 Apr. 1903, folder 28, box 3, ibid.
52. *Leader*, 23 Mar. 1889, 4.
53. Angell, *Bishop Henry McNeal Turner*, 160–61.
54. Cromwell, *History of the Bethel Literary*, 3–4.
55. Ibid., 6.
56. Ibid., 15–24, 27; *Colored American*, 14 May 1898, 6.
57. Harlan, *Booker T. Washington*, 37–38; *Colored American*, 17 Jan. 1903, 9, and 31 Jan. 1903, 5.
58. *Colored American*, 14 Feb. 1903, 11.

59. Harlan, *Booker T. Washington*, 38. See also Thomas J. Calloway to Emmett J. Scott, 12 Jan. 1903, and Richard W. Thompson to Scott, 4 Feb. 1903, both in Washington, *BTW Papers*, 7:45, 33–35.

60. Program, 19 Mar. 1912, scrapbook 3, box 1, Thomas H. R. Clarke Collection, MSRC; *Bee*, 29 Apr. 1919, 5.

CHAPTER 4. *The Church*

1. Higginbotham, *Righteous Discontent*, 23, 52–53; Montgomery, *Under Their Own Vine and Fig Tree*, 241, 244.

2. Higginbotham, *Righteous Discontent*, 64–65.

3. Montgomery, *Under Their Own Vine and Fig Tree*, 242–43. See also Woodson, *History of the Negro Church*, 238. For a discussion of the development of the National Baptist Publishing House see Elias C. Morris, "1899 Presidential Address to the National Baptist Convention," in Sernett, *Afro-American Religious History*, 280–81.

4. John Wesley Cromwell Sr., "First Negro Churches in the District of Columbia," 12–13, folder 37, box 2, Cromwell Family Papers, MSRC.

5. Sluby, *Sessional Minutes of the Fifteenth Street Presbyterian Church*, 157–65, 170, 184, 193, 205, 210–11.

6. FJG, "Equality of Rights for All Citizens, Black and White Alike," sermon delivered 27 Mar. 1909, in Grimké, *Works*, 1:418–19.

7. FJG, *A Look Backward*, 2–3.

8. FJG, "The Afro-American Pulpit in Relation to Race Elevation," in Grimké, *Works*, 1:229–33.

9. FJG, *A Look Backward*, 7; FJG sermons, 7 Apr. 1895, folder 663; 16 June 1895, folder 665; 14 July 1895, folder 667, all in FJG Papers, MSRC. In the latter sermon, Grimké crossed out a section that specifically accused white northern teachers of bowing to popular opinion and not associating with their students. Whether or not he read this part to his congregation is not clear, but it seems that, upon reflection, he thought the passage inappropriate.

10. FJG, "Discouragements: Hostility of the Press Silence and Cowardice of the Pulpit" and "Sources from Which No Help May Be Expected—The General Government, Political Parties," in Grimké, *Works*, 1:237–46, 252–54.

11. FJG, "God and Prayer as Factors in the Struggle," ibid., 274–90.

12. FJG, "God and the Race Problem," "Christianity and Race Prejudice," and "The Race Problem—Two Suggestions as to Its Solutions," ibid., 364–74, 461–64, 591–96.

13. Handy, *Social Gospel in America*, 6, 11.

14. See 25 Mar. 1889, in "Records of the Session and the Church Records, 1874–1890," II, folder 2, box 1, Records of the Fifteenth Street Presbyterian Church, MSRC.

15. See 6 Apr. 1885, ibid.; FJG, "The Attitude of the Home on the Temperance Question," in Grimké, *Works*, 2:472. For a sample of Grimké's sermons on this subject see ibid., 2:471–538.

16. See 25 Mar. 1889, in "Records of the Session and Church Records, 1874–1890," II, folder 2, box 1, Records of the Fifteenth Street Presbyterian Church, MSRC. Angelina Weld Grimké, Francis's niece, seems not to have taken a temperance pledge, or if she did, she did not keep it. In 1931 Angelina had to pay a fine of $15 for the transportation and possession of three pints of French wine. United States Custom Service Notice and Account of Fines, Penalties, and Forfeitures and Receipt, folder 130, box 8, AWG Papers, MSRC.

17. See 25 Mar. 1889, in "Records of the Session and the Church Records, 1874–1890," II, folder 2, box 1, Records of the Fifteenth Street Presbyterian Church, MSRC.

18. See 7 May 1880, 18 Nov. 1886, 28 Mar. 1887, ibid.

19. "Minutes of the Official Board [of Trustees], 20 January 1879 to July 1884," folder 46; 28 July 1884–23 Apr. 1894 and 8 Jan. 1894, folder 47; 14 May 1901, folder 48, all in box 3, Records of the Metropolitan AME Church, MSRC.

20. See 25 Mar. 1889, in "Records of the Session and the Church Records, 1874–1890," II, folder 2, box 1, Records of the Fifteenth Street Presbyterian Church, MSRC.

21. "Minutes of the Official Board [of Trustees]," 16 Mar. 1885, folder 47, and 3 Sept. 1895, folder 48, both in box 3, Records of the Metropolitan AME Church, MSRC.

22. Ibid., 6 Aug. 1895.

23. Annual Reports of the Metropolitan AME Church, 1898–1903, folder 48, box 3, Cromwell Family Papers, MSRC.

24. Higginbotham, *Righteous Discontent*, 174, 143, 177.

25. Hine, *Black Women in America*, 1:201–5.

26. Cromwell, "First Negro Churches," 30–33; "Address of the Congress to Their Catholic Fellow-Citizens of the United States," in Sernett, *Afro-American Religious History*, 267–69.

27. MCT to Miss Coveney, 10 Mar. 1918, box 5, MCT Papers, MLC.

28. Grimké, *Works*, 4:160n; Frederick Douglass to J. W. Beckett, 28 Oct. 1891, in *AME Church Review*, January–March 1963, 57, found in folder 63, box 2, Simms Family Papers, MSRC.

29. Charles R. Winthrop to FJG, 2 Feb. 1916, in Grimké, *Works*, 4:158. Wood-

son, the editor, commented in a footnote: "The Negro ministry has had much difficulty in holding their congregations in the last quarter of a century, inasmuch as young people question the Church because of its shortcomings."

30. Alice M. Dunbar to FJG, 14 Feb. 1916, ibid., 159; MCT Diary, 18 Jan. 1915, reel 1, MCT Papers, MLC; AJC to A. G. Comings, 1 Oct. 1928, folder 5, box 1, AJC Papers, MSRC.

31. St. Clair Drake and Horace Cayton, "The Churches of Bronzeville," in Sernett, *Afro-American Religious History*, 349–63; Woodson, *Negro Professional Man*, 79.

32. Boyd, *A Love That Equals My Labors*, 18, 27; Frederick Douglass to J. W. Beckett, 28 Oct. 1891, *AME Church Review*, January–March 1963, 57, found in folder 63, box 2, Simms Family Papers, MSRC.

33. Gatewood, *Aristocrats of Color*, 289–90; JWB to RCB, 22 Jan. 1897, folder 42, box 2, RCB Papers, MSRC.

34. MCT Diary, 9 May, 26 Sept., 3 and 10 Oct., and 26 Dec. 1909, reel 1, MCT Papers, MLC.

35. Ibid., 12 and 19 Mar. 1905, 28 June 1908; Mary Terrell to Mary Church Terrell, 11 May 1919, box 5, MCT Papers, MLC.

36. FJG to P. B. S. Pinchback, 28 June 1916, and Pinchback to FJG, 12 July 1916, in Grimké, *Works*, 4:171–72, 179.

37. Hine, *Black Women in America*, 1:63–64; *Chicago Defender*, undated clipping, scrapbook 3, box 1, Thomas H. R. Clarke Papers, MSRC; J. H. Hannen to FJG, 19 Mar. 1918, in Grimké, *Works*, 4:209–10.

38. Booker T. Washington, "The Religious Life of the Negro," in Nelsen, Yokley, and Nelsen, *Black Church in America*, 43.

CHAPTER 5. *Primary and Secondary Education*

1. Report of the Board of School Trustees, 18 Nov. 1885, 145–46; 1885–86, 347–63; 1886–87, 224–25, 306; 1888–89, 980; 1890–91, 903–6, 927, all in U.S. Congress, *Annual Report of the Commissioners* (hereafter cited as Report of the Board of Trustees or Report of the Board of Education).

2. Ibid., 1891–92, 822, 973; 1892–93, 591–92, 604.

3. Hundley, *Dunbar Story*, 66; Report of the Board of Trustees, 1895–96, 930; J. C. Wright to F. R. Lane, 3 Sept. 1900, folder 81, box 2, James C. Wright Papers, MSRC.

4. Report of the Board of Trustees, 1894–95, 1029.

5. Ibid., 1908–9, 215.

6. Report of the Board of Education, 1914–15, 269.

7. Terrell, "History of the High School for Negroes," 252–53; Report of the Board of Education, 1919–20, 366–69.

8. Undated memo [27 Sept. 1915?], folder 66, box 2, James C. Wright Papers, MSRC.

9. Harley, "Black Women in the District of Columbia," 188.

10. J. C. Wright, J. F. Allen, Charles M. Thomas, and William A. Joiner, petition to Congressional Committee on Schools for the District of Columbia, 12 Mar. 1900, folder 80, box 2, James C. Wright Papers, MSRC.

11. *Bee*, 24 Feb. 1883, 3, and 21 July 1883, 2; *National Leader*, 16 Feb. 1889, 4.

12. JWB to RCB, 23 Nov. 1897, folder 44, box 2, RCB Papers, MSRC.

13. *Bee*, 9 Apr. 1898, 4.

14. W. E. B. Du Bois to BTW, 17 Feb. 1900, in Washington, *BTW Papers*, 5: 443–44. See also Du Bois to BTW, 26 Feb. 190[0], ibid., 450. David Levering Lewis gives a detailed account of Du Bois's involvement in the District schools in *W. E. B. Du Bois*, 233–37, 241, 246.

15. BTW to Emmett J. Scott, 11 Mar. 1900, in Washington, *BTW Papers*, 5:457–58; BTW to T. Thomas Fortune, 14 Mar. 1900, ibid., 460–61; BTW to Du Bois, 11 Mar. 1900, ibid., 458–59; Fortune to BTW, 16 Mar. 1900, ibid., 5:465. See also William A. Pledger to BTW, 16 Mar. 1900, ibid., 466.

16. RHT to BTW, 25 Mar. 1900, ibid., 471–73, 465n.

17. Ursuline V. Brooks Notes, 22 Nov. 1916, folder 93, box 2, James C. Wright Papers, MSRC.

18. MCT Diary, 18 June 1908, reel 1, MCT Papers, MLC. The creation of Armstrong Manual Training School was an attempt to force blacks into industrial education. Although educational reformers considered manual training a revolutionary educational method, ultimately it trained blacks to be laborers rather than skilled professionals. With the creation of Armstrong, complaints of overcrowding at M Street could be countered by the argument that many more students could now attend school beyond the elementary level.

19. Undated memo, folder 179, box 4, James C. Wright Papers, MSRC; undated memo [27 Sept. 1915?], folder 66, box 2, ibid.

20. *Citizen*, 1 Feb. 1909, 3.

21. Hundley, *Dunbar Story*, 64.

22. Robinson, "M Street High School," 122–23; Gabel, *From Slavery to the Sorbonne*, 53.

23. Report of the Board of Education, 1902–3, 196–97; 1903–4, 187–88.

24. P. M. Hughes to A. T. Stuart, 14 Dec. 1904, folder 43, box 1, James C. Wright Papers, MSRC.

25. P. M. Hughes to Edward DeV. Morrell, 2 Mar. 1906, folder 112, box 2, ibid.

26. AJC to William A. Joiner, 26 Sept. 1902, folder 6, box 3, William A. Joiner Papers, MSRC.

27. *Bee,* 14 Jan. 1905, 4; 21 Jan. 1905, 4.

28. Ibid., 24 June 1905, 4; *Washington Post,* 19 Sept. 1905, quoted in Hutchinson, *Anna J. Cooper,* 73–75.

29. *Bee,* 5 Aug. 1905, 4.

30. Hutchinson, *Anna J. Cooper,* 75–76.

31. See *Bee,* 9 Dec. 1905, 4; 30 Dec. 1905, 1, 4; 20 Jan. 1906, 4; 17 Feb. 1906, 4; 14 Apr. 1906, 4; 28 Apr. 1906, 4; 12 May 1906, 4; 19 May 1906, 1, 4; 16 June 1906, 4.

32. Ibid., 7 July 1906, 1, 4. See also ibid., 14 July 1906, 1.

33. James A. Cobb to Emmett J. Scott, 3 Sept. 1906, in Washington, *BTW Papers,* 9:68; Pielmeier, "Roscoe Conkling Bruce," 14–21.

34. BTW to William E. Chancellor, 4 Sept. 1906, in Washington, *BTW Papers,* 9:68. Chancellor insisted that he chose Bruce on his merits, not because of Washington's recommendation. See Chancellor to BTW, 29 Nov. 1906, ibid., 150–51.

35. *Evening Star,* 1 Sept. 1906, 2.

36. Ibid., 31 Aug. 1906, 4; 5 Sept. 1906, 4; 10 Sept. 1906, 2; 13 Sept. 1906, 2; 14 Sept. 1906, 1; 16 Sept. 1906, 2; *Bee,* 1 Sept. 1906, 1; 8 Sept. 1906, 4; 15 Sept. 1906, 1, 4, 5.

37. *Evening Star,* 15 Sept. 1906, 4; 14 Sept. 1906, 4; 21 Sept. 1906, 10.

38. Ibid., 15 Sept. 1906, 6; 18 Sept. 1906, 3; 17 Sept. 1906, 3.

39. Washington, *BTW Papers,* 7:219n; Melvin Jack Chisum to BTW, 16, 17, and 19 Feb. 1906, ibid., 8:522–24, 526–27.

40. BTW to Chisum, 24 Feb. 1906, ibid., 8:534; Chisum to BTW, 26 Feb. 1906, ibid., 534–35; Emmett J. Scott to John A. Lankford, 12 Apr. 1906, ibid., 576; Lankford to Scott, 14 Apr. 1906, ibid., 581; Scott to Lankford, 16 Apr. 1906, ibid., 583–84, and 4 June 1906, ibid., 9:26; BTW to Chisum, 5 June 1906, ibid., 9:26; Chisum to BTW, 11 Oct. 1906, ibid., 9:94.

41. *Bee,* 22 Sept. 1906, 4, 5; 24 Nov. 1906, 4; 22 Dec. 1906.

42. Quoted in Hutchinson, *Anna J. Cooper,* 83.

43. See unidentified writer to James F. Oyster, 11 May 1911; Oyster to AJC, 5 July 1911; AJC to Oyster, 9 July 1911, all in folder 90, box 4, AHG Papers, MSRC. Cooper also implied that the 1906 offer to remain as a principal of a graded school was never properly delivered to her, nor was it offered in earnest; AJC to F. W. Ballou, 6 Feb. 1921 and 8 Mar. 1922, ibid.; AJC to Garnet C. Wilkinson, 24 May 1925, quoted in Hutchinson, *Anna J. Cooper,* 148–52; Survey of Negro College Graduates [1932], folder 1, box 1, AJC Papers, MSRC.

44. Evans claimed that Grimké, a noted poet and playwright, had no competence to teach English. AHG to AWG, 16 Sept. 1906, and extract from W. S. Mont-

gomery to William E. Chancellor, 12 Mar. 1908, folder 75, box 4; W. B. Evans to RCB, 29 Jan. 1908, and W. T. S. Jackson to RCB, 29 Jan. 1908, folder 30, box 3, all in AWG Papers, MSRC.

45. Neval H. Thomas to RCB, 17 June 1908, box 4, MCT Papers, MLC.

46. *Evening Star,* 26 Sept. 1906, 2; 30 Sept. 1906, 3; *Bee,* 17 Nov. 1906, 4, 5.

47. U.S. Congress, *Historical Sketch of Education,* 130.

48. Report of the Board of Education, 1907–8, 106–7.

49. Ibid., 107, 111. See, for example, RCB to A. T. Stuart, 16 Feb. 1909, box 4, MCT Papers, MLC.

50. Report of the Board of Education, 1908–9, 128.

51. RCB to Special Committee to investigate charges preferred by W. Calvin Chase Esq. against the Assistant Superintendent, 25 Oct. 1907, folder 49, box 3, RCB Papers, MSRC; Pielmeier, "Roscoe Conkling Bruce," 42–46.

52. Report of the Board of Education, 1907–8, 3. Chancellor continued his special brand of troublemaking well into the 1920s. During the 1920 presidential election campaign, it was Chancellor who first spread the rumors of Warren G. Harding's black ancestry.

53. Pielmeier, "Roscoe Conkling Bruce," 46–48.

54. MCT Diary, 1908: 20–24 June; 7, 8, and 18 July; 27 and 30 Nov.; 1, 5, and 8–9 Dec., reel 1, MCT Papers, MLC.

55. Undated clipping, John W. Cromwell Sr. Scrapbook, 1889–90, folder 53, box 3, Cromwell Family Papers, MSRC; RCB to A. T. Stuart, 13 July 1909, box 4, MCT Papers, MLC. Bruce did not always back down. In October 1909 he dismissed a teacher when Richard Horner, William V. Tunnell, and Mary Church Terrell, the black board members, all opposed this action. Bruce told the board that actually all three had agreed reluctantly. Terrell, at least, was not amused. MCT Diary, 11 and 28 Oct. 1909, reel 1, MCT Papers, MLC.

56. MCT Diary, 20 July 1909, reel 1, MCT Papers, MLC; Pielmeier, "Roscoe Conkling Bruce," 53–54. In November 1910, for example, Angelina Grimké reported to her father on the ongoing saga. "I don't know anything especial going on about Roscoe Bruce. That crowd that hates him is still working against him. . . . I don't know of anything in particular though." She also criticized Du Bois for joining the mudslingers against Bruce in the pages of the *Crisis;* there was little good blood between the two men. AWG to AHG, 13 Nov. 1910, folder 62, box 3, AHG Papers, MSRC.

57. BTW to James F. Oyster, 11 Sept. 1911, in Washington, *BTW Papers* 11: 301–2; BTW to Whitefield McKinlay, 11 Sept. 1911, ibid., 303–4, 304 n; McKinlay to BTW, 14 Sept. 1911, ibid., 311.

58. Unidentified clipping, folder 101, box 4, RCB Papers, MSRC.

59. "The Washington Public School Situation," extracts from the Hearing Before the Select Committee of the United States Senate, Res. 310 [1919], folder 10, box 1, Daniel P. Murray Papers, MSRC.

60. Pielmeier, "Roscoe Conkling Bruce," 95–97.

61. Terrell, *Colored Woman in a White World,* 243; AWG to AHG, 19 June 1895, folder 66, box 4, AWG Papers, MSRC.

62. Charles M. Thomas, "A Theory of Study," 29 Mar. 1916, folder 103, box 2, James C. Wright Papers, MSRC.

63. J. C. Wright to Garnet C. Wilkinson, 12 Feb. 1917, folder 37, box 1, ibid.; Robert N. Mattingly to MCT, 26 July 1906, box 4, MCT Papers, MLC; Hundley, *Dunbar Story,* 133–35. See also MCT Diary, 23 May 1911, box 1, MCT Collection Additions, MSRC; John W. Cromwell Sr., biographical sketch of Martha B. Briggs, undated, folder 34, box 2, Cromwell Family Papers, MSRC.

64. Washington, *BTW Papers,* 5:431n; Goggin, *Carter G. Woodson,* 30.

65. Charles R. Drew to Edwin B. Henderson, 31 May 1940, folder 15, box 3, Charles R. Drew Papers, MSRC.

66. Janken, *Rayford W. Logan,* 22.

67. Student essays, Dunbar High, 1922, folder 151, box 9, AWG Papers, MSRC.

68. Frederick Douglass speech, undated typescript, folder 351, box 19, AHG Papers, MSRC.

69. Report of the Board of Education, 1906–7, 93, 102.

70. Ibid., 1914–15, 248–50.

71. Ibid., 1915–16, 249–50; Arthur Schomburg to John Wesley Cromwell Sr., 19 Mar. 1918, folder 21, box 1, Cromwell Family Papers, MSRC; Bell, "Teaching of Negro History," 123–27.

72. Quoted in Hundley, *Dunbar Story,* preface.

73. Charles M. Thomas, "Occasional Papers of the Science Department of the M Street High and Armstrong Manual Training Schools" [1901], folder 177, box 4, James C. Wright Papers, MSRC.

74. *Dunbar Observer,* 10 Dec. [1925?], ibid.

CHAPTER 6. *Howard University and Higher Education*

1. MCT to Florence M. Fitch, October 1913, box 4, MCT Papers, MLC; Oswald Garrison Villard to MCT, 13 Jan. 1914; MCT to Henry C. King, 26 Jan. 1914; King to MCT, 4 Feb. 1914, all in box 5, ibid.; Charles B. Purvis to FJG, 15 Nov. 1920, in Grimké, *Works,* 4:290.

2. Rayford W. Logan, autobiographical typescript, "Chapter IV: A Freshman at the University of Pittsburgh, 1913–1914," folder 7, box 31, Rayford W. Logan Papers, MSRC.

3. See, for example, George J. Clarke to William A. Joiner, 20 June 1905, folder 5, box 3, William A. Joiner Papers, MSRC; Charles W. Stone to RHT, 18 May 1899, box 1, RHT Papers, MLC; biographical notes, "Living Roots" folder 2, box 1, Thomas W. Turner Papers, MSRC; RCB to BKB, [8] May 1897, folder 3, box 1, RCB Papers, MSRC.

4. Logan, *Fifty Years of Progress*, 2; Wesley, *History of Alpha Phi Alpha*, 24, 40, 59.

5. Peters, Wilson, and Crump, *Story of Kappa Alpha Psi*, 2–3, 10–11.

6. Wesley, *History of Alpha Phi Alpha*, 100, 128, 140, 176; Peters et al., *Story of Kappa Alpha Psi,* 19. A 1914 edition of the fraternity's journal listed the purposes of the organization as encouraging debate and oratory, providing sanitary housing, stimulating intellectual growth when the school did not meet the needs of its African American students, teaching social graces to prepare members for leadership positions, and encouraging larger attendance at integrated colleges. See Peters et al., *Story of Kappa Alpha Psi,* 174–75.

7. Gill, *Omega Psi Phi Fraternity,* 1–3, 5–6, 8; Dreer, *Omega Psi Phi Fraternity,* 10–11.

8. *Founders, Incorporators and Past Supreme Basilei,* iii.

9. Ibid., 9, 12, 19, 33–36.

10. Giddings, *In Search of Sisterhood,* 48–49, 55–60.

11. *Howard University Record,* January 1914; Proceedings of the Second Hampton Negro Conference, 25 May 1894, in Washington, *BTW Papers,* 3:434.

12. Thomas W. Turner, typescript memoirs, 36–37, 42, 59, folder 3, box 8, Thomas W. Turner Papers, MSRC.

13. Obituary, Kelly Miller, unidentified clipping, scrapbook 5, box 1, Thomas H. R. Clarke Papers, MSRC.

14. Dyson, *Howard University,* 94, 178–81, 287–88, 291–92.

15. Duncan, "History of Howard University Library," 41–42, 72, 82, 86–90.

16. Dyson, *Howard University,* 112; Turner, typescript memoirs, 46, folder 3, box 8, Thomas W. Turner Papers, MSRC.

17. Dyson, *Howard University,* 64, 169, 391–92.

18. Typescript, "(From the Press Bureau)" [1907], folder 698, box 34, Jesse E. Moorland Papers, MSRC.

19. Harlan, *Booker T. Washington,* 177–80.

20. Dyson, *Howard University,* 413–21, 66–68, 368–75.

21. George W. Cook to Thomas W. Turner, 4 Dec. 1914, folder 16, box 16, Thomas W. Turner Papers, MSRC.

22. Winston, *Howard University Department of History,* 3, 5–9, 13, 17–18, 20–24, 26–30. See also Goggin, *Carter G. Woodson,* 48–49.

23. Biographical notes, folder 1, box 1, Thomas W. Turner Papers, MSRC.

24. Logan, *Howard University*, 187–88; Dyson, *Howard University*, 396; Charles B. Purvis to FJG, 12 June 1919, in Grimké, *Works*, 4:240–41.

25. Thomas W. Turner, typescript memoirs, 130, folder 3, box 8, Thomas W. Turner Papers, MSRC.

26. See the correspondence from 1920 to 1924 in folder 1, box 17, Thomas W. Turner Papers, MSRC; for example, Turner to Isaac R. Sherwood, 24 Aug. 1920; Turner to Gale H. Stalker [1923]; Turner to Monsignor C. F. Thomas, 23 Aug. 1920.

27. CGW to Jesse E. Moorland, 15 May 1920, folder 695, box 34, Jesse E. Moorland Papers, MSRC. For a fuller story of the dispute between Durkee and Woodson, see Goggin, *Carter G. Woodson*, 50–53.

28. Charles B. Purvis to FJG, 10 Sept. 1920, in Grimké, *Works*, 4:287.

29. Obituary, Ernest Everett Just, undated typescript, folder 1, box 1, Ernest E. Just Papers, MSRC.

30. Quoted in Davis, "Ernest Everett Just," 3.

31. Obituary, Ernest Everett Just, undated typescript, folder 1, box 1, Ernest E. Just Papers, MSRC.

CHAPTER 7. *Occupation and Enterprise*

1. Schweninger, *Black Property Owners*, 221.

2. Ibid., 217–18.

3. *Bee*, 29 Oct. 1898, 4. See also ibid., 23 June, 1906, 5; Cantwell, "Anacostia," 359; program [1916], folder 13, box 1, Simms Family Papers, MSRC.

4. Joseph A. Pierce, "The Evolution of Negro Business," in Bailey, *Black Business Enterprise*, 29–30, 32; Fitzpatrick, "'A Great Agitation,'" 60; program [1916], folder 13, box 1, Simms Family Papers, MSRC.

5. Robert Kinzer and Edward Sagarin, "Roots of the Integrationist-Separatist Dilemma," in Bailey, *Black Business Enterprise*, 52–53, 55–56; Pierce, "Evolution of Negro Business," 36.

6. *Leader*, 9 Feb. 1889, 6.

7. AFH, "Washington Men and Women of Means," paper read at Hampton Institute Conference, 1898, folder 10, box 1, AFH Papers, MSRC.

8. See, for example, *Colored American*, 6 Aug. 1898, 5.

9. *Bee*, 4 June 1898, 4.

10. *Colored American*, 19 Nov. 1898, 5; Fitzgerald, "'A Great Agitation,'" 69.

11. Program [1916], folder 13, box 1, Simms Family Papers, MSRC.

12. Ibid.; Fitzpatrick, "'A Great Agitation,'" 59.

13. Levey, "Scurlock Studio," 41–43.

14. Fitzpatrick, "'A Great Agitation,'" 61–62.

15. Harris, *Negro as Capitalist*, 104–7.
16. Unidentified clipping [1913], folder 87, box 4, AHG Papers, MSRC; RHT to T. E. Davis, 16 Sept. 1915, box 2, RHT Papers, MLC.
17. Harris, *Negro as Capitalist*, 111–15.
18. Fitzpatrick, "'A Great Agitation,'" 50, 53, 55–56, 58, 64, 71, 73.
19. See Spear, *Black Chicago*, 71–89; Drake and Cayton, *Black Metropolis*, 543; Meier, *Negro Thought in America*, 156–57; Katzman, *Before the Ghetto*, 124–34; Kusmer, *A Ghetto Takes Shape*, 190–205.
20. Undated clipping [18 July 1927], scrapbook 3, box 1, Thomas H. R. Clarke Papers, MSRC.
21. Woodson, *Negro Professional Man*, 27.
22. Kenney, *Negro in Medicine*, 7, 35. See also Washington, *BTW Papers*, 4:274n.
23. *Bee*, 12 Mar. 1898, 4.
24. *Colored American*, 2 July 1898, 4; *Bee*, 2 July 1898, 4.
25. *Colored American*, 9 July 1898, 1, 5; *Bee*, 25 June 1898, 4, and 2 July 1898, 4.
26. *Bee*, 2 July 1898, 4.
27. Kenney, *Negro in Medicine*, 20, 33–34.
28. Washington, *BTW Papers*, 9:401n. Williams retained his interest in affairs at Freedmen's and in 1908 lobbied Booker T. Washington to have one of his candidates appointed to the position of surgeon-in-chief. Among those whom Washington ultimately recommended for the position were Charles I. West, John R. Francis, and Williams himself. See Williams to Emmett J. Scott, 5 Apr. 1908, ibid., 492–93; BTW to Williams, 9 Apr. 1908, ibid., 493–94; Scott to Williams, 9 Apr. 1908, ibid., 496–97; Williams to BTW, 18 Apr. 1908, ibid., 503; BTW to James R. Garfield, Secretary of the Interior, 21 Apr. 1908, ibid., 506–7.
29. *Colored American*, 2 July 1898, 1.
30. Ibid., 14 May 1898, 4.
31. Letterhead, J. R. Francis Private Sanatorium, 2112 Pennsylvania Ave NW, 1903, folder 25, box 3, AFH Papers, MSRC; Woodson, *Negro as Professional Man*, 120–21, 124.
32. Woodson, *Negro as Professional Man*, 97, 107, 113, 103–5, 116, 124.
33. Program [1916], folder 13, box 1, Simms Family Papers, MSRC.
34. Unidentified clipping, scrapbook 4, box 1, Thomas H. R. Clarke Papers, MSRC; *Colored American*, 19 Nov. 1898, 5.
35. Woodson, *Negro as Professional Man*, 176–78, 181–83, 168–69.
36. Ibid., 149–53, 162–63.
37. *Bee*, 9 Jan. 1886, 2.

38. Ibid., 29 Nov. 1919, 3.

39. Washington, *BTW Papers,* 8:401n. See also articles on Lankford in the *Bee,* 30 June 1906, 1; 17 Nov. 1906, 1; 22 Dec. 1906, 2.

40. Washington, *BTW Papers,* 2:236–37n. See also articles on the Jamestown Exposition in the *Bee,* 14 July 1906, 5, 20: 27 Oct. 1906, 1. Pittman's father-in-law often recommended him for projects, emphasizing the racial pride that could result from saying that a black architect had designed a building that would be used by the race. He also mentioned to the contractors that Pittman was his son-in-law, but specified that "I do not want this fact to weigh in his favor or against him." BTW to Loring Wilbur Messer, 14 Feb. 1911, in Washington, *BTW Papers,* 10:586–87.

41. *Bee,* 2 July 1898, 4.

42. Washington, *BTW Papers,* 6:345n, 379n.

43. *Bee,* 4 June 1898, 4; *Colored American,* 16 Apr. 1898, 4.

44. Woodson, *Negro as Professional Man,* 190, 196. For more about James H. Smith and John F. Cook see *Bee,* 21 July 1883, 2.

45. Woodson, *Negro as Professional Man,* 198, 213, 221, 231, 236.

46. Ibid., 199, 243–44, 246–47, 224, 241, 237, 229, 326–27.

47. AWG to AHG, 16 Nov. 1908, folder 62, box 3, AHG Papers, MSRC; AHG to AWG, 21 Nov. 1908, folder 67, box 4, AWG Papers, ibid.

48. See BKB to BTW, 4 Feb. 1897 and 15 Apr. 1897, in Washington, *BTW Papers,* 4:261–62, 271.

49. Charles W. Anderson to BTW, 27 May 1907, ibid., 9:274–76. Anderson spent the next two years trying to have Murray, who published the *Horizon* jointly with Hershaw and W. E. B. Du Bois, fired from his position in the War Department. Ibid., 9:277n.

50. Ralph W. Tyler to Emmett J. Scott, 4 Jan. 1914, ibid., 12:401–3.

51. James A. Cobb to Emmett J. Scott, 10 June 1914, ibid., 13:57–58; Scott to Cobb, 13 June 1914, ibid., 62; Cobb to Scott, 16 June 1914, ibid., 65–66; Scott to Cobb, 18 June 1914, ibid., 66; BTW to Joseph Patrick Tumulty, 4 Aug. 1914, ibid., 108.

52. BTW to AFH, 6 Aug. 1914, ibid., 113–14.

53. Mrs. Samuel A. Browne to AHG, 5 July 1914, folder 86, box 4, AHG Papers, MSRC.

54. W. T. Andrews to Whitefield McKinlay, 11 May 1903, reel 1, Whitefield McKinlay Collection, CGW Papers, MLC.

55. Boyd, *A Love That Equals My Labors,* 42.

56. Hayes, "Negro Federal Government Worker," 153; memo, R. W. Woolley to Chiefs of Divisions and Employees, 16 July 1913, folder 87, box 4, AHG Papers, MSRC.

57. Hayes, "Negro Federal Worker," 38–40, 46, 51; *Boston Record,* 16 Oct. 1913.

58. Hayes, "Negro Federal Worker," 43; Rolf Cobleigh to AHG, 13 Oct. 1913, folder 89, box 4, AHG Papers, MSRC.

59. FJG to U. S. Employment Services, Department of Labor, 24 Sept. 1917, in Grimké, *Works,* 4:197–98.

60. FJG to Ormond A. Forte, 2 Sept. 1918, in Grimké, *Works,* 4:221–22.

61. Hayes, "Negro Federal Worker," 153.

62. Grimké, *Works,* 4:260n.

CHAPTER 8. *Charitable, Professional, and Fraternal Organizations*

1. *Colored American,* 3 Sept. 1898, 8.

2. Harley, "Black Women in the District of Columbia," 283–84, 293–98. For more on Burroughs, see the discussion of the social welfare activities of the Nineteenth Street Baptist Church in Chapter 4.

3. Willard B. Gatewood notes in *Aristocrats of Color,* 242, that by the end of the nineteenth century upper-class black women's clubs had shifted their focus from domestic concerns and self-culture to civic reforms and racial uplift efforts.

4. Salem, *To Better Our World,* 13–28.

5. Ibid., 91; *Bee,* 8 Oct. 1898, 4.

6. Salem, *To Better Our World,* 94–95.

7. *The Colored Social Settlement* (pamphlet), 1913–14, 3, folder 83, box 7, Cromwell Family Papers, MSRC.

8. Ibid., 5–10; Salem, *To Better Our World,* 94–95; Hutchinson, *Anna J. Cooper,* 120–21; George W. Cook, open letter [ca. 31 Dec. 1918], box 5, MCT Papers, MLC.

9. Mary E. Cromwell, "Efforts for Social Betterment in Washington, D.C.," 4, 7, 13, typescript, folder 76, box 7, Cromwell Family Papers, MSRC; Jones, *Recreation and Amusement,* 37, 40.

10. Cromwell, "Efforts for Social Betterment," 11.

11. Ibid., 11–12; Jones, *Recreation and Amusement,* 45.

12. Jones, *Recreation and Amusement,* 46–49; Associated Charities/Citizen's Relief Association Joint Annual Report for the year ending 30 Sept. 1909, 31, folder 84, box 7, Cromwell Family Papers, MSRC; Cromwell, "Efforts for Social Betterment," 12.

13. Borchert, *Alley Life in Washington,* 45–47.

14. Cromwell, "Efforts for Social Betterment," 13–15; letterhead, folder 83, box 7, Cromwell Family Papers, MSRC.

15. Associated Charities/Citizen's Relief Association Joint Annual Report, July 1902, folder 84, box 7, Cromwell Family Papers, MSRC; Cromwell, "Efforts for Social Betterment," 7, 15–16.

16. Cromwell, "Efforts for Social Betterment," 10. According to the Associated Charities' 1903–4 annual report, in actuality it was not the student who died but a child in the family he visited; but since Cromwell, an active participant in alley work, cites the story in her manuscript, it is safe to assume that the general perception was that the volunteer had died, and perhaps that story made for better propaganda. The report is in folder 84, box 7, Cromwell Family Papers, MSRC.

17. Associated Charities/Citizen's Relief Association Joint Annual Report, 1905–6, folder 84, box 7, Cromwell Family Papers, MSRC.

18. "The City and Organized Good Will," joint yearbook of Associated Charities and Citizen's Relief Association, 1913, ibid.; Reed, *Racial Adjustments*, 52.

19. Cromwell, "Efforts for Social Betterment," 8.

20. *Bee*, 15 Oct. 1898, 4.

21. Mjagkij, *Light in the Darkness*, 18, 51, 59, 65–66.

22. Ibid., 69–73; Roosevelt had also inquired as to the status of the District YMCA building in 1908. At that time he was considering reopening the Brownsville case, in which he had given dishonorable discharges to all members of a unit of black soldiers for the actions of a few in a racially motivated fight, and wanted to bring public attention to positive efforts of African Americans to soften the blow. See BTW to Theodore Roosevelt, 2 Nov. 1908, and Roosevelt to BTW, 5 Nov. 1908, in Washington, *BTW Papers*, 9:685, 686.

23. Jones, *Recreation and Amusement*, 55–56; Colored Young Christian Women's Association fifth- and sixth-year annual reports, May 1909–May 1911, 26, folder 125, box 11, Cromwell Family Papers, MSRC.

24. Jones, *Recreation and Amusement*, 57–58, 60–61.

25. Hutchinson, *Voice of the South*, 123–25.

26. Colored Young Christian Women's Association fifth- and sixth-year annual reports, May 1909–May 1911, 8, 10, 11–13, 16, folder 125, box 11, Cromwell Family Papers, MSRC.

27. *Bee*, 4 Mar. 1899, 5; 8 Apr. 1899, 4; Woodson, *Negro Professional Man*, 199. Nonetheless, the organization did participate in efforts for racial uplift, as we saw in Chapter 7.

28. Woodson, *Negro Professional Man*, 118–19.

29. Cobb, *First Negro Medical Society*, 6, 18–19.

30. Ibid., 21–26, 29, 35–36, 16.

31. Ibid., 1, 40, 42–43.

32. *Crisis* 12 (May 1916): 11; *Bee*, 29 Nov. 1919, 3; Cobb, *First Negro Medical Society*, 63.

33. *Proceedings of the Most Worshipful Grand Lodge*, 1891–99.
34. Quoted in Cass, *Negro Freemasonry and Segregation*, 69.
35. Dumenil, *Freemasonry and American Culture*, 10, 122–23.
36. *Proceedings of the Most Worshipful Grand Lodge*, 1896, 55–69. See also *Bee*, 5 Nov. 1898, 8, and 22 Nov. 1898, 8; *Colored American*, 29 Apr. 1899, 6.
37. *National Leader*, 10 Aug. 1901, clipping, box 1, RHT Papers, MLC; Samuel Hill to RHT, 31 Jan. 1917, box 2, ibid.
38. The sociologist Loretta J. Williams suggests that the black Masons were never assimilationist in outlook but took pride in the achievements of the race. In addition, the Masonic lodges were in accord with the accepted values of society as a whole and thus provided a way to insulate blacks from society without raising much opposition. See Williams, *Black Freemasonry*, 4, 9.
39. *Colored American*, 5 Nov. 1898, 6.
40. *Constitution of Free Grace Lodge*, 7–9.
41. Brooks, *History and Manual of the Grand Order of Odd Fellows*, 5.
42. Ibid., 5–6.
43. John A. Simms Sr. to George A. Carter, 3 Sept. 1902, folder 2, box 1, Simms Family Papers, MSRC; program [1916], folder 13, box 1, ibid.
44. Unidentified clipping [1914], John W. Cromwell scrapbook, 1915, folder 54, box 3, Cromwell Family Papers, MSRC.

CHAPTER 9. *Race and Racial Uplift*

1. *Colored American*, 2 Apr. 1898, 4.
2. Quoted in Thomas H. Henriksen, "African Intellectual Influences on Black Americans: The Role of Edward W. Blyden," in Burkett and Newman, *Black Apostles*, 19.
3. *New York Age*, 29 Mar. 1906, clipping in John W. Cromwell Sr. scrapbook, 1915, folder 54, box 3, Cromwell Family Papers, MSRC.
4. RHT to William A. Joiner, 16 Apr. 1895, folder 10, box 3, William A. Joiner Papers, MSRC.
5. L. Lansburgh to MCT, 13 Dec. 1915, box 5, MCT Papers, MLC; Thomas J. Calloway to BTW, 2 May 1894, in Washington, *BTW Papers*, 3:415–16.
6. Ida Gibbs Hunt to Harriet Gibbs, 1 Jan. 1898, folder 28, box 1, William H. Hunt Papers, MSRC.
7. Gatewood, *Aristocrats of Color*, 142.
8. AWG Diary, 31 July 1903, folder 248, box 15, AWG Papers, MSRC. I have inserted a period after the uncertain word "small" and capitalized the first letter of "what" in the interest of legibility.
9. *Colored American*, 11 Nov. 1898, 6. Since most black papers could not afford

to employ enough reporters to fill six pages of print, boilerplate material was common in the black press. Typically it consisted of human interest stories, tips for gardening, poems, and short works of fiction. Whether or not editors made a practice of reading this material before printing it is not clear, but the fact that stories such as this one were repeated in multiple issues suggests that few complained of their inclusion.

10. Ibid., 26 Mar. 1898, 6.

11. "Questionnaire Survey of Negro College Graduates" [1932], folder 1, box 1, AJC Papers, MSRC.

12. FJG sermon, 14 July 1895, folder 667, box 15, FJG Papers, MSRC.

13. MCT Diary, 24 March 1908, reel 1, MCT Papers, MLC.

14. Boyd, *A Love That Equals My Labors*, 18.

15. MCT to RHT, 10 June 1919, box 3, MCT Papers, MLC.

16. William H. Hunt to Ida Gibbs Hunt [8 Feb. 1904], folder 16, box 1, William H. Hunt Papers, MSRC.

17. MCT Diary, 4 Feb. 1909, reel 1, MCT Papers, MLC. See, for example, ibid., 25, 28, and 30 Jan. 1908.

18. RHT to MCT, 24 Feb. 1919, box 3, MCT Papers, MLC.

19. P. B. S. Pinchback to BKB, 25 June 1879, folder 68, box 2, BKB Papers, MSRC.

20. *Leader*, 14 Sept. 1889, 2.

21. Schweninger, *Black Property Owners*, 231–32; *Colored American*, 5 Nov. 1898, 4.

22. Charles S. Hunt to AWG, 2 Jan. 1902, folder 31, box 3, AWG Papers, MSRC.

23. AFH, "An Address on the Union League and the Industrial and Organized Status of the Colored People of the District of Columbia," April 1893, folder 4, box 1, AFH Papers, MSRC.

24. *New York Age*, 29 Mar. 1906, clipping, John Wesley Cromwell Sr. scrapbook, 1915, folder 54, box 3, Cromwell Family Papers, MSRC.

25. Charles S. Johnson, ed., *The Story of Opportunity, Journal of Negro Life* (New York: National Urban League [1922]), pamphlet in folder 51, box 3, AWG Papers, MSRC.

26. Quoted in Meier and Rudwick, *Black History*, 7.

27. See Woodson, *Mis-education of the Negro*, 1–3, 132–43.

28. Wesley, "Racial Historical Societies," 14–15, 27; Dorothy Porter Wesley, "Black Antiquarians and Bibliophiles Revisited, with a Glance at Today's Lovers of Books and Memorabilia," in Sinnette, Coates, and Battle, *Black Bibliophiles*, 5.

29. *Colored American*, 1 Jan. [possibly 3 Jan. but incorrectly dated] 1903, 1.

30. Unidentified clippings, folder 38, box 2, Cromwell Family Papers, MSRC.

See, for example, Arthur Schomburg to John W. Cromwell Sr., 19 Mar. and 18 Apr. 1918, folder 21, box 1, ibid.

31. Unidentified clipping [1916], John W. Cromwell Sr. scrapbook, 1915, folder 54, box 3, ibid.

32. Unidentified clipping [28 Dec. 1916], ibid.; Woodson, "Ten Years," 600, 605.

33. Schomburg to John W. Cromwell Sr., 23 Feb. 1915, folder 18, box 1, Cromwell Family Papers, MSRC.

34. Quoted in Meier and Rudwick, *Black History,* 9.

35. William H. Crogman to FJG, 24 Aug. 1894, in Grimké, *Works,* 4:34.

36. Moss, *American Negro Academy,* 63–67, 165–68, 290–304; unidentified clipping, folder 756, box 38, AHG Papers, MSRC.

37. Terrell, *Colored Woman in a White World,* 172–74.

38. Ibid., 160–63.

39. See correspondence, 1917–19, box 5, MCT Papers, MLC.

40. FJG to BTW, 20 Sept. 1895, in Washington, *BTW Papers,* 4:25; FJG to BTW, 7 Nov. 1895, ibid., 74.

41. *Bee,* 2 Nov. 1895, 4; Edward E. Cooper to BTW, 2 Nov. 1895, in Washington, *BTW Papers,* 4:69–70.

42. See Timothy Thomas Fortune to BTW, 2 Mar. 1899, and BTW to Fortune, 7 Mar. 1899, ibid., 5:48–49, 52–53.

43. AHG to BTW, 6 June 1903, and Louis G. Gregory to BTW, 15 Jan. 1904, ibid., 7:170–71, 391–92.

44. Press release [ca. 8 Aug. 1903], in Washington, *BTW Papers,* 7:258. Angelina Grimké gives an excellent eyewitness account of events; see AWG Diary, 31 July 1903, folder 248, box 15, AWG Papers, MSRC.

45. See BTW to Hollis Burke Frissell, 3 Nov. 1903, in Washington, *BTW Papers,* 7:325–26.

46. BTW to FJG, 5 Dec. 1903; FJG to BTW, 9 Dec. 1903; BTW to Whitefield McKinlay, 2 Jan. 1904; RHT to BTW, 31 Jan. 1904, ibid., 359, 363, 383–84, 390n, 420–21.

47. Washington was addressing the Metropolitan AME Church. His speech may be found ibid., 468–76.

48. See BTW to AHG, 8 July 1904, and AHG to BTW, 13 July 1904, ibid., 8:9, 16–17.

49. W. E. B. Du Bois to AHG and Kelly Miller, 21 Mar. 1905, folder 91, box 4, AHG Papers, MSRC.

50. BTW to Charles W. Anderson, 26 Sept. 1904, in Washington, *BTW Papers,* 8:74–75. See, for example, Edward E. Cooper to RHT, 11 Aug. 1904, box 1, RHT Papers, MLC.

51. See Du Bois to William Hayes Ward, 10 Mar. 1905, in Du Bois, *Correspondence,* 96; Du Bois to Oswald Garrison Villard, 24 Mar. 1905, in Washington, *BTW Papers,* 8:224–42.

52. Thurber, *Negro at the Nation's Capital,* 10–49.

53. Ibid., 62–65; Ralph W. Tyler to BTW, 6 Jan. 1914, in Washington, *BTW Papers,* 12:404–5.

54. Charles W. Anderson to BTW, 6 Mar. and 3 Apr. 1906, in Washington, *BTW Papers,* 8:539–40, 560–61. Anderson said that his relationship with P. B. S. Pinchback had become strained because the Terrells had told Pinchback that Anderson had been in the District without contacting him. Washington advised Anderson to be sensitive to Pinchback's feelings, and stated that he would be more careful with the Terrells. See BTW to Anderson, 10 Apr. 1906, ibid., 8:574–75.

55. Anderson to BTW, 25 Feb. 1907, ibid., 9:223–25.

56. BTW to RHT, 27 Apr. 1910, ibid., 10:323. See BTW to Emmett J. Scott, 12 Dec. 1910, ibid., 504–5.

57. "An Admirer" to BTW, 15 Apr. 1911, ibid., 11:103.

58. J. G. Schmidlapp to MCT, 9 Apr. and 26 Dec. 1917, box 5, MCT Papers, MLC. With a true sense of noblesse oblige Schmidlapp also talked about the severe weather and how his tenants had particularly suffered when the gas ran out and they had no heat. "Whenever it gets cold I always feel more for them than I do for myself."

59. Ida Husted Harper to Elizabeth C. Carter, 18 Mar. 1919, ibid.

60. Thurber, *Negro at the Nation's Capital,* 90–91, 118.

61. House Resolution 948, 62d Cong., 1st sess.; House Resolution 1486, 62d Cong., 3d sess.; House Resolution 1710, 62d Cong., 2d sess.

62. MCT Diary, 18–19 Jan. 1915, reel 1, MCT Papers, MLC; petition, Jan. 1915, box 5, ibid.

63. Thurber, *Negro at the Nation's Capital,* 118.

64. See, for example *Bee,* 26 Mar. 1898, 2; 9 Apr. 1898, 4; 4 June 1898, 2; *Colored American,* 4 June 1898, 6; William C. Harris, "Blanche K. Bruce of Mississippi: Conservative Assimilationist," in Rabinowitz, *Southern Black Leaders,* 33.

65. *Bee,* 9 Apr. 1898, 4; Washington, *BTW Papers,* 4:447n.

66. See, for example, *Colored American,* March–April 1898, and *Bee,* March–April 1898. The *Bee* was more critical of the Spanish-American War at first but ultimately supported the efforts of the black troops.

67. Kennedy, *Over Here,* 160–63, 177.

68. U.S. Army certificate of honorable discharge issued to Napoleon B. Marshall, 16 May 1919, folder 54, box 2, Washington Conservatory of Music Records, MSRC.

69. Kennedy, *Over Here,* 199–200.

Notes to Pages 210–12 ▪ 239

70. Louis R. Mehlinger to FJG, 19 Nov. 1918, in Grimké, *Works*, 4:228, 230.

71. Ibid., 228–30.

72. Janken, *Rayford W. Logan*, 36.

73. Unidentified clipping [1917], folder 54, box 3, Cromwell Family Papers, MSRC; FJG to Joseph H. Odell, 13 Apr. 1918, in Grimké, *Works*, 4:213.

74. William H. Crogman Sr. to FJG, 20 Aug. 1919, in Grimké, *Works*, 4:246–47.

75. Charles B. Purvis to FJG, 17 Aug. 1919 and 20 Jan. 1920, ibid., 243–45, 268–70.

76. Thurber, *Negro at the Nation's Capital*, 291–93.

77. Arthur A. Schomburg to John W. Cromwell, 28 July 1919, folder 23, box 1, Cromwell Family Papers, MSRC.

78. Charles B. Purvis to FJG, 17 Aug. 1919, in Grimké, *Works*, 4:244–45.

79. William H. Crogman Sr. to FJG, 20 Aug. 1919, ibid., 246; FJG sermon, "The Race Problem as It Respects the Colored People and the Christian Church, in the Light of the Developments of the Last Year," 27 Nov. 1919, ibid., 1:606–8. In 1906 Francis J. Garrison, son of the famous abolitionist, had praised Grimké for his attempt to dissociate those blacks who had participated in the Atlanta riot from more law-abiding blacks, but he criticized Grimké's sermon, which advised African Americans to arm themselves in self-defense, with rifles if necessary. See Garrison to FJG, 6 Nov. 1906, ibid., 102.

80. Thurber, *Negro at the Nation's Capital*, 320.

BIBLIOGRAPHY

Manuscript Collections and Documents

Bruce, Blanche K., Papers. Manuscript Division, Moorland-Spingarn Research Center, Howard University, Washington, D.C. (MSRC).
Bruce, John E. "Washington's Colored Society." [1877.] John E. Bruce Papers, Schomburg Center for Research in Black Culture, New York Public Library.
Bruce, Roscoe Conkling, Sr., Papers. MSRC.
Cary, Mary Ann Shadd, Papers. MSRC.
Clarke, Thomas H. R., Papers. MSRC.
Colored Young Christian Women's Association. Fifth- and sixth-year annual reports, May 1909–May 1911. N.d., n.p.
Cooper, Anna J., Papers. MSRC.
Cromwell Family Papers. MSRC.
Drew, Charles R., Papers. MSRC.
Grimké, Angelina Weld, Papers. MSRC.
Grimké, Archibald H., Papers. MSRC.
Grimké, Francis J., Papers. MSRC.
Hilyer, Andrew F., Papers. MSRC.
Hunt, William H., Papers. MSRC.
Joiner, William A., Papers. MSRC.
Just, Ernest E., Papers. MSRC.
Logan, Rayford W., Papers. MSRC.
McKinlay, Whitefield, Collection. In Carter G. Woodson Papers, Manuscript Division, Library of Congress, Washington, D.C. (MLC).
Moorland, Jesse E., Papers. MSRC.
Murray, Daniel, Collection. MSRC.
Records of the Fifteenth Street Presbyterian Church. MSRC.
Records of the Metropolitan AME Church. MSRC.
Simms Family Papers. MSRC.
Terrell, Mary Church, Papers. MLC.
Terrell, Mary Church, Collection Additions. MSRC.
Terrell, Robert H., Papers. MLC.

Turner, Thomas W., Papers. MSRC.
Washington Conservatory of Music Records. MSRC.
Wright, James C., Papers. MSRC.

Newspapers and Periodicals

AME Church Review, 1963
Bee (Washington, D.C.), 1880–1920
The Citizen (Washington, D.C.), 1909
Colored American (Washington, D.C.), 1894–1904
Dunbar Observer (Washington, D.C.), 1925
Evening Star (Washington, D.C.), 1906
Howard University Record, 1914
National Leader (Washington, D.C.), 1888–89
New York Age, 1906
Opportunity, 1927
Washington Post, 1906

Published Works

Allen, Walter R. "The Search for Applicable Theories of Black Family Life." *Journal of Marriage and the Family* 40 (February 1978): 117–29.
Angell, Stephen Ward. *Bishop Henry McNeal Turner and African-American Religion in the South.* Knoxville, Tenn., 1992.
Baer, Hans A., and Merrill Singer. *African-American Religion in the Twentieth Century: Varieties of Protest and Accommodation.* Knoxville, Tenn., 1992.
Bailey, Ronald W., ed. *Black Business Enterprise: Historical and Contemporary Perspectives.* New York and London, 1971.
Bell, J. W. "The Teaching of Negro History." *Journal of Negro History* 8 (April 1923): 123–27.
Bernard, Jessie. *Marriage and Family Among Negroes.* Englewood Cliffs, N.J., 1966.
Billingsley, Andrew. *Climbing Jacob's Ladder: The Enduring Legacy of African-American Families.* New York, 1992.
Borchert, James. *Alley Life in Washington: Family, Community, Religion, and Folklife in the City, 1850–1970.* Urbana, Ill., 1980.
Boyd, Norma E. *A Love That Equals My Labors: The Life Story of Norma E. Boyd.* [Washington, D.C.], 1980.
Brooks, Charles H. *A History and Manual of the Grand Order of Odd Fellows in America.* Philadelphia, 1893.

Bruce, Dickson D., Jr. *Archibald Grimké: A Portrait of a Black Independent*. Baton Rouge and London, 1993.
Burkett, Randall K., and Richard Newman, eds. *Black Apostles: Afro-American Clergy Confront the Twentieth Century*. Boston, 1978.
Cantwell, Thomas J. "Anacostia: Strength in Adversity." *Records of the Columbia Historical Society* 73–74 (1976): 330–70.
Carnes, Mark C. *Secret Ritual and Manhood in Victorian America*. New Haven and London, 1989.
Cass, Donn A. *Negro Freemasonry and Segregation: An Historical Study of Prejudice Against American Negroes as Freemasons, and the Position of Negro Freemasonry in the Masonic Fraternity*. Chicago, 1957.
Clarke, Nina Honemond. *History of the Nineteenth-Century Black Churches in Maryland and Washington, D.C.* New York, 1983.
Cobb, William Montague. *The First Negro Medical Society: A History of the Medico-Chirurgical Society of the District of Columbia, 1884–1939*. Washington, D.C., 1939.
Constitution of Free Grace Lodge, No. 1343, of the G.U.O. of O.F. Washington, D.C., 1891.
Dabney, Lillian Gertrude. *The History of Schools for Negroes in the District of Columbia: 1807–1947*. Washington, D.C., 1949.
Cromwell, John Wesley, Sr. *History of the Bethel Literary and Historical Association*. Washington, D.C., 1896.
Davis, Arthur J. *'The Missing Link' and the Howard Theatre*. Washington, D.C., 1911.
Davis, Arthur P. "Ernest Everett Just (1883–1941)." *Profiles* 1 (May 1979): 1–8.
Drake, St. Clair, and Horace Cayton. *Black Metropolis: A Study of Negro Life in a Northern City*. New York, 1945.
Dreer, Herman. *The Omega Psi Phi Fraternity: A Brotherhood of Negro College Men, 1911–1939*. 1940.
Du Bois, W. E. B. *The Correspondence of W. E. B. Du Bois*. Edited by Herbert Aptheker. 3 vols. Amherst, Mass., 1973–78.
———. *Writings by W. E. B. Du Bois in Non-Periodical Literature Edited by Others*. Edited by Herbert Aptheker. New York, 1982.
Dumenil, Lynn. *Freemasonry and American Culture: 1880–1930*. Princeton, 1984.
Dunbar, Paul Laurence. "Negro Life in Washington." In *Black Literature: Essays*, ed. Darwin T. Turner. Columbus, Ohio, 1969.
Dyson, Walter. *Howard University, the Capstone of Negro Education, a History: 1867–1940*. Washington, D.C., 1941.
Fitzpatrick, Michael Andrew. "'A Great Agitation for Business': Black Economic Development in Shaw." *Washington History* 2 (Fall/Winter 1990–91): 48–73.

Founders, Incorporators and Past Supreme Basilei. Heritage Series no. 6. [Washington, D.C.], 1976.

Frazier, E. Franklin. *Black Bourgeoisie: The Rise of a New Middle Class.* New York, 1957.

———. *The Negro Family in the United States.* Chicago, 1939.

Gabel, Leona C. *From Slavery to the Sorbonne and Beyond: The Life and Writings of Anna J. Cooper.* Northampton, Mass., 1982.

Gatewood, Willard B. *Aristocrats of Color: The Black Elite, 1880–1920.* Bloomington and Indianapolis, 1990.

Giddings, Paula. *In Search of Sisterhood: Delta Sigma Theta and the Challenge of the Black Sorority Movement.* New York, 1988.

Gill, Robert L. *The Omega Psi Phi Fraternity and the Men Who Made Its History: A Concise History.* 1963.

Goggin, Jacqueline. *Carter G. Woodson: A Life in Black History.* Baton Rouge and London, 1993.

Green, Constance McLaughlin. *The Secret City: A History of Race Relations in the Nation's Capital.* Princeton, 1967.

Grimké, Francis J. *A Look Backward over a Pastorate of More than Forty-two Years over the Fifteenth Street Presbyterian Church, Washington, D.C.* Sermon delivered 14 Oct. 1923. N.p. Moorland-Spingarn Collection, Howard University.

———. *The Works of Francis J. Grimké.* Edited by Carter G. Woodson. 4 vols. Washington, D.C., 1942.

Handy, Robert T., ed. *The Social Gospel in America: 1870–1920.* New York, 1966.

Harlan, Louis R. *Booker T. Washington: The Wizard of Tuskegee, 1901–1915.* New York and Oxford, 1983.

Harris, Abram L. *The Negro as Capitalist: A Study of Banking and Business Among American Negroes.* Philadelphia, 1936.

Higginbotham, Evelyn Brooks. *Righteous Discontent: The Women's Movement in the Black Baptist Church, 1880–1920.* Cambridge, Mass., and London, 1993.

Hine, Darlene Clark, ed. *Black Women in America.* 2 vols. Brooklyn, 1993.

Hughes, Langston. "Our Wonderful Society, Washington." *Opportunity* 5 (August, 1927): 226–27.

Hundley, Mary G. *The Dunbar Story, 1870–1955.* New York, 1965.

Hutchinson, Louise Daniel. *Anna J. Cooper, a Voice from the South.* Washington, D.C., 1981.

Ione, Carole. *Pride of Family: Four Generations of American Women of Color.* New York, 1991.

Janken, Kenneth Robert. *Rayford W. Logan and the Dilemma of the African-American Intellectual.* Amherst, Mass., 1993.

Johnson, Charles S., ed. *The Story of Opportunity, Journal of Negro Life*. New York, [1922].
Johnson, Clifton H. "Mary Ann Shadd: Crusader for the Freedom of Man." *Crisis* 78 (April–May 1971): 89–90.
Jones, Beverly Washington. *Quest for Equality: The Life and Writings of Mary Eliza Church Terrell, 1863–1954*. Brooklyn, 1990.
Jones, William H. *Recreation and Amusement Among Negroes in Washington, D.C.: A Sociological Analysis of the Negro in an Urban Environment*. [1927.] Westport, Conn., 1970.
Katzman, David M. *Before the Ghetto: Black Detroit in the Nineteenth Century*. Urbana, Ill., 1973.
Kennedy, David M. *Over Here: The First World War and American Society*. Oxford and New York, 1980.
Kenney, John A. *The Negro in Medicine*. [1912.] Ann Arbor, 1973.
Kusmer, Kenneth L. *A Ghetto Takes Shape: Black Cleveland, 1870–1930*. Urbana, Ill., 1976.
Levey, Jane Freundel. "The Scurlock Studio." *Washington History* 1 (Spring 1989): 41–57.
Lewis, David Levering. *W. E. B. Du Bois: Biography of a Race, 1868–1919*. New York, 1993.
Logan, Rayford W. *Fifty Years of Progress in Greek Letter Societies*. Pittsburgh, 1950.
———. *Howard University: The First Hundred Years, 1867–1967*. New York, 1969.
Mays, Benjamin E., and Joseph W. Nicholson. *The Negro's Church*. [1933.] New York, 1969.
Meier, August. *Negro Thought in America, 1880–1915*. Ann Arbor, 1963.
Meier, August, and Elliott Rudwick. *Black History and the Historical Profession, 1915–1980*. Urbana, Ill., 1986.
Mintz, Steven, and Susan Kellogg. *Domestic Revolutions: A Social History of American Family Life*. New York, 1988.
Mjagkij, Nina. *Light in the Darkness: African Americans and the YMCA, 1852–1946*. [Lexington, Ky.], 1994.
Montgomery, William E. *Under Their Own Vine and Fig Tree: The African-American Church in the South, 1865–1900*. Baton Rouge and London, 1993.
Moss, Alfred A., Jr. *The American Negro Academy: The Voice of the Talented Tenth*. Baton Rouge and London, 1981.
Muraskin, William A. *Middle-Class Blacks in a White Society: Prince Hall Freemasonry in America*. Berkeley and Los Angeles, 1975.

Nelsen, Hart M., Raytha L. Yokley, and Anne K. Nelsen, eds. *The Black Church in America.* New York and London, 1971.

Null, Druscilla J. "Myrtilla Miner's 'School for Colored Girls.'" *Records of the Columbia Historical Society* n.s.52 (1989): 254–68.

Peters, J. Jerome, C. Rodger Wilson, and William L. Crump. *The Story of Kappa Alpha Psi: A History of the Beginning and Development of a College Greek Letter Organization, 1911–1961.* Philadelphia, 1967.

Proceedings of the Most Worshipful Grand Lodge of Free and Accepted Masons for the District of Columbia. Washington, D.C., 1891–99.

Rabinowitz, Howard N., ed. *Southern Black Leaders of the Reconstruction Era.* Urbana, Ill., 1982.

Reed, John H. *Racial Adjustments in the Methodist Episcopal Church.* New York, 1914.

Roberts, J. Deotis. *Roots of a Black Future: Family and Church.* Philadelphia, 1980.

Robinson, Henry S. "The M Street High School, 1891–1916." *Records of the Columbia Historical Society* n.s.51 (1984): 119–43.

Salem, Dorothy. *To Better Our World: Black Women in Organized Reform, 1890–1920.* Brooklyn, 1990.

Schweninger, Loren. *Black Property Owners in the South: 1790–1915.* Urbana, Ill., 1990.

Sernett, Milton C., ed. *Afro-American Religious History: A Documentary Witness.* Durham, N.C., 1985.

Severson, William H. *History of Felix Lodge No. 3, F.A.A.M., or Freemasonry in the District of Columbia from 1825–1908.* Washington, D.C., 1908.

Sinnette, Elinor Des Verney, W. Paul Coates, and Thomas C. Battle, eds. *Black Bibliophiles and Collectors: Preservers of Black History.* Washington, D.C., 1990.

Sluby, Paul E., Sr., ed. *Sessional Minutes of the Fifteenth Street Presbyterian Church (First Colored Presbyterian Church).* 3 vols. Washington, D.C., 1981.

Smith, Jessie Carney, ed. *Notable Black American Women.* Detroit, London, 1992.

Smythe, Mabel M., ed. *Black American Reference Book.* Englewood Cliffs, N.J., 1976.

Spear, Allan H. *Black Chicago: The Making of a Negro Ghetto, 1890–1920.* Chicago and London, 1967.

Terrell, Mary Church. *A Colored Woman in a White World.* [1940.] Washington, D.C., 1968.

———. "History of the High School for Negroes in Washington." *Journal of Negro History* 2 (July 1917): 252–56.

———. "Society Among the Colored People of Washington." *Voice of the Negro* 1 (April 1904): 150–56.

Thurber, Bert Henry. *The Negro at the Nation's Capital, 1913–1921.* Ann Arbor, 1973.
U.S. Congress. *Annual Report of the Commissioners of the District of Columbia.* Washington, D.C., 1880–1920.
U.S. Congress. House. *Historical Sketch of Education for the Colored Race in the District of Columbia, 1807–1905.* Report prepared by William S. Montgomery. 59th Cong., 1st sess., 1906. H. Doc. 8.
———. 62d Cong., 1st sess., H.R. 948.
———. 62d Cong., 2d sess., H.R. 1710.
———. 62d Cong., 3d sess., H.R. 1486.
Washington, Booker T. *The Booker T. Washington Papers.* Edited by Louis R. Harlan and Raymond W. Smock. 14 vols. Urbana, Ill., 1972–1987.
Wesley, Charles H. *The History of Alpha Phi Alpha: A Development in Negro College Life.* Washington, D.C., 1939.
———. "Racial Historical Societies and the American Heritage." *Journal of Negro History* 37 (January 1952): 11–35.
Williams, Loretta J. *Black Freemasonry and Middle-Class Realities.* Columbia, Mo., and London, 1980.
Wills, David D., and Richard Newman, eds. *Black Apostles at Home and Abroad: Afro-Americans and the Christian Mission from the Revolution to Reconstruction.* Boston, 1982.
Winston, Michael R. *The Howard University Department of History: 1913–1973.* Washington, D.C., 1973.
Woodson, Carter G. *The History of the Negro Church.* 2d ed. Washington, D.C., 1945.
———. *The Mis-education of the Negro.* [1933.] Trenton, N.J., 1990.
———. *The Negro Professional Man and the Community, with Special Emphasis on the Physician and the Lawyer.* [1934.] New York, 1969.
———. "Ten Years of Collecting and Publishing the Records of the Negro." *Journal of Negro History* 10 (October 1925): 598–606.

Unpublished Works

Duncan, Anne McKay. "History of Howard University Library, 1867–1921." Master's thesis, Department of Library Science, Catholic University, 1951.
Harley, Sharon. "Black Women in the District of Columbia, 1890–1920: Their Economic, Social and Institutional Activities." Ph.D. diss., Howard University, 1981.
Hayes, Laurence John Wesley. "The Negro Federal Government Worker: A Study

of His Classification Status in the District of Columbia, 1881–1938." Master's thesis, Howard University, 1941.

Pielmeier, Douglas E. "Bruce and the District of Columbia's Public Schools, 1906 to 1921." Master's thesis, Department of History, University of Maryland, College Park, 1992.

Film

The Howard Theater District. Film shown at the Annual Meeting of the Organization of American Historians, Washington, D.C., Spring 1991.

INDEX

Alley Improvement Association, 169–70
alleys, 168, 169–70
Alpha Kappa Alpha, 117–18
Alpha Phi Alpha, 115, 116
American Baptist Home Mission Society, 71–72
American Negro Academy, 195–97
Anderson, Charles W., 56, 154, 204, 238 n. 54
architects, 148
Armstrong Manual Training School, 93–94, 118, 225 n. 18
assimilation, belief in, 3, 5, 31, 153, 188, 198, 213
Associated Charities, 170, 171
Association for the Study of Negro Life and History, 127, 129, 195
Atwood, Oliver M., 98
Augusta, Alexander T., 177

Bachelor's Club, 62
Baha'i movement, 83–84
Ballou, F. W., 107
banks, 137–39
bar association, 150, 151, 176–77
Bethel Literary and Historical Association, 16, 19–20, 66–69, 162, 194, 198
black history, 66–68, 110, 126–27, 193–95
board of education, 22, 91, 93, 96, 97–98, 99–100, 104–6, 107–8
"Boston Riot" (1903), 199–200
Bowen, Amanda R., 163, 166

Bowen, Anthony, 172
Boyd, Norma, 39, 82, 190
Briggs, Martha B., 109
Brooks, Charles H., 183
Brooks, Julia Evangeline, 118
Brooks, Walter H., 21, 71–73, 97, 170
Brown, Albertus, 140
Brown, Hallie Q., 162
Brown, Mary J., 143
Brown, Sterling N., 19, 97
Browne, Hugh M., 93, 108
Bruce, Blanche K., 12, 30, 158, 180, 207; family relationships, 37, 39, 45, 48; and racial uplift, 153, 192; and religion, 82–83
Bruce, Henry C., 37
Bruce, John E., 9–10, 188
Bruce, Josephine Willson, 12; family relationships, 39, 45, 48; reform activity of, 164, 165; and religion, 82–83; and school appointments, 91; and skin color of, 189
Bruce, Roscoe Conkling, 12, 92, 113, 181; career of, 99, 103, 104–8, 226 n. 34, 227 n. 55, 227 n. 56; family relationships, 39, 45, 48, 49, 114; and racial uplift, 34, 103–4, 110, 154, 202, 203–4
Bruce, William H., 14, 29
Bruce family, 12, 37, 39, 45
Burrill, Mary P., 64
Burroughs, Nannie Helen, 5, 30–31, 80–81, 92, 164

249

business enterprise: black capitalism, 58–60, 135–36, 139, 147; evolution of, 24–25, 134–39; impact of segregation on, 135; and racial uplift, 132; and white patronage, 24–25

Cabaniss, George W., 181
Calloway, Thomas J., 149, 154
Capital Savings Bank, 137–38
Cardozo family, 12
Carnegie Hall Conference of 1904, 200
Cary, Mary Ann Shadd, 11, 21, 162, 165
Chamberlain, John, 24–25
Chancellor, William E., 98, 100, 102–3, 104, 226 n. 34, 227 n. 52
charity. *See* social welfare
Chase, William Calvin, 98, 100–101, 104, 133, 136, 149, 176, 181, 199, 202
Chisum, Melvin Jack, 100–101
Church, Anna, 43
Church, Annette, 43
Church, Robert R., 11, 37, 40, 43, 116
Church, Robert R., Jr., 43
Church family, 37, 43, 56
churches: denominational loyalty, 82–84; discrimination in, 71, 81–82; forming elite congregations, 16–21, 70–71; financial difficulties among, 78–79; and fundamentalism, 81–82; and racial uplift, 73–75; and recreation, 60–61; secularization and response of, 75–82, 84, 223–24 n. 29; and separatism, 71–73; social welfare of, 76–78, 79–81
Clarke, Thomas H. R., 84, 203
Clifford, Carrie, 202
clubs: art, 63–64; literary, 15–16, 65–69; musical, 15, 64–65; social, 14–15, 62–63. *See also* Bethel Literary and Historical Association
clubwomen, 76, 80–81, 161–65, 233 n. 3
Cobb, James Adlai, 98–99, 149, 155, 207
Cobb, William Montague, 109, 178, 181
Colored American, 201, 236 n. 9

Colored Druggist's Association, 147–48, 179
Colored Social Settlement, 166–67
Colored Woman's League, 165
Committee of Twelve, 200–201
Cook, Charles C., 126
Cook, Coralie Franklin, 64, 84, 125
Cook, Elizabeth Appo, 126
Cook, George F. T., 11, 14, 22, 88, 91, 134
Cook, George W., 11, 84, 119, 124–25, 167, 168, 180, 203, 207
Cook, Helen Appo, 163, 165
Cook, John F., 11, 14, 21, 29, 73, 183
Cook, John F., Jr., 11, 98, 150
Cook, Samuel LeCount, 11
Cook family, 11
Cooper, Anna J., 29, 54, 82, 161, 190; and M Street controversy, 93, 95–97, 99–102, 107–8, 226 n. 43
Cooper, Edward E., 18, 154, 181, 199, 201
Cosmos Club, 62–63
Craig, Arthur U., 109
Crogman, William H., 195, 211, 212
Cromwell, John Wesley, 15, 36, 110, 121, 194, 196, 201, 212
Cromwell, John Wesley, Jr., 36–37
Cromwell, Mary E., 36, 37, 167, 168, 170, 173, 174, 234 n. 16
Cromwell, Otelia, 36, 113
Cromwell family, 36–37
Crummell, Alexander, 10, 16, 18, 180, 188, 195, 207
Curtis, Austin M., 141–43
Curtis, Naomi, 206

Dabney, James H., 134
Davis, Benjamin O., 92
Delta Sigma Theta, 118
dentists, 146, 178–79
divorce, 42–43
Douglass, Charles, 12, 30, 41–42

Douglass, Frederick D., 12, 30, 41–42, 81, 82, 109, 180, 207
Douglass, Helen, 30, 41–42
Douglass, Lewis H., 12, 30, 41–42, 66, 138
Douglass family, 12, 30, 41–42
Drew, Charles R., 109
Du Bois, W. E. B.: as president of American Negro Academy, 196; in black history, 194; and business support, 135–36; and conflict with Booker T. Washington, 68, 87, 91–92, 94, 95, 98–99, 122–24, 198–202, 232 n. 49
Dunbar, Alice M., 82
Dunbar, Paul Laurence, 188, 193
Dunbar High School, 89, 109, 111. *See also* M Street High School; Preparatory High School
Durkee, James Stanley, 128–30
Dyson, Walter H., 127, 181

education. *See* board of education; higher education; public schools; teachers
Elks, 182
employment. *See* occupation
etiquette, 12–13, 16–18, 52, 56–57
Europe, Mary L., 108–9
Evans, William Bruce, 62, 68, 73, 93–94, 102, 104, 226 n. 44
Evening Star, 100

family: and child rearing, 43–47; closeness of, 37–38; defense against discrimination of, 34, 48–49; educational strategies of, 47–49; extended, 37–38, 42, 43; as promoting racial uplift, 33–34, 37; social distinctions of, 35–37. *See also* marriage
Fernandis, Sarah Collins, 166
Fifteenth Street Presbyterian Church, 16, 17–18, 73–75, 76–77, 78
Flagg, Margaret, 117
Fleetwood, Christian A., 134
Fleetwood, Sara Iredell, 165
Fort Des Moines, 116, 209
Francis, Bettie Cox, 164, 174
Francis, John R., 124, 141, 145, 146, 177–78, 231 n. 28
Francis family, 11
fraternal organizations, 27–29, 150, 179–84, 218 n. 52. *See also* Elks; Masons; Odd Fellows
fraternities, 114–17
Freedmen's Hospital, 140–44
Freeman, Daniel, 63, 137
Frisby, Perri W., 4–5, 176

Garnet, Henry Highland, 73
Gibson, Mary Syphax, 104
government employment, 10, 26–27; discrimination against, 19, 156–58, 203; and patronage, 152–55; protest of treatment of, 157–59; and racial uplift, 132
Gray, Amanda, 147
Gray, Arthur S., 147
Gray family, 11
Greener, Richard T., 10, 30
Gregory, Louis G., 84, 199
Grimké, Angelina Weld, 11, 152; at "Boston Riot," 199–200; family relationships, 37–38, 41, 45–47, 48; as poet, 192–93; racial solidarity, 33–34; on skin color, 189; social activity of, 56; as teacher, 93, 102, 109, 226 n. 44, 227 n. 56; and temperance, 223 n. 16
Grimké, Archibald H., 11, 113, 149; and American Negro Academy, 196–97; on appearances, 13; family relationships, 37–38, 40–41, 45–47, 48, 106; and government appointments, 152, 156; and NAACP, 203; on riots and World War I, 212; social activities of, 54; and Washington–Du Bois conflict, 199–201
Grimké, Charlotte Forten, 11, 38, 46

Grimké, Francis J., 11, 83; American Negro Academy, 196; and Anna J. Cooper controversy, 97, 100; as board member of Howard University, 124; family relationships, 38, 46; and government appointments, 10; intellectual background of, 73–74; on interracial marriage, 30, 41; on morality, 17, 74; and NAACP, 203; on passing, 190; on patriotism, 210–11; protests segregation, 157; on racism, 74–75, 222 n. 9; on riots, 212, 239 n. 79; social activities of, 54; and social reform, 76–77, 78; on violence, 74–75, 239 n. 79; and Washington–Du Bois conflict, 198, 200, 201
Grimké, Sarah Stanley, 37–38, 40–41, 46
Grimké family, 11, 37, 40–41, 45–47

Harris, H. C., 26
Henderson, Edwin B., 109
Hershaw, Lafayette M., 149, 154, 158, 202, 203, 232 n. 39
Hewlett, Emmanuel M., 149, 150, 176, 181
higher education: costs of, 114; faculty experiences in, 121–22, 128–31; Greek organizations and, 114–18; segregation in, 113–14; student experiences of, 113–19; value of, 112–13. *See also* Howard University
Hilyer, Andrew F., 64–65, 155, 193
Hilyer, Mamie F., 64–65, 206
Holland, Milton M., 135
Horner, Richard R., 106, 227 n. 55
hotels, 24–25, 136
Houston, Charles, 93, 208
Howard Theater, 59
Howard University: advantages of, 118; curriculum struggles at, 23, 122–25; faculty and racial uplift at, 125–27; faculty recognition at, 121–22, 128–31; funding at, 121–22; graduate program at, 120–21; Greek organizations at, 115–18; improvement of, 119–21, 126–28; industrial education at, 122, 125; organization of, 119–20; role in community, 23, 134; student experience at, 116–19
Hughes, Percy M., 95–96, 99, 102
Hunt, Ida Gibbs, 189
Hunt, William Henry, 154, 191

Industrial Savings Bank, 139
institution building: in business enterprise, 135–39, 145–46; in churches, 70–73; fear of, 31; hospitals and, 144–45; necessity of, 61; and nonconfrontation, 192; organizational, 171–75, 176–79, 184–86, 213–14; in social activities, 69
insurance companies, 134–35
interracial marriage, 30, 40–42, 189–90, 206–7

Jackson, William T. S., 100, 102, 181
Jenifer family, 56–57
Johnson, Jerome A., 172, 176
Joiner, William A., 181, 188–89
Just, Ernest Everett, 130–31

Kappa Alpha Psi, 115, 116, 229 n. 6

Langston, John Mercer, 180, 207
Lankford, John Anderson, 133, 148
Lawson, Jesse, 68, 149, 154
Lawson, Rosetta, 56, 170, 207
lawyers, 25, 148–51
Lewis, Carole, 42
Lewis, Hylan Garnet, 38, 42
Lewis, John Whitelaw, 136, 137, 139, 208
Locke, Alain, 127, 197
Lofton, William S., 146
Logan, Rayford W., 92, 109, 114, 210
Lotus Club, 14
Love, John L., Jr., 97, 99
Lynch, John R., 134, 149

M Street High School: Anna J. Cooper controversy, 95–97, 99–102, 226 n. 43; discipline problems, 97; objective conditions, 89; quality of education, 92–93; racial uplift, 109, 111; scheduling problems, 89–90; teaching appointments, 93–95. *See also* Dunbar High School; Preparatory High School

marriage, 38–42. *See also* divorce; interracial marriage

Marshall, Harriet Gibbs, 64, 84, 209

Marshall, Napoleon B., 209

Masons, 28–29, 180–82, 235 n. 38

Matthews, William E., 134

Mattingly, Robert N., 108

McKinlay, Whitefield, 68, 134, 152, 154, 207

McKinlay family, 12

Medical Society of D.C., 177–78

Medico-Chirurgical Society, 31, 178, 179, 218 n. 62

Mehlinger, Louis R., 209–10

Menard family, 12

Meriwether, James H., 73, 117–18

Meriwether, Sarah, 117–18

Merritt, Emma F. G., 163, 173, 174

Metropolitan AME Church, 17–18, 20, 66, 77–79, 237 n. 47. *See also* Union Bethel AME Church

Miller, Kelly, 64, 69, 119, 123, 124, 127, 196, 199, 200, 207

ministers, 17, 25–26, 76

Monday Night Literary Society, 15

Monocan Club, 62–63

Montgomery, Winfield Scott, 92, 96, 99, 102–3, 111

Moore, Lewis B., 123, 124, 128, 170, 196

Moorland, Jesse, 123, 172–73, 181

Murray, Anna Evans, 56, 163, 165

Murray, Daniel, 56, 62

Murray, Freeman H. M., 154, 202, 232 n. 49

Murray family, 12, 56

Mu-So-Lit Society, 63

Myrtilla Miner Normal School, 22, 93

NAACP, 155, 158–59, 202–5

National Association for Colored Women (NACW), 162, 164–65

National Baptist Convention, USA, 72–73

National Medical Association, 177, 179

National Training School for Women and Girls, 80–81, 164

new leadership, 165, 207–8

Niagara Movement, 154, 201

Nineteenth Street Baptist Church, 16, 20–21, 71–73, 79–81

nonconfrontation, 67, 69, 172–73, 191–98, 213–14

occupation: business enterprise, 24–25, 134–39; changing nature, 25–26, 133; government employment, 26–27, 152–59; limited opportunities, 23–24; professionals, 25–26, 139–52; as racial uplift, 132, 151–52, 159–60

Odd Fellows, 182–84

Odd Fellows Association Hall, 183–84

Omega Psi Phi, 116

organizations: charitable, 161–75; discrimination in, 162, 170–71, 174, 175–76, 177–78, 180–81, 182; fraternal, 179–84; professional, 175–79; racial solidarity in, 163, 179; promote racial uplift, 161, 184

Parks, Edward L., 123

passing, 58, 190–91

Payne, Daniel Alexander, 19, 20, 65, 66

pharmacists, 146–48

physicians, 31, 140–46

Pinchback, Nina, 12

Pinchback, P. B. S., 12, 56, 83, 192, 238 n. 54

Pinchback family, 12, 56

Pittman, William Sidney, 148, 173, 232 n. 40
Plymouth Congregational Church, 19, 23, 82–83
Preparatory High School, 22, 25. *See also* Dunbar High School; M Street High School
President's Homes Commission, 168, 169
professionals, 25–26, 132, 133, 139–52, 175–79
protest, 55, 157–59, 196–97, 202–3, 206–7, 214
public schools: curriculum conflicts, 95–96, 101–2, 103–4; education, value of, 86–87; history of, 21–22; objective conditions, 87–89; struggle for control, 86, 87, 91–92, 94–95, 97–98, 99–100, 102–3, 105, 107–8; teaching appointments, 91, 93–95. *See also* board of education; Dunbar High School; M Street High School; Preparatory High School
Purnell, William V., 144
Purvis, Charles B., 30, 41, 91, 124, 129, 130, 144, 177, 211
Purvis family, 12, 41

Quander, Nellie, 92, 117, 118

racial discrimination: black on black, 14, 58, 189; in business, 135; in charity, 162, 170–71, 174; in churches, 71, 81–82, 84; at colleges, 49, 113–14; against foreigners, 58; in fraternal orders, 180–81, 182; at Freedmen's Hospital, 141, 142; in government employment, 27, 156–58, 203; laws and, 206–7; in the military, 205, 208–11; professional, 149–50, 175, 176, 177–78; in recreation, 14, 52, 55, 57–58, 61; Riot of 1919, 211–13; rise of, 5–6, 67; in schools, 91–92, 94–96, 99–100, 102–3, 105, 107–8; white attitudes toward, 192–93, 205, 238 n. 58; against women, 164–65, 205–6
racial pride: through black history, 66–68, 110, 126–27, 193–95; blackness, 29–30, 187–91; through charity, 163; in churches, 81; through cultural activities, 63–65, 66–68; through recreational activities, 51, 54; in schools, 109–11; as self-defense, 91
racial solidarity: through black history, 67–68; in business, 58–60, 135–36, 139; in charity, 163; in fraternal orders, 185; in organizations, 185–86; parents teaching, 6, 33–34; in professional activities, 145–46, 147, 151–52, 179, 185; in recreational activities, 51
racial uplift: through black history, 66–69; through charity, 161–63; church involvement in, 73–75, 84; through clubs, 63, 65; education as, 109–111; at Howard University, 125–26, 130; through institution building, 6, 213–14; marriage as strengthening, 39; occupation and, 132, 159–60; parents teaching, 6, 33–34, 37; professionals take up, 147, 149, 151, 179; women's role in, 39, 161–62. *See also* protest
recreation: automobiles as, 54–55; clubs, 62–69; commercial entertainment, 57–60; home entertainment, 53–54; outdoor activities, 52–53, 60–61; social distinctions, 13–16, 51; sports, 54, 61–62; vacations, 55–57
restaurants, 13, 55
Rice, Moses P., 137
Riot of 1919, 211–13
Rollin, Margarette, 42
Rollin, William, 12
Roosevelt, Theodore, 153, 154, 169, 173, 234 n. 22

St. Augustine Roman Catholic Church, 16, 81

St. Luke's Protestant Episcopal Church, 16, 18, 60–61
Samuel Coleridge-Taylor Choral Society, 64–65
Schomburg, Arthur A., 194, 195, 212
Scurlock, Addison N., 34, 37, 137
Scurlock, George, 34, 37
Scurlock, Henry, 181
Scurlock, Mamie, 34, 37
Scurlock, Robert, 34, 37
Scurlock family, 34, 37
segregation: in business, 135, 146; at colleges, 113–14; in government departments, 156–58; legislation, 206–7; rise of, 5–6; in theaters, 57–58
Settle, Josiah, Jr., 53
settlement house movement, 79–80, 166–67
Shadd, Furman J., 73, 141, 144, 177–78
Shadd, Marion P., 173
Shadd family, 11
Shaw District, 134, 136–37
Shiloh Baptist Church, 23, 80, 202
Shorter, Charles H., 195
Simms, George W., 180
Simms, John A., 19, 26, 183
Simms, John A., Jr., 19
Simms, John A., III, 26
Simms, Martha Ann, 19
Simms family, 18–19
Sinclair, William A., 124
skin color, 14, 29–31, 188–89
Slowe, Lucy Diggs, 117
Smith, George C., 26
Smith, James H., 91
social distinctions: in 1880s, 2–3, 31–32, 188; by 1920, 3–4, 213–14; appearances and, 13, 137; in churches, 16–21, 70–71; etiquette and, 12–13; between families, 35–37; in fraternal orders, 27–28, 179, 180; in higher education, 112–13; through occupation, 132–33; through recreational activities, 13–16, 62; skin color and, 14, 30–31, 62; and prejudice against working class, 58, 59, 189, 236 n. 9
social gospel, 75–78, 79–81
Social Settlement Centre, 79–80
social welfare: through churches, 77–78, 79–81; clubwomen and, 80–81, 161–65; and discrimination against workers, 162, 170–71, 174; effectiveness of, 167, 170; and health and sanitation, 168–69; housing and, 169–70; institution building and, 171–75; and juvenile reform, 167–68; and outdoor recreation, 167–69; umbrella organizations, 171–72; YMCA and YWCA work, 172–75
Sojourner Truth Home for Working Girls, 166
sororities, 117–18
Stevenson, John W., 19–20
Straker, D. Augustus, 149
streetcars, 55, 206–7, 211
Syphax, John E., 181
Syphax, William, 11
Syphax family, 10–11, 104

Tancil, Arthur W., 147, 178, 181
teachers, 22, 25–26, 90, 91, 99, 102, 104, 108–9
temperance, 77, 223 n. 16
Terrell, Harrison, 11
Terrell, Mary (daughter), 44–45, 47, 48, 49, 53, 83, 113, 219 n. 31
Terrell, Mary Church, 11; on appearances, 13; charity work of, 161, 164, 165; cultural activities of, 58, 64; family relationships, 37, 39–40, 43, 44–45, 47–48, 49, 106; financial difficulties of, 40; lectures by, 197–98; on passing, 58, 190–91; and protest, 55, 189, 206–7; and religion, 82, 83; and schools, 93, 98, 104–5, 108–9, 227 n. 55; social activities of, 53–55, 56, 57; and Washington–Du Bois conflict, 98,

Terrell, Mary Church (*continued*) 99, 204–5, 238 n. 54; and woman's suffrage, 205–6
Terrell, Phyllis, 44–45, 47–48, 49, 53, 58, 113, 191, 219 n. 31
Terrell, Robert H., 4–5, 113; black capitalism and, 59–60, 138; career of, 92, 134, 149; family relationships, 11, 37, 39–40, 44–45, 48; financial difficulty of, 40, 138; leadership qualities of, 207–8; as a Mason, 181–82; race pride of, 188–89; and religion, 82–83; on skin color, 191; social activities of, 53, 54, 56–57; and Washington–Du Bois conflict, 99, 153–54, 200, 204–5, 238 n. 54
Terrell family, 11, 39–40, 44–45, 47–48, 116
theaters, 57–60
Thirkield, Wilbur P., 122–24
Thompson, Richard W., 68, 154, 202
Tignor, Charles, 168
Toomer, Jean, 12
Treble Clef Club, 64
Tri-State Dental Association, 178–79
Trotter, William Monroe, 68, 157
Tunnell, William V., 97, 106, 118, 124, 126–27, 227 n. 55
Turner, Henry McNeal, 65–66
Turner, Thomas Wyatt, 114, 118–19, 122, 125, 128–29
Tyler, Ralph W., 98, 154, 155, 156, 203

undertakers, 134
Union Bethel AME Church, 16, 18–20, 66. *See also* Metropolitan AME Church
University Park Temple, 82–83

Waldron, John Milton, 80, 100, 170, 202–3
Warfield, William A., 138, 143–44, 181
Waring, James H. N. , 123, 169
Washington, Booker T.: "Atlanta Compromise," 198–99; and black capitalism,

135–36; on Committee of Twelve, 200–201; conflict with W. E. B. Du Bois, 68, 87, 91–92, 94, 95, 98–99, 122–24, 198–202, 232 n. 49; and Howard University, 122–24; and patronage, 10, 91–92, 106, 144, 152–55, 198, 231 n. 28; and press subsidies, 100–101, 104, 201–2; and racial uplift, 84; and son-in-law, 148, 232 n. 40
Washington, D.C., views of, 6–7, 9–10, 21
Washington Bee, 100–101, 201–2, 238 n. 66
Wesley, Charles H., 127
West, Charles I., 143–44, 231 n. 28
Wheeler, Virginia, 42
Whipper, Frances Rollin, 12, 36, 39, 42
Whipper, Ionia Rollin, 12, 34, 36, 42
Whipper, Leigh, 36, 37, 42
Whipper, Leighla, 42
Whipper, William J., 36, 39, 42
Whipper, Winifred, 36
Whipper family, 12, 36, 39, 42
Wilkinson, Garnet C., 107
Williams, Daniel Hale, 141, 142–43, 178, 231 n. 28
Williams, Edward C., 121, 203
Williams, Fannie Barrier, 162
Wilson, Ellen, 169
Wilson, Woodrow, 154–55, 156, 157, 158, 202, 203, 212
women: in the church, 80–81; clubwomen, 162–66; discrimination against, 164–65, 205–6; and marriage, 38–39; and racial uplift, 39; in social clubs, 63; and social welfare reform, 76, 161–62, 175; and woman's suffrage, 205–6
Woodson, Carter G.: and black history, 110, 195, 208; at Howard University, 116, 120–21, 127, 129–30; at M Street, 93, 109, 110
Woodson, Henry, 136

World War I, 208–11
Wormley, Charles Sumner, 64, 146, 181
Wormley, Clarence, 102
Wormley, James A., 24, 147, 180, 192
Wormley, James T., 181
Wormley family, 10, 56, 57

Wright, James C., 89–90, 94, 108
Wright, Thomas H., 183–84

YMCA, 79, 137, 172–73, 234 n. 22
YWCA, 173–75